a collection of recipes

RAVE REVIEWS

presented by

The Junior League of North Little Rock, Inc.

The purpose of the Junior League is exclusively educational and charitable and is to promote voluntarism; to develop the potential of its members for voluntary participation in community affairs; and to demonstrate the effectiveness of trained volunteers.

The proceeds from the sale of RAVE REVIEWS go into the North Little Rock Junior League's Community Trust Fund which supports its projects.

The Junior League of North Little Rock wishes to express appreciation to all members and friends for the many hours spent testing, typing, proofing and compiling the following sampling of Southern cuisine.

Copyright © 1982
Rave Reviews Publications
North Little Rock, Arkansas

First Edition	1982	10,000 copies
Second Edition	1983	10,000 copies
Third Edition	1984	10,000 copies

LIBRARY OF CONGRESS CATALOGUE CARD NUMBER 12-72354
INTERNATIONAL STANDARD BOOK NUMBER 0-961122404

Additional copies may be purchased for $11.95. Order forms are available in the back of this book, or write directly to:

RAVE REVIEWS
The Junior League of North Little Rock
P.O. Box 15753
North Little Rock, Arkansas 72231

Printed by
HART GRAPHICS, INC.
Austin, Texas

Table of Contents

Wining and Dining 5

Appetizers 41

Beverages 63

Breads 73

Salads and Dressings 91

Soups and Sandwiches 111

Eggs and Cheese 127

Condiments 137

Meats 145

Vegetables 197

Desserts 225

Microwave 285

Index 297

Foreword

The Junior League of North Little Rock was organized as a Junior Auxiliary in 1948 and obtained membership in the Association of Junior Leagues, Inc. in 1978. The primary purpose has been to promote voluntarism among members in order to improve our community, state and country. The money received from the sale of RAVE REVIEWS will be used to further that purpose.

North Little Rock, Arkansas, has a population of just over sixty thousand. Situated on the Arkansas River, North Little Rock has an abundance of lakes and rolling hills. The people are proud and hospitable. Their pride stems from the natural resources and their hospitality from their Southern heritage.

RAVE REVIEWS originated in the hearts and minds of Junior League members in 1979. Between these pages can be found over 600 recipes submitted and tested by Junior League members and friends. The recipes selected represent the best of "home cooking" in Central Arkansas. The dedication of the women of the Junior League of North Little Rock is apparent as these pages unfold. Many hours have been spent so that RAVE REVIEWS would become a reality. These hours were spent by busy women having in common the desire to give—give of their time, energy and creativity.

A feature in RAVE REVIEWS presents menus and recipes from some of the finest restaurants in the area. At the end of the section is a useful wine guide contributed by David Cone and Andrea Davenport. It is our hope that RAVE REVIEWS will be an asset for today's busy cook.

THE MATCHMAKERS' ART: PAIRING WINE WITH FOOD

At long last, Americans have finally come to understand and value the centuries-old tradition of drinking wine with meals. Somehow, in our task of building a new country, we laid aside this ancient practice; but recently we have learned, as our ancestors must have known, that there are, in addition to a pleasing taste, other sound reasons for pairing wine with food. In moderate amounts, wine aids in digestion, enhances the flavor of our foods, and promotes relaxation and lively conversation among those who are dining. What better reasons could we have for preserving a timeless tradition? With this in mind, we offer the benefit of our knowledge and experience as follows, and invite you to enjoy a glass of wine with your very next meal. Salute!

Serving Wine with Meals:

While the oft-repeated dictum "red wine with red meat and white wine with seafood and poultry" is a good rule-of-thumb, it surely is not absolute. In choosing which wine with which food, you should take into account the general characteristics of the food being served. If the food is "heavy" or highly seasoned, a relatively hearty wine is your best choice. If the food possesses a more subtle flavor, it requires a lighter, more delicate wine. After all, the wine you drink should enhance, not overpower, the flavor of your food; conversely, the food should not overpower the flavor of the wine. Your ultimate goal in pairing wine with food should be a balance of both flavor and body.

Equally important is the personal taste preferences of those who are dining. Common sense tells you it would be unwise to serve a full-bodied, dry red wine to your guests, knowing they find this type of wine distasteful. It would be far better to compromise by serving a lighter-bodied, slightly fruity red, or even a dry, full-bodied white wine, even if the main course is a heavy red meat, such as Beef Prime Rib. The flavor of the food that you have meticulously prepared will not be enhanced by a wine that is offensive to you or to your dinner guests. Remember, the key is balance.

When serving wine with meals there are two general rules that should be followed: 1. Never serve wine with any food that has a vinaigrette. The acid in the vinegar will bring out the acidity in any wine. (This is why the French and Italians serve a salad after the main course.) 2. Serve great, aged wines with fine, yet simple dishes to show off the wine. If the food is the main attraction, choose a sound, appropriate wine to complement the food, but do not steal the curtain calls from the "chef."

Cooking with Wine:

If your recipe calls for wine, it is usually best to serve the same or similar wine with that course. (Exception: Soups, meats, and fish prepared with Marsala, Port, Sherry, or Madeira.) For the wine novice, this is a good general serving guide, because if the food and wine are compatible for cooking, they are usually compatible for dining.

In cooking, the alcohol in both red and white wines should be allowed to cook out, leaving only the mellow essence of the wine. When wine is added early in the preparation of the dish, the alcohol is reduced by the long cooking. However, if wine is added toward the end of cooking, the wine should be boiled rapidly in a separate pan. (Use only a deep pan over a gas flame to prevent the alcohol from catching fire.) Red wine should usually be reduced by one-eighth and white wine usually by one-fourth.

Serving Wine to Large Groups:

When serving wine to large groups of people for an event such as a wine and cheese party, you may find it necessary to offer wines that are moderately priced and less complex in character. It probably would be more feasible to serve "middle-of-the-road" type wines to such a group, where taste preferences are likely to be widely varied.

With this in mind, and assuming that cost is also a factor to be considered, there are the "jugs," those big bottles of white, rosé, and red wines that run the spectrum from fruity to dry. Most large domestic wineries produce generic wines (those made with any number of grape types and labeled as Chablis, Burgundy, etc.), and more recently some varietals (those made primarily from the grape mentioned on the label), such as Chenin Blanc, French Columbard, Chardonnay, Zinfandel, etc. You will find surprisingly palatable wines at very reasonable prices in 1½ liter and 3 liter packages, all designed to meet what the individual vintner feels is *the* taste desired by the majority of the wine drinking public.

There are wines being produced today to satisfy everyone's tastes and needs. Experimenting with wines is a fascinating venture; finding the ones you like best will be a pleasurable experience. In doing so, you will enjoy one of the oldest traditions known to man.

Fortified Wine:

In addition to the natural wines previously listed, there are several "fortified wines" — natural wines to which brandy has been added — that are widely favored for flavoring meats, sauces, desserts, etc. Usually the domestic and foreign versions bear the same names. These wines possess a more pronounced flavor, due to the higher alcoholic content. This additional alcohol also makes them useful in flaming dishes. The principal fortified wines are Madeira, Marsala, Port, and Sherry. These are also known as "dessert wines."

Madeira—A sweet brown wine (from the Portuguese island of Madeira) whose rich flavors are a complement to braised meats, game sauces, etc.

Marsala—A sweet, strong Italian wine with a unique taste and bouquet, used in preparing such dishes as scalloped veal and zabaione.

Port—A sweet red wine that is widely served with or after dessert, and which sometimes is added to game sauces or served over fresh fruit.

Sherry—Probably the most universally known fortified wine, and one whose characteristics vary greatly. The sweeter varieties are especially suited for cooking with dark meats, sauces, and soups, and for flavoring desserts. This wine is also often served with or after dessert.

Champagnes and Sparkling Wines:

Since sparkling wines are widely accepted as the wines of celebration, you cannot ignore the subject of how they should be served. You purchase sparkling wines for these special occasions because their bubbles lend an air of gaiety and festiveness. Why then should they be abused by reducing them, or nearly reducing them, to still wines, by serving them in shallow, wide-mouthed, Champagne glasses or through a Champagne fountain? Since all sparkling wines contain gases, they immediately begin to unleash their effervescence once the bottle has been opened. So unless a person consumes his wine somewhat rapidly from a wide-mouthed Champagne glass, those precious bubbles go floating off through the air before he has had a chance to enjoy the wine's festive qualities. Also, since much of the wine is exposed to the warm air, the wine that you painstakingly chilled becomes warm before all of it is consumed. These same abuses take place through a Champagne fountain, with the bubbles escaping even faster, and the heating process being accelerated, due to the recycling motion of the fountain. Obviously, these utensils were invented for "show", and as a means of increasing sales. No winemaker would ever wish to see his wines abused in this fashion.

So the next time you serve a sparkling wine, serve it from the bottle into a tulip-shaped wine glass with a narrow mouth and a deep bowl; give it the respect that it deserves by preserving its lively and festive effervescent qualities.

David Cone
Andrea Davenport

9

SUGGESTED WINES TO ACCOMPANY FOODS

F—FRANCE, G—GERMANY
I—ITALY, P—PORTUGAL
S—SPAIN, Sw—SWITZERLAND
fb—FULL-BODIED

FOOD	DRY WHITE BORDEAUX (F)	CALIF. SAUVIGNON BLANC	SOAVE (I)	WHITE GRAVES (F)	WHITE RHONE (F)	CALIF. CHABLIS	VALPOLICELLA (I)	BEAUJOLAIS (F)	LIGHT RED BORDEAUX (F)	CALIF. LIGHT ZINFANDEL	BEAUJOLAIS-VILLAGES (F)	FRENCH SAUTERNES (F)	ALSATIAN RIESLING (F)	CHIANTI (I)	VOUVRAY (F)	CALIF. RIESLING	CALIF. CHARDONNAY	MOSEL (G)	CALIF. DRY ROSÉ	ORVIETO (SECCO) (I)	SPANISH WHITES (S)	CALIF. CHENIN BLANC	CALIF. SEMILLON	WHITE BURGUNDY (F)	VERDICCHIO (I)
STEAMED CLAMS	•	•	•																						
CHEESE FONDUE																•		•							
HORS D'OEUVRES				•	•	•	•	•																	
RAW OYSTERS		•															•								
PATE, COARSE								•	•	•															
PATE, FINE		•										•	•												
PIZZA									•					•											
QUICHE		•										•		•											
BOILED SHRIMP	•			•											•	•	•								
BOUILLABAISSE		•																	•	•	•				
COQUILLE ST. JACQUES			•														•					•			
STEAMED CRAB	•																•							•	
BROILED FISH																•	•			•				•	•
SAUTEED FLOUNDER		•		•												•	•			•				•	•
SAUTEED SOLE		•		•												•	•			•				•	•
SAUTEED TROUT		•		•												•	•			•				•	•
FISH AND CHIPS					•															•		•			
LOBSTER			•																			•			
SAUTEED FISH															•		•								
SAUTEED SCALLOPS															•		•								
OYSTERS & CREAM SAUCE																									
POACHED SALMON	•																•		•						
SHRIMP CREOLE															•					•	•				
BAKED CHICKEN					•												•								
BROILED CHICKEN					•												•								
ROAST CHICKEN					•												•								
BBQ CHICKEN																									
CURRIED CHICKEN																									
COQ AU VIN																									
FRIED CHICKEN					•		•																		
TURKEY					•											•									
DUCK A L'ORANGE										•															
ROAST GOOSE													•												
PHEASANT																									
GUINEA HEN																									
ROAST QUAIL																									

PORTUGUESE WHITES (P)	CALIF. JUG WHITES	GERMAN RIESLING (G)	CHAMPAGNE, EXTRA DRY	CALIF. PINOT NOIR BLANC	MACON BLANC (F)	BARDOLINO (I)	LIGHT RED RHONE (F)	LIGHT WHITE RHONE (F)	RHINE WINES (G)	HERMITAGE WHITE (F)	CAL. ROSÉ OF PINOT NOIR	RED BURGUNDY (F)	CALIF. CABERNET (fb)	BAROLO (I)	RED RHONE (F) (fb)	COTE ROTIE (F)	CHIANTI RISERVA (I)	RIOJA RED (S)	COTE DE BEAUNE (F)	BARBARESCO (I)	ST. EMILION (F)	POMEROL (F)	CLASSIFIED MEDOC (F)	CALIF. ZINFANDEL (fb)	CALIF. BURGUNDY	CALIF. PETIT SIRAH	HERMITAGE RED (F)	CALIF. GRIGNOLINO	ANJOU ROSÉ (F)	RIOJA WHITE (S)	FRASCATI (I)	CALIF. GEWURZTRAMINER	CHAMPAGNE, BRUT	SWISS WHITES (Sw)	MUSCADET (F)
		●							●																									●	
																																			●
																								●											
																																			●
																																			●
																																			●
●	●																																		
		●																																	
		●																																	
		●																																	
				●		●		●																											
					●																								●						
							●	●	●																										
							●	●	●																										
							●	●	●																										
		●							●	●																									
				●					●		●																								
												●		●	●																				
		●					●	●	●																										
									●																										
											●			●																					
																	●									●									
											●						●	●																	
												●							●	●															
											●			●																					

SUGGESTED WINES TO ACCOMPANY FOODS

F—FRANCE, G—GERMANY
I—ITALY, P—PORTUGAL
S—SPAIN, Sw—SWITZERLAND
fb—FULL-BODIED

FOOD	DRY WHITE BORDEAUX (F)	CALIF. SAUVIGNON BLANC	SOAVE (I)	WHITE GRAVES (F)	WHITE RHONE (F)	CALIF. CHABLIS	VALPOLICELLA (I)	BEAUJOLAIS (F)	LIGHT RED BORDEAUX (F)	CALIF. LIGHT ZINFANDEL	BEAUJOLAIS-VILLAGES (F)	FRENCH SAUTERNES (F)	ALSATIAN RIESLING (F)	CHIANTI (I)	VOUVRAY (F)	CALIF. RIESLING	CALIF. CHARDONNAY	MOSEL (G)	CALIF. DRY ROSÉ	ORVIETO (SECCO) (I)	SPANISH WHITES (S)	CALIF. CHENIN BLANC	CALIF. SEMILLON	WHITE BURGUNDY (F)	VERDICCHIO (I)
RABBIT																									
CHILI CON CARNE																									
BBQ BEEF																									
BEEF BOURGUIGNON										•				•											
BEEF CURRY																									
BEEF STEW																									
BEEF STROGANOFF										•															
HAMBURGERS							•	•		•															
MEATLOAF								•																	
PEPPERCORN STEAK																									
ROAST BEEF																									
LAMB PATTIES										•															
LAMB SHANKS										•															
LAMB STEW							•																		
LEG OF LAMB							•	•									•								
LIVER AND ONIONS							•		•	•															
BAKED HAM													•						•						
PORK CHOPS	•		•																	•					•
ROAST PORK	•		•																	•					•
PORK SAUSAGE	•												•								•				
VEAL CHOPS							•										•								
ROAST VEAL							•										•								
WEINER SCHNITZEL							•	•																	
PASTA & CREAM SAUCE																						•			
PASTA & CLAM SAUCE		•		•	•																				
MEAT-FILLED RAVIOLI							•																		
CHEESE-FILLED RAVIOLI				•	•																				
SPAGHETTI & MEAT SAUCE									•																
CANTONESE DISHES																									
CHICKEN CHOW MEIN																						•			
CHINESE ROAST DUCK							•																		
EGG FU YONG			•																						•
MO-SHU PORK			•																	•					
HUNAN-SZECHUAN DISHES																									
PEKING DISHES								•	•																
SHRIMP TEMPURA			•										•			•									

Wine columns (left to right):

1. PORTUGUESE WHITES (P)
2. CALIF. JUG WHITES
3. GERMAN RIESLING (G)
4. CHAMPAGNE, EXTRA DRY
5. CALIF. PINOT NOIR BLANC
6. MACON BLANC (F)
7. BARDOLINO (I)
8. LIGHT RED RHONE (F)
9. LIGHT WHITE RHONE (F)
10. RHINE WINES (G)
11. HERMITAGE WHITE (F)
12. CAL. ROSÉ OF PINOT NOIR
13. RED BURGUNDY (F)
14. CALIF. CABERNET (fb)
15. BAROLO (I)
16. RED RHONE (F) (fb)
17. COTE ROTIE (F)
18. CHIANTI RISERVA (I)
19. RIOJA RED (S)
20. COTE DE BEAUNE (F)
21. BARBARESCO (I)
22. ST. EMILION (F)
23. POMEROL (F)
24. CLASSIFIED MEDOC (F)
25. CALIF. ZINFANDEL (fb)
26. CALIF. BURGUNDY
27. CALIF. PETIT SIRAH
28. HERMITAGE RED (F)
29. CALIF. GRIGNOLINO
30. ANJOU ROSÉ (F)
31. RIOJA WHITE (S)
32. FRASCATI (I)
33. CALIF. GEWURZTRAMINER
34. CHAMPAGNE, BRUT
35. SWISS WHITES (Sw)
36. MUSCADET (F)

A GUIDE TO WINE AND CHEESE

	BANON (FRANCE)	BEL PAESE (ITALY)	BRIE (FRANCE)	CAMEMBERT (FRANCE)	CHEDDAR (GR. BRITAIN, U.S.)	DANABLU (DENMARK)	EDAM (NETHERLANDS)	FORTINA (ITALY)	GORGONZOLA (ITALY)	GOUDA (NETHERLANDS)	GRUYERE (FRANCE, SWITZERLAND)	FETA (GREECE)	LIEDERKRANZ (U.S.)	MOZZARELLA (ITALY)	MUNSTER (FRANCE, GERMANY)	PORT-SALUT (DENMARK, FRANCE)	ROQUEFORT (FRANCE)	STILTON (GR. BRITAIN)	TILSITER (GERMANY)
BEAUJOLAIS							●				●								
RED BORDEAUX			●				●			●									
RED BURGUNDY				●	●		●		●							●	●	●	
WHITE BURGUNDY				●															
CABERNET SAUVIGNON				●															
CHABLIS												●	●	●	●				●
CHATEAUNEUF-DU-PAPE																	●		
CHENIN BLANC												●	●	●	●				●
CHIANTI		●		●				●	●	●								●	
CLARET				●															
GAMAY																		●	
GEWURZTRAMINER												●			●				
MADEIRA					●														
PINOT NOIR			●	●				●								●	●		
PORT				●												●		●	
RED RHONE				●	●														
ROSÉ	●																		
SHERRY				●															
ZINFANDEL																			

ANDERSON'S CAJUN'S WHARF

Little Rock

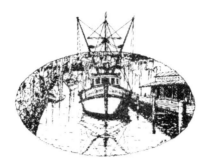

A Cajun Feast

Oysters Bienville*   Trout Broussard

Dirty Rice

French Bread   Cajun Cobbler

OYSTERS BIENVILLE

¼ **cup green onions, chopped**   ¼ **cup half and half**
¼ **cup mushrooms, chopped**   ¼ **cup flour**
⅛ **pound butter**   ½ **tsp. black pepper**
½ **tsp. chicken base**   **Dash of Tabasco**
½ **cup baby shrimp**   **2 dozen oysters on the half shell**
1 ounce Chablis   **1 pound Parmesan cheese**
2 egg yolks

Sauté green onions and mushrooms in butter until cooked. Add chicken base, shrimp and Chablis. Beat egg yolks with half and half. Add flour, egg yolks and spices to mixture. Top oysters with 2 to 3 ounces of sauce and bake 3 to 4 minutes. Sprinkle with Parmesan cheese and brown. Before serving, top each oyster with melted butter.

ANDRE'S

Little Rock

Dinner For Six

Fresh Mushroom Soup

Spinach Salade—Vinaigrette Dressing

Andean-Style Sweet Roast Pork*

Fruited Rice*

Black Forest Cake   Cafe au Lait

ANDEAN-STYLE SWEET ROAST PORK

3 pound pork loin*
1 Tb. salt
¼ cup melted butter
1 cup light cream or half and half
1 tsp. ground cinnamon
¾ tsp. nutmeg
1 cup seedless raisins

½ cup bread crumbs

Marinade:
  1 cup dry white wine
  5 whole cloves
  ⅓ cup brown sugar

*Pork must marinate 24 hours before preparation.

Rub the pork loin with salt; let stand for 20 minutes. In a large, non-metallic bowl or pan, combine the white wine, cloves and brown sugar. Add the pork loin, spooning marinade over meat to coat thoroughly. Cover and refrigerate 24 hours. Pre-heat oven to 350°. Remove meat from marinade and pat dry. Gradually add the melted butter, cream, cinnamon, nutmeg and raisins to the marinade. Whisk thoroughly. Place the pork in a roasting pan and sprinkle with bread crumbs. Cover with the marinade mixture and cook until tender (about 1½ hours or until internal temperature is 185°). Baste meat frequently. Serve at once, ladling the marinade mixture over the pork.

FRUITED RICE

7 ounces sliced carrots
2 ounces butter or margarine
5½ ounces chopped green onion
5 ounces unpeeled apples, thinly
  sliced and cored
1½ pounds rice cooked in 1½ quarts
  chicken broth

4 ounces seedless raisins
½ tsp. salt
½ tsp. black pepper
3 tsp. toasted sesame seeds

Cook carrots in butter, leaving stiff, about 3 minutes. Add onions and apples and cook 5 minutes longer. Stir in rice, raisins, salt and pepper. Stir over low heat until rice is thoroughly heated. Add sesame seeds and toss lightly.

THE CAPITAL CLUB

Little Rock

A Dinner By Candlelight

Fresh Spinach Leaf Salad & Hot Bacon Dressing

Buttered Asparagus

Boned Breast of Chicken Rochambeau
Set on Rusk with Grilled Ham Bearnaise

Mushroom Cap

Hot Rolls and Butter   Pumpkin Cream Pie*

PUMPKIN CREAM PIE

12 ounces cream cheese
⅔ cup sugar
3 eggs
½ tsp. cloves
1 tsp. cinnamon

1 tsp. nutmeg
1 tsp. ginger
1 tsp. vanilla
16-ounce can pumpkin

Beat cream cheese with sugar. Add eggs, one at a time, continuing to beat. Season with cloves, cinnamon, nutmeg, ginger and vanilla. Add pumpkin. Turn into a 10″ pie shell and bake for 40 minutes at 340° or until set. Let cool for 10 minutes.

Topping:

8 ounces sour cream
½ cup sugar

1 tsp. vanilla
Chopped pecans or walnuts

Mix sour cream with sugar and vanilla. Stir together and spread on pie and sprinkle with chopped walnuts or pecans. Bake 5 more minutes.

18

CHEERS!

Little Rock

Vegetarian Delight

Avocado Sandwich*

Potato Chips   Dill Pickles

Cheesecake

AVOCADO SANDWICH

2 slices dark rye bread
Mayonnaise
1 medium avocado, peeled and sliced
Shredded lettuce
Alfalfa sprouts
Purple onion slices

Slice of tomato
Cucumber slices
Fresh mushrooms, sliced
Oil and vinegar sauce
Provolone cheese slice

Spread mayonnaise on bread. Layer the sandwich with avocado, lettuce, alfalfa sprouts, onion, tomato, cucumber, mushrooms, oil and vinegar sauce and cheese.

THE COUNTRY CLUB OF LITTLE ROCK

A Spring Salad Luncheon

Spinach Cheese Salad*   Chicken Salad

Bacon and Cheese Quiche

Fresh Fruit Salad with Poppy Seed Dressing

Paradise Pie*

SPINACH CHEESE SALAD

1 three-ounce package lemon Jello
1 cup hot water
½ cup cold water
1½ Tb. vinegar
½ cup mayonnaise

Salt and pepper
1 cup raw spinach, finely chopped
¾ cup cottage cheese
1 Tb. onion, finely chopped

Dissolve Jello in hot water. Add cold water, vinegar, mayonnaise, salt and pepper. Blend well with rotary beater. Pour into refrigerator tray. Chill 15 to 20 minutes or until firm 1 inch from edge but soft in center. Turn into bowl and whip until fluffy. Add spinach, cottage cheese and onion and mix thoroughly. Pour into 1 quart mold or individual molds. Chill in refrigerator and set. To serve, top with mayonnaise.

PARADISE PIE

3 egg whites
1 cup sugar
20 soda crackers
1 cup chopped nuts

1 tsp. vanilla
½ pint whipped cream
Grated coconut

Beat egg whites. Gradually add sugar. Fold in crumbled crackers, nuts and vanilla. Bake 20 minutes at 325°. Cool and top with whipped cream and coconut. Refrigerate. Can be frozen.

COY'S

Little Rock/Hot Springs

A Holiday Dinner

Escargot*

Lamb with Mint Jelly   Au gratin Potatoes

Hot Biscuits

Cheese Cake

ESCARGOT

3 dozen escargot
½ pound butter
½ cup pale, dry sherry

¼ tsp. ground red pepper
1½ Tb. garlic powder
½ Tb. onion powder

Place all ingredients in sauce pan except escargot and simmer into sauce, stirring occasionally. Add escargot and simmer for ten minutes.

GONZALES' & GERTRUDE'S

Memphis

South of the Border Shrimp Dinner

Camerones Cancun*

Mexican Rice   Mexican String Beans

Garnish with:

Wedge of Romaine Lettuce   ½ Curl Orange Slice
Green and Red Bell Pepper   Ring of White Onion
                2 slices of Radish

CAMERONES CANCUN

6 ounces light vegetable oil
1-2 cloves garlic,
  finely diced
1 pimiento, finely diced

1 stalk of large green onion,
  finely diced
6 jumbo shrimp, butterflied and
  left in shell

Stir the oil and garlic together and pour a small amount onto a hot grill. Stir the pimiento and onion into the garlic oil mixture. Shrimp should be placed on the grill back to back and standing up. Baste the shrimp with the oil mixture and cook for approximately 5 minutes. Serve the shrimp on bed of Mexican rice.

JACQUES & SUZANNE

Little Rock

JACQUES & SUZANNE

A Post-Concert Dinner

Fresh Beefsteak Tomato Salad

Steak du Chef with Green Peppercorn Sauce*

Fresh Green Vegetable   Herbed Rice or Sautéed Potatoes

Rolls and Butter   Creamed Cheesecake

STEAK DU CHEF WITH GREEN PEPPERCORN SAUCE

1 pound unsalted butter
½ cup finely chopped parsley
1½ Tb. finely chopped shallots
¼ cup green peppercorns
  (Madagascar)

¼ cup Dijon (French) Mustard
2 Tb. freshly squeezed lemon juice
2½ tsp. salt
1½ cups whipping cream

Whip the butter until it is light and fluffy. Finely chop the parsley, shallots and green peppercorns. Add to the beaten butter. Add the mustard, lemon juice and salt, and mix until well blended. This makes 18 ounces of butter which can be kept under refrigeration for two weeks, or it can be frozen.

To prepare butter sauce for 8 portions, reduce, over heat, 1½ cups of whipping cream (30% butterfat) to ¾ cup. Set aside until it has cooled to approximately 120°F. Using a French whip, gradually beat in, tablespoon by tablespoon, 2 cups of green peppercorn butter (firm, but not refrigerator cold). Hold the sauce in a warm, but not hot place, as for a hollandiase. Grill, broil or sauté steak and slice diagonally; nap with green peppercorn sauce.

LEATHER BOTTLE

Little Rock

A Beefeater's Repast

Spinach and Mushroom Salad;
Honey and Mustard Dressing

Steak Oscar   Stuffed Potato

Soda Bread   Cheesecake*

CHEESECAKE

Crust:

½ cup butter   **1¼ cup graham cracker crumbs**
¼ cup sugar

Melt butter and combine with graham cracker crumbs and sugar. Pressing on sides and bottom of 8" springform pan.

Filling:

5 eight-ounce packages cream cheese
1¾ cups sugar
3 Tb. flour
½ tsp. vanilla
¼ tsp. orange rind

¼ tsp. lemon rind
5 eggs and 2 egg yolks
¼ cup heavy cream
Cinnamon sugar

Preheat oven to 500°. Have all ingredients at room temperature. Whip cream cheese until soft and fluffy. Combine sugar, flour, vanilla, orange and lemon rind with cream cheese and mix well. Add eggs and yolks one at a time and mix thoroughly after each addition. Pour in heavy cream; mix well. Pour in prepared springform pan and bake at 500° for 12 minutes. Reduce heat to 200° and bake for 1 hour. Turn off oven and let cool for 1 hour. Refrigerate overnight or for several hours. Sprinkle top with cinnamon sugar.

LITTLE ROCK CLUB

THE LITTLE ROCK CLUB

A Special Steak Dinner

Crabmeat de Jonghe en Coquille

Hearts of Romaine Salad with Oil and Vinegar Dressing

Lemon Sorbet (Lemon Ice)

The Little Rock Club Special Steak*

Potato Balls Sautéed in Butter   Asparagus

Gateau Riche

THE LITTLE ROCK CLUB SPECIAL STEAK

12-14 ounce New York Sirloin	**¾ tsp. finely minced garlic**
Salt and pepper	**2 Tb. chopped parsley**
Fresh mushrooms, sliced	**¾-1 cup espagnole sauce***
3 Tb. butter	

Pat the steak dry with a towel. Season with salt and pepper. Broil steak to its desired doneness. Remove outer skin completely. Slice steak across in a slant, ½ inch apart. Cover the steak with slices of fresh mushrooms. Set aside. In a sauté pan melt the butter. Add the garlic. While it is bubbling, add the parsley. Let it cook until the garlic begins to change color. At this time, add the espagnole sauce*. Swirl it around a few times and simmer for 3 minutes; cover the already warm steak. Glaze under the broiler and serve.

*Espagnole Sauce — Any enriched brown sauce of your choosing, or from the following recipe.

ESPAGNOLE SAUCE

(Rich Brown Sauce)

½ cup fat (fresh unsalted beef,
  veal or pork
1 small carrot, coarsely chopped
2 onions, coarsely chopped
½ cup flour
8 cups brown stock
3 sprigs parsley

1 stalk celery
1 small bay leaf
1 garlic clove
Pinch of thyme
¼ cup tomato sauce
  (or ½ cup tomato puree)

Melt the fat in a heavy sauce pan. Add carrot and onions and cook them until they just start to turn golden, shaking the pan to insure even cooking. Add flour and cook the vegetables, stirring until they are a rich brown. Add 3 cups of boiling brown stock, parsley, celery, bay leaf, garlic and thyme and cook the mixture, stirring frequently until it thickens. Add 3 more cups of stock and simmer the sauce, slowly stirring occasionally for 1 to 1½ hours, or until it is reduced to about 3 cups. Skim off the fat as it accumulates on the surface. Add tomato sauce or tomato puree, cook the sauce for a few minutes longer, and strain it through a fine sieve. Add 2 more cups of stock and continue to cook the sauce slowly for about 1 hour, skimming from time to time, until it is reduced to about 4 cups. Cool the sauce stirring occasionally. Seal it with a layer of melted fat for storing.

MEXICO CHIQUITO

North Little Rock

Pescados Mexicanos

(Mexican Seafood)

Pezcado a la Veracruzano Chuachinango*

Mexican or White Rice   Carrot and Zucchini Combination

Garnish with Lemon Wheels or Parsley

PEZCADO A LA VERACRUZANO CHUACHINANGO
(Individual Serving)

3 ounces oil for frying   **Pinch of pepper**
6 ounces fish fillet (ocean variety)   **Pinch of garlic powder**
Milk   **3 ounces seafood filling***
1 ounce flour   **4 ounces Veracruz sauce***
Pinch of Salt

Seafood Filling:

Seafood combination (King crab,
bay shrimp, red snapper, etc.)
Lemon

Salt
Onion
Shrimp sauce

Combine equal parts of any seafood combination. Fill a saucepan with water.
Add lemon, salt and onion to water and bring to a rolling boil. Remove water
from heat. Add fish. Leave for 5 minutes. Remove fish; debone. Add 5 ounces
of shrimp sauce per pound of seafood combination.

Veracruz Sauce:

1 pound white onion julienne
1 pound green pepper julienne
¼ pound fresh mushrooms, sliced
½ cup crushed tomatoes
½ ounce Chablis
1 ounce MSG
1 ounce capers

Dash of white pepper
Dash of cayenne
¼ ounce granulated garlic
½ ounce salt
Dash of oregano
Dash of paprika

Sauté the white onions, green peppers and mushrooms. Add the remaining
ingredients and heat. Add additional crushed tomatoes to make the sauce
more "tomato-ee".

To Prepare:

Place oil in frying pan or on griddle. Dip fish fillet in milk. Mix the flour, salt,
pepper and garlic powder. Dip fish fillet in flour mixture. Place in pan or griddle
and saute. Cut the fillet into 2 pieces. Place 1 piece on plate and cover with 3
ounces of seafood filling. Place second piece on top. Cover with Veracruz
Sauce.

"NU DELI" LTD.

North Little Rock

A Classic French Dinner

Rainbow Omelet

(Spinach, Cheese & Tomato Omelet, served cold)

Bouchee á la Reine
(Fluffy pie crust filled with chicken,
mushrooms and green peas and
covered with bechamel sauce)

Chocolate Mousse*

CHOCOLATE MOUSSE

1 bar of German chocolate
1 tsp. cocoa powder
3 tsp. coffee, strong and hot

8 egg whites
Pinch of salt
2 ounces sugar

In a large double boiler, mix chocolate, cocoa powder and coffee. Egg whites should be at room temperature. Put them in a bowl and add just a pinch of salt. With a whip beat the egg whites until they start to rise. At that time, add the sugar. Keep beating until mixture is very consistent. Mix ¼ of the egg white mixture with the warm chocolate. Incorporate the rest gently with a spatula. Keep the mousse in the refrigerator for 1 or 2 hours before serving. Serves 4 or 5.

PERCITO'S

North Little Rock

Dinner Italian Style

Green Salad   Eggplant Parmigiano*

Pasta with White Clam Sauce*

Garlic Bread   Spumoni

EGGPLANT PARMIGIANO

1 large eggplant
1 Tb. salt
⅛ tsp. pepper
2 eggs, well beaten
1 cup bread crumbs

¼ cup Parmesan cheese, grated
1 tsp. basil
Enough oil for deep frying
Mozzarella cheese slices

Cut eggplant in slices, about 1 inch thick. Salt and pepper both sides. Let stand for 30 minutes. Dip each slice in eggs, and then roll in bread crumbs mixed with Parmesan cheese and basil. Fry until golden brown. Melt 1 thin slice of mozzarella cheese over each slice of eggplant. Drain.

PASTA WITH WHITE CLAM SAUCE

¼ cup olive oil
1 clove garlic (thinly sliced)
¼ cup water
½ tsp. chopped parsley

½ tsp. salt
¼ tsp. oregano
¼ tsp. black pepper
1 cup small clams with juice

Sauté garlic in oil until brown. Add water. Stir in remaining ingredients. Cook until clams are heated thoroughly. Serve hot over favorite pasta.

PLEASANT VALLEY COUNTRY CLUB

Little Rock

A Lake Trout Dinner for Six

Caesar Salad   Sheepshead Chowder*

Sauteed Lake Trout Topped with Crawfish Etoufee*

Candied Carrots

Turnip Greens with Smoked Pork   Snap Beans with Red Onions

Praline Cheesecake

SHEEPSHEAD CHOWDER

¼ pound salt pork
4 medium onions, chopped
4 medium potatoes, diced
1 quart fish stock
2 Tb. butter

2 Tb. flour
3 pounds sheepshead fillets
1 quart milk (or 1 pint cream and
  1 pint milk)
Salt and freshly ground black pepper

When buying sheepshead fillets, ask at the fish market for the heads, tails, bones and trimmings, and use them to make a good fish stock (enough for the one quart needed here).

Have a soup pot ready. Fry the diced pork in a skillet with a little water, and remove the pieces when they are opaque white and firm but not browned. Add to the soup pot. Put the onions in the pan and cook until golden brown. Drain off the fat and put the onions in the pot. Put the potatoes and fish stock in the pot. Cook slowly until the potatoes are done. Rub the butter and the flour together thoroughly and add to the pot. Cut the sheepshead fillets into one-inch pieces and add them. Bring to a boil, lower the heat and cook for about 15 minutes more. Add milk or milk-cream mixture just before serving. Heat the chowder through gently, being careful not to let boil. Add salt and pepper to taste.

CRAWFISH ETOUFFEE

1 stick butter
3 Tb. flour
1 medium onion, chopped
3 scallions with 3 inches of their
green leaves, thinly sliced
2 cloves garlic, minced
2 Tb. fresh parsley, chopped
½ cup tomato sauce (purée)
½ tsp. grated lemon peel
¼ tsp. cayenne

¼ tsp. thyme
1 Tb. lemon juice
⅓ cup crawfish fat
1 cup chicken broth
1 ounce brandy
¼ cup sherry
2 cups crawfish tails
1 cup fish stock
Salt and freshly ground
black pepper

Melt the butter in a saucepan and add the flour. Cook over low heat, stirring constantly, for 20 minutes to make a brown roux. Add the onion, scallions, garlic and parsley, and cook until the vegetables are soft and transparent. Add the tomato sauce, lemon peel, cayenne, thyme, lemon juice, crawfish fat, chicken broth and brandy. Cover and cook slowly for 20 minutes. Add the sherry, and then the crawfish tails. Stir in the fish stock and simmer. Add salt and pepper to taste. Serve over sauteed lake trout.

THE RED APPLE INN

Eden Isle/Heber Springs

A Patio Luncheon for Twelve

Fresh Fruit Salad with Poppyseed Dressing

Hot Chicken Loaf with Mushroom Sauce*

Buttered Broccoli

Hot Rolls   Apple Pie*

HOT CHICKEN LOAF WITH MUSHROOM SAUCE

1 hen
1 onion
2 celery stalks
2 bay leaves
Whole pepper corns
2 Tb. salt
2 Tb. flour
2 Tb. butter
2 beaten eggs
1 cup milk
1 Tb. chopped parsley

1 cup cooked rice
1 Tb. pepper
1 tsp. paprika
1 can chopped pimiento
1 cup chopped celery
1 large chopped onion
1 clove garlic, finely chopped
6 hard boiled eggs, finely chopped
1 cup rich chicken stock
Buttered cracker crumbs
1 cup chopped pecans

Cut up the meat from a hen that has been boiled with an onion, celery stalks, bay leaves, whole pepper corns and 1 Tb. salt. Brown the flour in melted butter. Add beaten eggs and milk. Cook gently until thick. Pour over chicken. Add the parsley, cooked rice, pepper, paprika, 1 Tb. salt, pimiento, celery, onion, garlic, eggs and chicken stock. Pour into a buttered rectangular pan. Sprinkle top with buttered cracker crumbs and pecans. Bake at 350° for 45 minutes or until firm.

Mushroom Sauce:

2 Tb. butter	1 can cream of mushroom soup
2 Tb. flour	Salt and pepper to taste
1 onion, finely chopped	Thin cream
¼ tsp. Beau Monde	1 can chopped mushrooms

Melt butter and brown flour in it. Add the onion, Beau Monde, cream of mushroom soup, salt, pepper, and enough thin cream to make a thin sauce. Add the mushrooms. Serve over each serving of chicken loaf which has been cut into squares.

APPLE PIE FILLING

1½ cups sugar	Grated rind of 1 orange
Juice of 1 orange	½ stick butter
Juice of 1 lemon	1 pound apples, peeled and sliced
½ tsp. cinnamon (scant)	Cream

Mix the first six ingredients in saucepan and bring to a boil. Place a layer of apples in a pie pan lined with a partially cooked pastry. Pour some of the mixture over the apples, continuing layers until the center of the pie is higher than the rim in a rounded fashion. Put strips of pastry, in checked pattern, on top. Brush with cream. Bake at 325° until brown. Turn the temperature down and cook until done.

SHORTY SMALL'S

Little Rock

Soup and Sandwich Special

Judge Roy Bean Soup*   Grilled Cheese Sandwich

Dill Pickle   Green Onion

Cheesecake

JUDGE ROY BEAN SOUP
(Senate Bean Soup)

2 pounds dry Great Northern Beans   1 stalk celery, chopped
1½ pounds ham   1¼ Tb. white pepper
1 Tb. MSG   1¼ Tb. celery salt
1 pound white onions, chopped

Cook beans in water and salt according to package directions (may add ham bone). In a separate pan, cover ham with water. Add MSG and onions and cook until ham is tender. Remove ham from heat and chop. Place ham back in stock, add celery and cover (not over heat), and let it stand until celery is tender. Meanwhile, remove the lid on the beans and continue to cook on low until the stock is thicker. When the beans and the ham stock are ready, pour together, draining the beans first to desired thickness. Add seasonings and return to heat to simmer for 30 minutes. Makes approximately 2½ gallons.

S.O.B.
SHRIMP, OYSTER & BEERHAUS

Little Rock

A Seafaring Feast

Baked Oysters S.O.B.*   Salad Boat with Garlic Dressing*

Deviled Crab*

Baked Potato or French Fries   Hushpuppies

BAKED OYSTERS S.O.B.

1 dozen fresh shucked oysters   **Cocktail sauce (your favorite)**
   on the half shell   **Parmesan cheese**
Lemon juice   **Bacon**

Squeeze lemon juice over oysters. Cover with cocktail sauce (your favorite or a combination of Heinz Ketchup, a dash of Worcestershire Sauce, a squeeze of lemon and prepared horseradish to taste). Sprinkle with Parmesan cheese. Place a 1" strip of bacon over oysters. Bake in the oven at 450° until the bacon is crisp. (May be broiled.)

GARLIC DRESSING

1 quart mayonnaise
4-6 large cloves, peeled and
   finely chopped
3 celery ribs, finely chopped

5 parsley sprigs, finely chopped
4 green onions, finely chopped
4 boiled eggs, finely chopped
¼ cup lemon juice

Place all ingredients in mixer or food processor until thoroughly blended. This is best when stored in the refrigerator for 3 days. It is excellent with spinach salad.

DEVILED CRAB
OR
CRAB STUFFING FOR ANY SEAFOOD

1 pound white fish (cod, perch,
   etc.)
2 pounds of yellow onions, chopped
3 ribs of celery, chopped
3 medium bell peppers, chopped
3 Tb. butter or margarine
2 ounces Worcestershire sauce
¼ cup chopped parsley
1 tsp. black pepper
1½ tsp. salt (or to taste)

¼ tsp. garlic powder
¼ tsp. dry mustard
1 pinch of crushed red pepper
1 twelve-ounce bag English muffins
½ loaf day-old bread
¾ pound snow or king crab meat
   or lump crab
1 egg, beaten
3 Tb. salad dressing
2 dozen crab shells

Cook fish in boiling water about 10 minutes. Drain and flake. Sauté onions, celery and bell peppers in butter until soft. Add Worcestershire sauce and spices and cook 2 minutes longer. Crumble muffins and bread. Cut crab into fine pieces. Mix breads, fish, sautéed vegetables and crab. Add egg and salad dressing. Mix thoroughly. Put 3 or 4 ounces of deviled crab mix into crab shells. Deep fry at 350° until brown (approximately 3 minutes), or bake at 350° approximately 15 minutes. If crab shells are not available, shape mixture into balls and deep fry or bake. Makes 2 dozen. Garnish with lemon wedges and parsley. This crab mix can also be used as a stuffing for any type seafood, such as fish, shrimp or lobster.

THE VILLA

Little Rock

A Fettuccini Dinner

Antipasto Tray
(Selection of Meats, Cheese, Olives, Peppers)

Salad

Fettuccini*

Bread   Marinated Mushrooms

FETTUCCINI

10-12 ounces green spinach noodles   1½ tsp. pepper
   (may substitute egg noodles)   1½ tsp. garlic powder
½ cup melted butter   1 tsp. parsley
2 cups whipping cream   ½ tsp. chicken base
2 cups grated Parmesan cheese

Boil green spinach noodles or egg noodles. Rinse and set aside. Melt butter in skillet. Add whipping cream. Mix and heat slightly. Add Parmesan cheese, pepper, garlic, parsley and chicken base. Stir with wire whisk or fork until creamy. Cook until cheese melts or it is boiling, stirring occasionally. Add noodles and mix until hot and creamy. More cheese can be added to make it thicker. Serves 4.

TORTA RISO (NORTHERN ITALY)

2¾ cups raw rice
9 average-size cloves of garlic,
  finely chopped
¾ cup olive oil (do not use
  vegetable oil)
¼ cup parsley flakes (fresh may
  be used)

2 cups grated Parmesan cheese
12 eggs, well beaten
Salt
Pepper

Cook rice according to package directions. In a small pan, lightly toast the chopped garlic in the olive oil. Remove pan from heat. Combine the parsley and Parmesan cheese with the beaten eggs. Mix well. To this mixture, add the garlic, olive oil and rice. Mix well. Add salt and pepper to taste. Mix again. Empty mixture into a 1 inch deep cookie sheet that has been lightly coated with olive oil. Distribute evenly in pan and pack down lightly with the back of a spoon. Bake at 400° about 35-40 minutes or until very lightly browned. Cool and cut into squares. These are best when served at room temperature. (Refrigeration changes the texture and alters flavor unfavorably.)

This recipe was one of my Grandmother Cassinelli's, who came to this country from Terminago in the Italian Alps.

Yield: 48

Andrea Davenport

CREAM CHEESE —THE INSTANT APPETIZER

The need for an instant appetizer or snack always seems to arise when the "cupboard is bare." The solution is a block of cream cheese and your favorite variety of snack crackers. There are as many possibilities as your imagination will allow. Use the following as a guide and add your own creative talents to get great results. You are guaranteed to get RAVE REVIEWS with little effort.

SEAFOOD SPREAD—Spread 1 small can of crab or shrimp over block of cream cheese. Cover this with your favorite cocktail sauce.
PICKAPEPPA SAUCE—Use a fork or a knife to make diagonal cuts in the cream cheese. These cuts only need to be ⅛ inch deep. Pour Pickapeppa Sauce over cream cheese.
PEPPER JELLY—The recipe for this versatile jelly can be found in the condiment section of RAVE REVIEWS. Spread the jelly over the block of cream cheese. Be sure to allow for jelly to go over the top and sides.
JEZEBEL SAUCE—This very special sauce is great spread over cream cheese. The recipe is in the condiment section of RAVE REVIEWS.
SPECIAL HINTS—The cream cheese will slice and spread better if it is at room temperature.

CHEESE BALL

8 ounces Velveeta cheese, grated
1 four-ounce package bleu cheese, crumbled
1 three-ounce package Philadelphia brand cream cheese

2½ ounces Cheddar cheese, grated
½ small onion, finely grated
1 Tb. parsley flakes
2 tsp. Worcestershire sauce
½ tsp. garlic powder
½ tsp. red pepper

Mix softened cheeses and other ingredients together. Shape into ball. Roll in parsley flakes, paprika, or finely chopped nuts. Serve with snack crackers.

Becki Vassar

DRIED BEEF CHEESE BALL

2 eight-ounce packages cream cheese
6 to 8 green onions, chopped
2 two and ½ ounce-jars Armour Dried Beef

2 to 3 tsp. Accent
1 tsp. Worcestershire sauce

Let cream cheese soften at room temperature. Chop onion and cut up dried beef into small pieces. Combine all ingredients using about ¾ of the beef. Roll ball in remaining ¼ beef for outside coating. Refrigerate. Serve with assorted crackers.

Variation: may add chopped ripe olives.

Judy Wilson
Susan Eanes

HAM BALL

4 cups ground baked ham
4 Tb. chopped sweet pickles
1 Tb. chopped onion
4 Tb. mayonnaise
1 tsp. Worcestershire

1 tsp. prepared mustard
1 tsp. chili powder
6 ounces cream cheese
1-3 Tb. cream

Grind enough cold baked ham to make 4 cups. Add pickles and onion. For easier blending, mix mayonnaise, mustard, Worcestershire and chili powder together. Add to ham mixture. Blend well, adding more mayonnaise if necessary. Chill several hours. Form into ball and spread with cream cheese which has been whipped until fluffy with a little cream. Keep both parts stiff enough so they will keep their shape in a warm room. Serve as a dip or spread.

Charlotte Lloyd

HAM CHEESE BALL

1 eight-ounce package cream cheese
½ cup Miracle Whip
2 cups ham, ground in blender

2 Tb. chopped parsley
1 Tb. chopped onion
1 cup chopped pecans

Mix softened cream cheese and Miracle Whip together. Add other ingredients. Place in refrigerator until firm. Shape into a ball and then roll in pecans. Serve with assorted crackers.

Serves 15-20   Carole Hoofman

JALAPEÑO CHEESE BALL

4 ounces Velveeta cheese
8 ounces cream cheese
1 roll Kraft Jalapeño cheese
1 roll Kraft Garlic cheese,
    spread or squeeze variety

½ tsp. garlic powder
½ tsp. chili powder
½ stick oleo
1 tsp. horseradish
1 jalapeño pepper

Let cheese and oleo stand until they reach room temperature. Chop jalapeño pepper reserving 1 slice for garnish. Mix all ingredients and form into a ball. Sprinkle with paprika and garnish with pepper slice. Serve with crackers. Better if prepared a few hours in advance.

Bobbie McKenzie

JALAPEÑO CHEESE SQUARES

½ stick butter
3 jalapeño peppers,
    chopped

1 pound sharp
    Cheddar cheese, grated
6 eggs, beaten

Mash and spread softened butter with fork over the bottom of an 8 x 8-inch square casserole. Layer peppers and cheese in dish so peppers are evenly distributed throughout the cheese. Pour beaten eggs over entire casserole. Bake at 350° for 30 minutes. Cut in squares. Serve warm.

Adjust amount of peppers to taste.

Serves 4-6   Carolyn Waddington

45

PINEAPPLE CHEESE BALL

2 eight-ounce packages cream cheese
1 eight-ounce can crushed pineapple,
   well-drained
1 cup chopped pecans
¼ cup chopped green pepper

2 Tb. green onion
   or dried onion flakes
1 tsp. Lawry's Seasoned Salt

Leave cream cheese out of refrigerator for about 2 hours so that it will be soft. Stir. Mix pineapple, ¾ cup of the pecans, green pepper, onion, and Seasoned Salt in large mixing bowl. Form two small balls or one large ball and roll in remaining pecans.

Variation: can be used as a spread

SHRIMP LOG

2-eight ounce packages of
   cream cheese
¼ cup chives

2 Tb. sour cream or mayonnaise
2 cups chopped shrimp, canned or
   fresh

Soften cream cheese and mix with other ingredients. Shape in form of a log. Roll in finely chopped pecans. Chill and serve with cocktail crackers.

Variation: Add Worcestershire sauce to taste.

Serves 20

Donna Bosley

SHRIMP BALL

2 large packages cream cheese
2 Tb. chili sauce or to taste
¼ tsp. salt
1 clove garlic, minced

2 ounces Bleu Cheese
1 can shrimp, minced
Paprika
Chopped nuts

Mix all ingredients together. Shape into a ball and roll in paprika. Roll in nuts. Let stand overnight.

Jo Johnson

ARTICHOKE DIP

1 fourteen-ounce can artichoke hearts,
   drained and chopped
1 cup mayonnaise

1 cup Parmesan cheese
Garlic powder to taste

Mix all ingredients. Heat in oven at 350° for 20 minutes. Spread on crackers. Mixture may be stored up to 12 hours in refrigerator before heating.

Mrs. James Mosley

BLACK-EYED PEA DIP

4 cups black-eyed peas, cooked
   and drained
5 jalapeño peppers
1 Tb. jalapeño juice
½ medium onion, chopped

4-ounce can green chilies
1 clove garlic
½ pound Old English
   sharp cheese
¼ pound butter

Mix black-eyed peas, jalapeño peppers and juice, onions, chilies and garlic in blender. Work with 1 to ¼ the measure at a time if the load is too much for the blender. Heat cheese and butter in double boiler until melted. Stir in pea mixture. Serve in chafing dish with chips. (Adjust peppers and chilies measurement to personal taste.)

Serves 25-30

Hazel Hurst

CHEESE DIP

1 pound sausage
1 pound ground beef
2 pounds Velveeta cheese

4 ounces taco sauce
1 ten and ¾-ounce can cream of
   mushroom soup

Cook sausage and ground beef. Drain. Melt Velveeta cheese. Stir in taco sauce and mushroom soup. Add meat and heat until warmed through.

Suzie Thompson

HOT CHEESE DIP WITH CRAB MEAT

1 pound box Velveeta cheese
¼ pound Kraft Old English cheese
1 can Ro-tel tomatoes and green
  peppers
1 tsp. onion juice

1 tsp. seasoned salt
1 garlic button (squeeze
  into sauce through
  garlic press)
1 six-and-½-ounce can crab meat

Melt cheese in double boiler. Add remaining ingredients except crab meat and mix well. Just before serving add crab meat.

Serves 12

Margaret Kennedy

JALAPEÑO CHEESE DIP

1 large onion
¼ cup jalapeño peppers or
  to taste
1 five-ounce can evaporated milk

1 pint Hellman's mayonnaise
2 pounds Velveeta

In blender, purée onion and peppers in the milk. Pour into a large mixing bowl and add mayonnaise and cheese. Beat with a mixer for 30 minutes. Heat in the microwave oven or double boiler before serving. Serve with corn chips.

This dip makes a lot and keeps up to 6 months in refrigerator. Also, it is very good used as a spread, if not heated.

Brenda Cerrato

CRAB MEAT DIP

8 ounces cream cheese
1 Tb. milk
1 six and ½-ounce can of crab meat
2 Tb. chopped onion

½ tsp. horseradish
¼ tsp. salt
Dash Tabasco sauce
⅓ cup toasted almonds

Blend all ingredients except almonds well. Spoon into oven-proof dish. Sprinkle with almonds. Bake at 375° for 15 minutes or until hot and bubbly.

Wanda Blodgett

CUCUMBER DIP

1 eight-ounce package cream cheese,
  softened
1 medium cucumber, chopped
½ small white onion, grated
1 eight-ounce carton sour cream

½ to 1 cup Miracle Whip
Dash of cayenne pepper
Dash of salt
Dash of green food coloring

In medium or large mixing bowl, blend all ingredients together on low speed of mixer until thoroughly blended. If using for finger sandwiches, lessen this amount. Food coloring depends on personal preference.

People who don't like cucumbers usually like this recipe.

Becky Witcher

CURRY DIP

1 cup mayonnaise
1 tsp. curry powder
1 tsp. dry horseradish
1 tsp. tarragon vinegar

Dash of Worcestershire
  sauce
Dash of garlic salt
Dash of onion salt

Mix all ingredients well. Cover and chill 12 hours. Serve with raw vegetables.

Serve 8

Mrs. Paul J. Moses

DELICIOUS COCKTAIL DIP

8 ounces cream cheese
1 two and ½-ounce jar dried beef,
  finely chopped
2 Tb. milk
2 Tb. finely chopped green
  pepper

2 Tb. instant minced
  onions
⅛ tsp. pepper
½ cup sour cream
¼ cup chopped walnuts
  or pecans

Blend all ingredients together except nuts. Put into 9-inch pie plate and sprinkle with nuts. Bake in 350° oven for 15 minutes. Serve on crackers.

49

DIP FOR RAW VEGETABLES

1 package Original Hidden Valley
  Ranch Dressing Mix
1 cup sour cream
1 cup mayonnaise
1 Tb. garlic powder

1 Tb. onion flakes
¾ Tb. dill weed
1 tsp. ground parsley or flakes
1 or 2 dashes Tabasco sauce

Mix all ingredients very well. Refrigerate for at least 1 hour. Suggested vegetables: cauliflower, celery sticks, carrot sticks, bell pepper strips and cucumbers. Dorito brand chips may be used.

Dip gets better as it sits and will keep well for at least a week.

Serves 10-15

Darby Blair

GOOD SEASONS ITALIAN DIP

½ pint sour cream
1 six-ounce package Good Seasons
  Italian Dressing Mix
1 Tb. mayonnaise

Juice of ½ lemon
½ avocado, finely chopped
½ tomato, chopped
Dash of Tabasco

Mix sour cream, dressing mix powder, and mayonnaise. Add lemon juice, avocado, tomato and Tabasco. Chill. Serve with chips, vegetables or crackers.

Donna Bosley

FIESTA APPETIZER PIE

3 avocados
1 Tb. lemon juice
1 eight-ounce carton sour cream
2 green onions

1 eight-ounce bottle of Mild
  Old El Paso Taco Sauce
6 ounces Monterey Jack cheese,
  grated

Mash avocados and mix with lemon juice. Spread across the bottom of a glass pie pan. Spread sour cream on top of avocados, extending the layer completely to the edge of the pan. Chop onions using 4 inches of green tops. Sprinkle this over the sour cream. Spread the taco sauce to cover the sour cream and onions completely. Top with grated cheese. Refrigerate a minimum of 6 hours. To serve, scoop portions onto individual plates and serve with chips or crackers.

Best if made the night before serving.

Serves 8

Michelle Kavanaugh

GUACAMOLE DIP

2 medium avocados, ripened
1 Tb. green chilies, chopped
1 Tb. onion juice or grated onion
2 tsp. lemon juice

½ tsp. salt
1 clove garlic, crushed
　or ⅛ tsp. garlic powder

Cut avocados in half; seed and peel. Sieve avocados or blend in an electric blender until smooth. Add remaining ingredients and blend well. Cover and chill. Makes about 1¼ cups. Serve as appetizer, meat accompaniment or salad. Top with chopped tomatoes, croutons, corn chips or Parmesan cheese.

Serves 4-6

Marcella Nofziger

MEXICO CHIQUITO CHEESE DIP

½ cup oleo
4 Tb. flour
1 heaping tsp. paprika
1 heaping tsp. salt
¼ tsp. dry mustard
1 tsp. chili powder
½ tsp. cumin powder

1 Tb. catsup
1 tsp. jalapeño juice
1 pod jalapeño pepper, chopped
2 cups milk
1 clove garlic
8 ounces Velveeta cheese

Mix oleo and flour to paste in a double boiler. Add remaining ingredients and bring to a boil. You may use more jalapeño peppers for a hotter dip. Serve with chips.

Serves 8-10

MEXICAN PIZZA DIP

2 Ten and ½-ounce cans bean dip
3 medium ripe avocados
¼ tsp. pepper
½ tsp. salt
½ cup lemon juice
1 cup sour cream
½ cup mayonnaise

1 package taco seasoning
½ bunch green onions
3 medium tomatoes
2 four and ¼-ounce cans ripe
　olives, chopped
½ cup shredded
　Cheddar cheese

Use a 9 x 12-inch pan. Spread bean dip evenly over bottom of container. Mix together mashed avocados, pepper, salt and lemon juice. Spread over bean dip. Mix together sour cream, mayonnaise and seasonings and spread over avocado mixture. Cut up green onions, olives and tomatoes. Sprinkle over top of sour cream mixture. Sprinkle with Cheddar cheese. Serve with chips.

Nedra Wood

51

SHRIMP DIP

1 large package cream cheese
Juice of 1 lemon
1 medium onion, finely chopped
  with juice

3 heaping Tb. mayonnaise
1 tsp. Worchestershire sauce
1 can shrimp, drained

Using electric mixer, cream softened cheese. Add lemon juice, onion, mayonnaise and Worcestershire sauce. Stir in shrimp. Refrigerate for 1 hour. Serve with king-sized Fritos.

Francille Turbyfill

TAMALE DIP

1 medium onion, chopped
1 pound Velveeta cheese
1 fifteen-ounce can chili without beans

1 thirteen and ½-ounce jar Derby Brand
  tamales, chopped

Sauté onion in butter. Drain off butter. Add cheese, chili and chopped tamales. Heat thoroughly. Serve in a crock pot to keep warm. Serve with Fritos or Doritos.

Serves 6

Valarie Garland

WATER CHESTNUT DIP

1 eight-ounce can water chestnuts,
  chopped
1 cup sour cream
1 cup mayonnaise
1 Tb. soy sauce

3 or 4 green onions, including tops,
  chopped
2 or 3 dashes of Lea and Perrin
  Tabasco sauce
Salt to taste

Drain water chestnuts. Mix all ingredients together and refrigerate.

Atheta Ball

HOT SAUCE

1 twenty-eight-ounce can Hunts
   tomatoes
2 cloves garlic or garlic powder
   to taste
¼ tsp. salt

¼ tsp. minced onion
1 or 2 fresh jalapeño
   peppers, chopped

Drain tomatoes. Put juice from tomatoes and all other ingredients into blender. Blend for about 30 seconds. Add tomatoes and just turn blender on and then off. Let stand in refrigerator for a couple of hours to season.

Great with any kind of chips!

Vikki Koch

BAKED STUFFED MUSHROOMS

1 pound large mushrooms (fresh)
½ stick butter
½ tsp. garlic salt
¼ tsp. pepper

1 tsp. parsley
2 Tb. seasoned bread crumbs
2 Tb. grated mozzarella cheese

Wash the mushrooms well, remove stems and chop the stems fine. Sauté the stems in 2 Tbs. butter. Sprinkle with garlic salt and pepper. Add parsley and bread crumbs to make a light stuffing. Fill the mushroom caps with the stuffing. Melt remaining butter in baking dish. Place stuffed mushroom caps in melted butter. Sprinkle caps with cheese and bake 350° for 10 to 15 minutes. Do not overcook. Cheese should be melted and lightly browned.

Serves 8

Sandra Cook

CURRIED MUSHROOMS

1 Tb. instant minced onion or
   ¼ cup finely chopped onion
1 Tb. curry powder
2 Tb. lemon juice

½ cup salad oil
1-½ cups button mushrooms,
   drained

In fruit jar combine onion, curry powder and lemon juice. Add oil. Shake well to mix. Put mushrooms or olives in a large jar. Pour curry mixture over them. Cover and refrigerate at least 3 days for mellow flavor. Drain before serving.

Variation: Substitute green olives for mushrooms.

Serves 6-8

Wanda Blodgett

STUFFED MUSHROOMS

36 small fresh mushrooms
½ cup butter, melted
Garlic powder to taste
¾ cup Monterey Jack Cheese

1 package toasted onion dip mix
1 Tb. soy sauce
2 Tb. dry red wine
1 two and ¾-ounce package Fritos,
   finely crushed

Remove stems. Wash, pat dry and brush caps with part of melted butter. Combine rest of butter with garlic powder. Add cheese and onion dip mix. Mix well. Add soy sauce, wine and corn chips. Fill mushroom caps with paste. Place on cookie sheet and broil only about 3 minutes.

Serves 9-12

Saundra Hatch

STUFFED MUSHROOMS WITH BACON

1 pound fresh mushrooms
1 eight ounce package of cream cheese, softened
1 twelve to sixteen ounce package bacon

Quickly rinse mushrooms under cold running water. Remove stems (save for soup or other dishes). Fry bacon until crisp. Crumble into softened cream cheese. Fill each mushroom cap with bacon cream cheese mixture. Bake at 350° on cookie sheet for approximately 15 minutes. Turn on broiler for a second to brown if necessary.

Serve Hot!!! These can be made ahead and baked at the last minute.

Variation: May substitute sausage and Cheddar cheese for bacon and cream cheese.

Ginger Bailey

FROSTED NUTS

1 cup sugar
½ cup sour cream
1 Tb. light corn syrup

1 Tb. butter
½ Tb. vanilla
2 cups nuts, halves or large pieces

Bring first three ingredients to a soft boil. Using a candy thermometer, boil until mixture reaches a firm ball stage. Add butter and vanilla. Cool. Beat and add nuts, coating each nut well with candy. Place on waxed paper and separate with fork or fingers when cool. Lay out until completely cooled and firm. It sometimes takes overnight to cool.

Serves 12

Agnes G. Dean

GLAZED PECANS

3 Tb. light karo syrup
¼ cup vegetable oil

1 quart pecan halves
Salt

Preheat oven to 300°. Heat karo and oil in cast iron skillet. Stir to mix. Add pecans and stir thoroughly. Place skillet in oven and bake for 35 minutes. Stir occasionally. Remove from oven and place pecans on wax paper. Separate pecans and salt thoroughly. These become crisp as they cool.

Serves 10-12   Atheta Ball

GRANOLA

1 tsp. cinnamon
¼ tsp. salt
2½ cups old-fashioned oats
½ cup coconut
½ cup chopped nuts
¼ cup sesame seeds

½ cup brown sugar, firmly packed
1 tsp. vanilla
½ cup honey
2 Tb. water
½ cup raisins

Mix all dry ingredients in a large mixing bowl. Mix all liquids in a small bowl. Combine mixtures and blend thoroughly. Spread on a cookie sheet and bake at 300° for approximately 30 minutes, until light brown. Stir occasionally while baking. Remove from oven and add ½ cup raisins. After cooling, store in a tightly covered container.

"May be served as a cereal"

Yield: 5-6 cups   Marcella Nofziger

NIX-NAX PARTY MIX

1 stick oleo
½ cup bacon drippings
2 Tbs. Worcestershire sauce
1 tsp. garlic salt
1 tsp. celery salt
1 tsp. seasoned salt
1 tsp. red pepper

½ twelve-ounce box Wheat Chex
½ twelve-ounce box Rice Chex
½ twelve-ounce box Cheerios
1 ten-ounce box pretzels, broken
1 seven-ounce can peanuts
2 cups pecan halves

Melt oleo and bacon drippings in sauce pan. Add seasonings and simmer. Mix cereal and nuts together in large roaster pan. Pour oleo mixture over cereal mixture and mix gently. Heat at 250° for 1 hour. Stir every 20 minutes.

Mary Anne Salmon

PARTY NUTS

1 cup sugar
½ cup water

2 cups raw peanuts
Pam

Mix sugar and water. Add nuts and cook in a skillet until water is gone. Spray a cookie sheet with Pam. Bake 20 minutes at 300°.

Madeline Johnson

CAJUN MISTAKES

1 pound ground beef
1 pound hot pork sausage
1 pound Velveeta cheese
1 tsp. oregano
Salt
Pepper
Tabasco to taste

Garlic salt
Lemon pepper
Accent
Dash of Worcestershire sauce
Melba Rounds, garlic
 or plain

Brown ground beef and sausage. Drain all grease. Stir in cheese until it melts. Add seasonings. Mound mixture on Melba Rounds. At this point Melba Rounds may be frozen on cookie sheets and then transferred to plastic bag for cooking at a later date. To cook, place in preheated 400° oven. Heat until bubbly.

Variation: Substitute nachos or English muffins for Melba Rounds.

Ann Carruth Logan

CUCUMBER SANDWICHES

3 cucumbers, sliced
1 Tb. vinegar
Water
Salt and peper to taste

½ onion, sliced
1 eight-ounce package cream cheese,
 softened
½ to 1 cup mayonnaise

Soak sliced cucumbers in vinegar, water, salt, pepper and onions for 1 to 2 hours or overnight. Remove ½ cup of onions and cucumbers from liquid. Put in blender and puree. Combine this mixture with cream cheese and mayonnaise. Mix until of spreading consistency. If too thick, add juice from cucumbers to thin. Spread over bread. Place cucumbers on 4 corners, and cut in fourths. Place between damp cloths in closed container. Refrigerate.

Yield: 32

Marcella Nofziger

HOMEMADE PARTY SALAMI

2 pounds ground beef
2 tsp. liquid smoke
⅛ tsp. garlic powder
2 to 3 Tb. Quick Salt (cure salt)

½ tsp. mustard seed
½ cup water
½ tsp. coarse ground pepper

1st morning: Mix all ingredients together by hand in large mixing bowl. Cover and refrigerate.

2nd and 3rd mornings: Mix again and set back in refrigerator.

4th morning: Mix again and form into 2 small rolls. Bake on broiler pan for 8 hours at 150°.

Cure in refrigerator 2 more days.

This is great served as summer sausage would be. Serve with cheese and crackers. This freezes well.

Serves 24   Ann Wittkamp

OLIVE-TUNA CANAPÉ SPREAD

1 cup creamed cottage cheese
1 six and ½-ounce can tuna, drained
½ cup stuffed olives, chopped
2 Tb. chopped green onions

2 Tb. chopped celery
2 Tb. mayonnaise
¼ cup chopped pecans
Salt and pepper to taste

Mix all ingredients for a delicious sandwich, salad or canapé.

Eloise Evans

PARTY RYE BREAD

1 cup Hellman's mayonnaise
2 cups grated sharp Cheddar cheese
1 two and ½-ounce can ripe olives,
   chopped

2 Tb. chopped onion
Bacon bits

Mix all ingredients together. Spread on party rye bread. Sprinkle top with bacon bits. Bake at 300° for 15 to 20 minutes.

Irma Dumas

PATÉ

1 eight-ounce roll Braunschweiger
1 eight-ounce package cream cheese,
  softened
¼ cup finely chopped onion

6 slices bacon, cooked and crumbled
2 Tb. minced parsley
2 tsp. Worcestershire sauce

Combine Braunschweiger and cream cheese until well blended. Add onion, bacon, parsley and Worchestershire sauce. Mix well. Serve on party rye bread. Paté improves if refrigerated at least one day before serving.

Yield: 2 cups

Mrs. Forrest Penny

PIZZA SPREAD

2 eight-ounce packages cream cheese
1 cup seafood cocktail sauce
2 four and ¼-ounce cans small shrimp
2 green onions, chopped

2 green peppers, chopped
1 cup mushrooms, chopped
1 cup ripe olives, chopped
6 ounces mozzarella cheese, grated

Slice cream cheese and place on large plate. Smooth to form a crust. Layer remaining ingredients in order listed. Chill and serve with crackers.

Variation: may also add layers of fresh tomatoes and top with Parmesan cheese and paprika.

Jean Edwards

SMOKEY SALMON CHEESE SPREAD

8 ounces softened cream cheese
2 drops Liquid Smoke
4½-ounce can flaked salmon,
  reserve liquid

3 Tb. thinly sliced green onions
2 Tb. thinly sliced celery
½ cup finely chopped parsley

Blend cream cheese with Liquid Smoke and salmon liquid. Stir in onions and celery. Fold in salmon. Refrigerate at least 4 hours. Shape into a ball and roll in parsley. Serve with assorted crackers.

E. G. Finch

HOT SPICED MEAT BALLS

MEAT BALLS:

¾ to 1 pound ground beef
¾ cup fine dry bread crumbs
1½ Tb. minced onion
½ tsp. prepared horseradish

3 drops Tabasco sauce
2 eggs, beaten
¾ tsp. salt
½ tsp. pepper

Combine ingredients. Form into small meat balls the size of a heaping teaspoonful. Cook in hot skillet. Pour off drippings.

SAUCE:

¾ cup catsup
½ cup water
¼ cup vinegar
1 tsp. dry mustard
1½ tsp. salt

1 Tb. onion, minced
2 Tb. brown sugar
2 tsp. Worcestershire sauce
¼ tsp. pepper
3 drops Tabasco

Mix all ingredients. Pour over cooked meat balls. Cover and cook 10 minutes. Stir occasionally. Serve hot.

Colleen Wallace

DRUNKEN MEAT BALLS

3 pounds ground beef
1 large onion, grated
Salt and pepper to taste
Garlic powder to taste

¼ cup water
1 fourteen-ounce bottle catsup
1 twelve-ounce can beer

Combine meat and seasonings. Form into bite-sized balls. Heat water, catsup and beer in saucepan. Carefully drop balls into liquid. Boil slowly for 1 hour. Serve in sauce in chafing dish.

Yield: 50-55 meatballs

Pat Stanger

SAUSAGE BALLS

3 cups Bisquick
1 pound hot sausage
1 ten-ounce package Cheddar cheese, grated
1 tsp. minced onion

1 tsp. garlic powder
1 tsp. oregano
1 tsp. black pepper
1 Tb. Worcestershire sauce
2 Tb. parsley flakes

Mix all ingredients thoroughly and roll into small balls. Place on greased baking sheet and bake 15 to 18 minutes at 375°. Serve warm.

Yield: 100 Balls

Becki Vassar

SWEET AND SOUR MEATBALLS

MEATBALLS:

3 pounds ground beef
3 cups soft bread crumbs
3 eggs
¾ cup onion

3 Tb. parsley
1 Tb. salt
1 tsp. pepper

SAUCE:

1 sixteen-ounce jar apricot preserves   ¾ cup hot barbecue sauce

Mix first seven ingredients together and form into small meatballs. Brown meatballs in large skillet. Put browned meatballs in a 9 x 13-inch baking pan. Mix apricot preserves and barbecue sauce and pour over meatballs. Bake at 350° uncovered for 30 minutes. Serve hot in chafing dish.

Ann Cornwell

COCKTAIL WEINERS

1 twelve-ounce jar plum jam
1 cup mustard

2 packages all-beef weiners

Cook and stir jam and mustard over medium heat until jam is dissolved. Slice weiners into bite-sized pieces. Add to jam mixture and heat. To serve, place in serving bowl on warming tray and use cocktail toothpicks.

Sheila Hammonds

HOT DOGS

3 pounds hot dogs
1¼ cups brown sugar
32 ounces catsup

3 Tb. minced onions
1½ cups vinegar

Slice hot dogs crosswise and drop in pan with other ingredients that have been mixed and heated. Let simmer at least 1 hour. To serve, leave meat in liquid and use toothpicks.

Serves 30   Nedra Wood

LITTLE LINKS IN ORIENTAL SAUCE

1 cup firmly packed brown
   sugar
3 Tb. flour
2 tsp. dry mustard
1 cup pineapple juice
½ cup vinegar

1½ tsp. soy sauce
2 one-pound packages
   little wieners
2 one-pound packages
   cocktail smoked sausages

Combine brown sugar, flour and mustard in saucepan. Add pineapple juice, vinegar and soy sauce. Heat to boiling, stirring constantly. Boil 1 minute. Add weiners and sausages. Stir. Cook slowly 5 minutes or until heated thoroughly. Keep warm in a chafing dish over low heat. To serve, use wooden toothpicks.

Yield: 64

CHEESE KRISPIES

2 sticks butter or margarine
2 cups grated cheese
2 cups flour
¼ tsp. salt

¼ tsp. onion salt
¼ tsp. white pepper
⅛ tsp. red pepper
2 cups Rice Krispies

Cream butter and cheese. Add flour and other ingredients. Mix thoroughly. Put Rice Krispies in last. Make into marble-size balls. Place on ungreased cookie sheet and mash with a fork. Bake at 325° 10-15 minutes or until lightly browned. Store in air tight container.

These freeze well.

Variation: substitute 1 cup of cheese with a 6-ounce roll of Kraft Jalapeño Cheese.

Yield: 3 to 4 dozen   Carol Williamson
                                                          Bobbie McKenzie

CHEESE PUFFS

1 cup butter or oleo
4 cups Cracker Barrel Sharp
   cheese, shredded

2 cups flour
1 tsp. salt
½ tsp. paprika

Cream butter and add cheese. Mix well. Add flour, salt and paprika. Mix and shape into marble size balls. Freeze on a cookie sheet. After freezing, place in containers. Defrost ½ hour. Bake 15 minutes at 350°. If cooked straight from freezer, the cooking time will be longer.

Variation: Wrap 1 tsp. mixture around stuffed green olives.

Pam Gustavus

CHINESE EGG ROLL CRÊPES

2 Tb. oleo
1 green onion, chopped
1 cup chopped celery
2 Tb. soy sauce
1 cup chopped bean sprouts
8 ounces of shrimp, chicken or pork

1 Tb. corn starch
2 Tb. cold water
1 egg, beaten
1 recipe basic crêpe batter

Sauté chopped onion and celery in oleo until slightly tender. Add soy sauce, chopped bean sprouts and shrimp, chicken or pork. Mix well. Combine water and corn starch. Pour into saucepan and stir. Add beaten egg and cook until thick. Remove from heat. Place ¼ cup of mixture into each crêpe. Brush with egg and water mixture. After folding and sealing edges, fry in hot oil until golden brown. Drain. Serve with hot mustard or sweet and sour sauce.

Serves 10

Cathy Simpson

CHICKEN LIVER AND
WATER CHESTNUT HORS D'OEUVRE

½ pound chicken livers
¼ cup soy sauce
1 clove garlic minced

15 slices of bacon, cut in half
1 five-ounce can (⅔) cup
   water chestnuts, cut in thirds

Marinate chicken liver pieces in mixture of soy sauce and garlic for 3 hours at room temperature or overnight in refrigerator. Wrap a piece of water chestnut and a piece of chicken liver with a half slice of bacon. Secure with toothpick. Place on broiler pan and cook, turning occasionally, at 425° about 25 minutes or until bacon is crisp.

Variation: Marinate whole water chestnuts and cook them without the chicken livers.

Yields: 30

Susan Plunkett

Beverages

BERMUDA CRUSH

4 ounces pineapple juice
2 ounces orange juice
2 ounces grapefruit juice
2 ounces cream of coconut (Coco Lopez)

4 ounces white rum
1 ounce grenadine
Crushed ice to the level of the mix

Mix and serve in a tall glass.

Serves 4   Rosemary Russell

BRANDIED CIDER

1 orange
1 lemon
1½ quarts unsweetened apple cider
   (forty-eight-ounce bottle)

3 cinnamon sticks
1 Tb. cloves
1 Tb. allspice
Peach brandy

Slice orange and lemon in rings. Place spices in cheesecloth bag or prepare to strain. Add all ingredients except brandy to crockpot. Turn to low setting. Let simmer for at least 2 hours. Flavor is enhanced by additional time in crockpot. When ready to serve, pour jigger of peach brandy into cup and fill with cider.

Especially nice for winter holiday meals, as the spices impart a wonderful fragrance to kitchen. Any remaining cider may be refrigerated and reheated or served without brandy over ice.

Serves 10-12   Betty Pullam

D.J.'s DELIGHT

3 ounces Kahlua
1½ ounces light crème de cacao
1 tsp. instant coffee

Vanilla ice cream
Nutmeg

In blender add Kahlua, crème de cacao, and coffee. Fill blender with ice cream and blend thoroughly. It probably will be necessary to add more ice cream and blend more. Mixture should be thick. Serve in martini glasses and lightly sprinkle nutmeg over top.

Once you try this, you'll always use it to follow a heavy meal at your dinner party.

Serves 5-6   Joyce Hall
                                                          Deborah Carmen

65

EGGNOG

12 eggs, separated	1 cup brandy
1½ cups sugar	1 quart whole milk
1 tsp. vanilla	1½ pints heavy cream
½ tsp. ground nutmeg	6 Tb. sugar
¾ cup Jamaican rum	Ground nutmeg

Beat yolks until light. Add sugar, vanilla, and nutmeg. Beat well. Place in bowl. Add rum gradually, stirring constantly. Add brandy and continue to stir until wellblended. Let mixure stand overnight, stirring occasionally. Add milk and cream a little at a time. Beat egg whites with 6 Tb. sugar. Fold in. Sprinkle ground nutmeg and serve.

Serves 40   Florene Tyler

FOG CUTTER

1 ounce lime juice	1 ounce vodka
1 ounce orange juice	1 ounce brandy
1 ounce pineapple juice	1 ounce gin
*1½ ounce simple syrup	1 ounce rum
1½ ounce orgeat syrup	

*Simple syrup can be bought as bar syrup or made by heating ½ cup water to ½ cup sugar.

Combine all ingredients in a shaker or small pitcher. Blend, shake, or stir well. Serve over ice cubes and decorate with fruit if desired. For a sweeter taste, add more simple syrup.

Serves 1-2   Joanne Ellison

FRUIT PUNCH TROPICANA

1 twelve-ounce can frozen orange juice	1½ twelve-ounce cans water
1 twelve-ounce can frozen lemonade	1 quart strawberries, fresh or frozen
1 fifteen-ounce can crushed pineapple	Ginger ale
2 or 3 large bananas	Red food coloring

Thaw frozen juices and strawberries. Combine pineapple, bananas, and strawberries in blender, using water to aid blending. Mix all ingredients except ginger ale in a punch bowl. Dilute punch with ginger ale about half and half before serving. Add food coloring to reach desired color.

Serves 25-30   Edwina Whalen

FROZEN MARGARITAS

1 six-ounce can frozen limeade
Juice from 3 limes
1 cup tequila

⅓ cup Triple Sec
¼ cup sugar
Ice

Pour above ingredients into blender. Fill with ice until blender is ⅔ full. Blend until well-blended and ice is crushed. Squeeze lime around rims of glasses, and then turn glasses upside down into a thin layer of salt to salt rim. Pour liquid into glasses. Store unused portion in freezer.

Serves 8   Susan Eanes

GLÖGG — TRADITIONAL CHRISTMAS PARTY PUNCH

3 cups water
1½ cups sugar
In cheesecloth bag:
    10 open cardamon seeds
    10 whole cloves
    Thin peel of 1 lemon
1 cinnamon stick

½ cup golden raisins
1 cup almonds
1 six-ounce package dried apricots
¼ small ginger root
1 large bottle dry red wine
2 cups brandy

Heat water and sugar to boil. Put in a crockpot on low; add cheesecloth bag with spices and peels. Continue by adding cinnamon, raisins, almonds, fruit, ginger, and liquids. Heat slowly for 8 hours. Serve warm in punch cups or wine glasses with spoon to eat fruits.

Serves 12-16   Signa Bodisbaugh

GOLDEN SUMMER PUNCH

3 cups sugar
3 cups water
1 six-ounce can frozen lemonade

1 twelve-ounce can frozen orange juice
1 forty-six-ounce can pineapple juice
2 quarts ginger ale

Boil sugar and water for 7 minutes. Set aside to cool. Mix lemonade, orange juice, and pineapple. Stir in syrup mixture when ready to serve. Add ginger ale.

Serves 30   Francille Turbyfill

Use grated lemon rind instead of juice to flavor tea. Serve rind in a dish and let each person help himself.

HOT BUTTERED RUM

1 one-pound box Fleischmann's
  margarine
1 one-pound box brown sugar
1 one-pound box powdered sugar
2 tsp. ground cinnamon

2 tsp. ground nutmeg
1 one-quart vanilla ice cream, softened
Rum
Whipped cream or Cool Whip
Cinnamon sticks

Combine margarine, sugar and spices; beat until light and fluffy. Add ice cream, stirring until well blended. Spoon mixture into a 2-quart freezer container. Freeze. To serve, thaw slightly. Place 3 Tb. margarine mixture and 1 jigger of rum into a large mug; fill with boiling water. Stir well. Top with whipped cream and serve with a cinnamon stick. Unused margarine mixture may be refrozen.

Serves 25

Sue Moore

HOT CHOCOLATE

1 eight-quart size box Carnation
  powdered milk
1 six-ounce jar Coffeemate

1 one-pound box Nestle's Quick
1¼ cups powdered sugar

Mix all the ingredients together. Keep in a plastic container. When ready to serve, use ½ cup mix to 1 cup boiling water.

Serves 15

Pam Gustavus

HOT MULLED PARTY PUNCH

1½ quarts cranberry juice
2 quarts apple juice or cider
½ cup brown sugar

½ tsp. salt
4 cinnamon sticks
1½ tsp. whole cloves

Pour fruit juices into 30-cup coffee maker. Place the remaining ingredients in the basket. Plug in coffee maker and perk. Add sugar to pot if more is desired.

Serves 20-25

Marianne Gosser

Orange marmalade is a tasty sweetener for a cup of hot tea.

HOT SPICED CIDER

1 gallon apple cider (not apple juice)   **½ tsp. allspice**
1 six-ounce package red hots   **3 cinnamon sticks**
½ tsp. nutmeg

Warm cider in Dutch oven. Add red hots and stir until dissolved. Add other ingredients in order given. Mixture may be kept in refrigerator and reheated.

Children love it!

Serves 25

Brenda Cerrato
Dallas, Texas

KAHLUA

4 cups water   **1 chopped vanilla bean**
4 cups sugar   **1 fifth of vodka**
¾ cup instant coffee

Boil sugar and water for 10 minutes. Cool. Add the next 3 ingredients. Put mixture into a container with a top. Let stand for 3 weeks. Shake daily.

Serves 12-15

Nancy Peters
Ft. Smith, Ark.

MILK PUNCH

1½ gallons milk   **1 fifth bourbon**
1½ gallons vanilla ice cream   **Nutmeg**

Put ice cream into punch bowl and break into several pieces with a spoon. Pour in bourbon and then milk. Stir to mix. Sprinkle with nutmeg.

Serves 15

Wanda Blodgett
Sylvia Cavin

If instant tea crystals have turned to solid rock, put a slice of fresh bread in the jar and leave overnight.

ORANGE FLIP (ENERGY DRINK)

2 heaping Tb. orange juice
   concentrate
1-2 tsp. honey (more or less to taste)
2 tsp. wheat germ

1-2 eggs
1 tsp. vanilla
½ cup milk and 5-8 ice cubes
   or ice cream to desired consistency

Blend ingredients in a blender for 40-90 seconds, until malt-like.

Good for breakfast or as a pick-me-up between meals.

Variation: Grapefruit concentrate or pineapple concentrate can be sub-stituted for orange juice concentrate.

Serves 1-2

Marcella Nofziger

ORANGE JULIUS

1 six-ounce can frozen orange juice
1 cup milk
1 cup water

½ cup sugar
1 tsp. vanilla
11-12 ice cubes

Combine all ingredients in blender. Cover and blend until smooth, about 30 seconds.

Serves 6

Marsha Elliot

SANGRIA

2 fifths Burgundy
1 six-ounce can orange juice
   concentrate

2 quarts club soda
Approximately 1 cup sugar
Ice ring (optional)

Chill wine and club soda. Mix fruit juice with wine. Add club soda and sugar. Pour over ice ring and serve.

Ice ring: Mix orange juice and strawberries or other fruits in ring mold; freeze.

Rosemary Russell

To remove mineral rings from inside glass coffee pots, fill with 3 parts vinegar to 1 part water. Let stand until ring dissolves.

SPICED TEA

12 cups water:
In cheesecloth bag:
   3 sticks cinnamon
   2 Tb. whole cloves
   2 Tb. whole allspice
5 regular tea bags

1½ cups sugar
Juice of 3 lemons
Juice of 3 oranges
2 twelve-ounce cans unsweetened
   pineapple juice

Bring water to boil in a large pot. Tie spices in 8-inch square of cheesecloth. Drop into boiling water and continue to let water boil for 15 minutes. Remove from heat and put in tea bags. Cover and steep for 5 minutes. Remove tea bags and spice bag. Stir in sugar and juices. Store in glass jar in refrigerator. Heat to serve.

Serves 15-20

Mary Jo Oliver

RUM WASSAIL

1 cup sugar
In cheesecloth bag:
   1 tsp. ground allspice
   20 whole cloves
   8 sticks cinnamon
4 cups cranberry juice

4 twelve-ounce cans frozen apple
   juice concentrate, diluted
   according to directions
   on can
1 cup rum (optional)

Tie allspice, cloves, and cinnamon together in cheesecloth. Combine sugar and juices in 2-gallon container and simmer for 30 minutes. Remove spice bag and add rum just before serving.

Serves 30

Jo Cobb

BLOODY MARYS

3 quarts tomato juice
3 cups vodka
⅓ cup steak sauce
¼ cup Worcestershire sauce
2½ Tb. salt

3 tsp. sugar
½ tsp. hot sauce
Juice of 12 limes
Lime slices
Celery sticks

Combine first 8 ingredients, stirring well. Pour into punch bowl. Float lime slices on top. To serve, pour Bloody Marys into ice-filled glasses and garnish with celery sticks.

Yield: 4 quarts
Serves 20-25

Ann Cornwell

Breads

CRESCENT ROLLS

1 cake yeast	2 eggs
3 Tb. warm water	½ cup raw brown sugar
½ cup shortening	4 cups unbleached flour
1 tsp. salt	Soft butter
1 cup boiling water	

Dissolve yeast in warm water; set aside. Place shortening and salt in boiling water. Let stand until lukewarm. Beat eggs and mix in sugar. Add water mixture to eggs. Add yeast. Stir in 2 cups flour and beat well. Gradually add remaining flour. Place in bowl and cover. Refrigerate overnight. Round out dough in shaped wedges. Brush dough with softened butter, starting at wide end. Let rise three hours on cookie sheet. Bake at 400° for 6-10 minutes.

Yield: 24-36 rolls
Terri Caple

DILLY BREAD

1 package active dry yeast	2 tsp. dill
¼ cup warm water	1 tsp. salt
1 cup creamed cottage cheese	¼ tsp. soda
2 Tb. sugar	1 egg, unbeaten
1 Tb. butter	2¼ to 2½ cups flour

Soften yeast in water. Combine in mixing bowl creamed cottage cheese, sugar, butter, dill, salt, soda, egg, and softened yeast. Add flour to form a stiff dough. Cover and let rise until light and double in size (about an hour). Stir dough down and turn into well-greased loaf pan or 2-quart casserole. Let rise again. Bake at 350° for 45 minutes.

Charlotte Murray

HOMEMADE ROLLS

1 package of yeast	3 Tb. cooled, melted shortening
2 cups lukewarm water	or liquid shortening
½ cup sugar	4½ - 4¾ cups flour
1 tsp. salt	

Dissolve yeast in 2 cups lukewarm water. Add ½ cup sugar, 1 tsp. salt, and 3 Tb. shortening. Stir. Add flour gradually, beating as you add. When enough flour has been added, the mixture turns loose from side of the bowl. Pour out on floured board and knead a few times. Place in greased bowl, cover and let rise 2 hours. Knead again, roll out and cut with cookie cutter. Place on greased pan, fold over and brush with butter. Let rise about 2 more hours. Bake at 425° until brown, about 10 minutes.

Yield: 36
Sue Dean

MONKEY BREAD

1 package dry yeast
¼ cup warm water
1 tsp. sugar
1 egg
½ cup sugar

¼ cup vegetable oil
1 tsp. salt
1 cup water
4½ cups flour
1 stick oleo

Dissolve 1 package dry yeast in ¼ cup warm water. Add 1 tsp. sugar. Let rise while preparing the remainder. Beat 1 egg; add to it sugar, vegetable oil, and salt. Add yeast and 1 cup water. Add approximately 4½ cups flour, until it makes a stiff dough. Knead dough. Cover and let rise, or put in the refrigerator overnight to rise. When dough has doubled in size, punch down and let rest a few minutes. Roll dough out and cut into strips. Drip each strip into melted oleo. Place the strips in a Bunt pan and pour the remaining oleo on top. Let rise for about 30-45 minutes. Bake at 350° for 20-25 minutes or until brown on top.

Serves 6-8

Susan Plunkett

REFRIGERATOR ROLLS

1 cup shortening
½ cup sugar
1 heaping tsp. salt
2 cups water

2 eggs
6 cups flour
2 packages yeast

Dissolve yeast in 1 cup of warm water. Set aside. Pour 1 cup boiling water over shortening, sugar and salt. Set aside. When these mixtures have cooled, mix together and add eggs. Add flour, 1 cup at a time. Dough may require hand mixing. Put into greased mixing bowl. Spread a thin coat of oil on dough and cover bowl loosely with damp cloth. Place in refrigerator for at least 3 hours before using. Remove part of dough, place on floured surface and roll out. Cut in 3-inch circles. Brush circles with warm melted butter, and place on cookie sheet or in greased muffin tins to rise (about 3 hours). Bake 8 to 10 minutes at 400°. These rolls can be rolled out the night before and removed from refrigerator to rise at least 4 hours before baking.

Gerrie Fletcher

When making bread, grease bowls and pans with butter or shortening, not oil.

SIMPLE CROISSANTS

1 package yeast	⅓ cup sugar
1 cup warm water	½ stick oleo, melted
1 cup flour	1½ tsp. salt
¾ cup Pet milk	4 cups flour
1 egg	2 sticks oleo

Dissolve yeast in water, and mix with next six ingredients. Put 4 cups flour and 2 sticks of cold oleo into bowl. With pastry blender cut in butter until size of kidney beans. Add yeast mixture and stir to mix. Cover tight and refrigerate 4 hours or longer. Take out and divide into 4 parts. On a floured surface, roll each part into a 17-inch circle. Cut into 8 wedges. Roll, starting from broad end. Let rise on ungreased sheets about 1 hour. Brush top with 1 egg and mix with 1 tablespoon of water. Bake at 350° for 30 minutes.

Gerrie Fletcher
Pine Bluff, Ark.

WHOLE WHEAT BREAD WITH HONEY

2 cups unbleached all-purpose flour	3 Tb. honey
1 cup whole wheat flour	1 package active dry yeast
1 tsp. salt	1 cup warm water (110°)

Preheat oven to 375°. Oil large bowl and 1 loaf pan with unsaturated cooking oil. Combine 2 cups unbleached flour and 1 cup whole wheat flour. Put 2 cups of flour mixture into the bowl of the food processor, using the steel knife. Add salt, honey, and yeast. Gradually add water with the machine running. Dough will be gooey. Next add half of remaining flour, turning processor on and off. Continue to add flour by tablespoonfuls. Process until dough forms a ball and is smooth and elastic. After dough has formed a ball, process for another 30 seconds for kneading. Roll dough in oiled bowl and cover with a cloth. Let rise for 2 hours with bowl sitting in pan of warm water. Remove dough, beat down, and put into loaf pan. Bake at 375° for 30 minutes. Cool on rack, remove from pan, and slice.

Yield: 1 loaf

Anne Glover

Bread dough has been kneaded enough when you press it with your knuckles and the dents spring back.

APPLE BREAD

1 cup shortening (melted) or oil
2 cups sugar
3 eggs
2 cups peeled, chopped apples
2 tsp. vanilla

3 cups flour
1 tsp. soda
½ tsp. salt
1½ tsp. cinnamon
1 cup chopped pecans

Beat shortening, sugar and eggs. Stir in apples, vanilla and combined dry ingredients. Mix in nuts and pour into two ungreased loaf pans. Bake in preheated 350° oven for about 1 hour. Cool 10 minutes. Remove from pan to cool on wire rack.

Freezes well!

Yield: 2 loaves

Debbie Deacon

HAWAIIAN BANANA NUT BREAD

3 cups flour
2 cups sugar
1 tsp. soda
1 tsp. salt
1 tsp. ground cinnamon
1 cup chopped nuts (or ½ cup
  each nuts and dates)

3 eggs, beaten
1½ cups oil
2 cups mashed ripe bananas
1 eight-ounce can crushed pineapple,
  drained
2 tsp. vanilla

Combine dry ingredients. Stir in nuts. Combine remaining ingredients and add to dry ingredients. Stir only until batter is moistened. Spoon into 2 greased and floured 9 x 5 x 3-inch loaf pans. Bake at 350° for 1 hour or until done. Cool 10 minutes in pan. Remove to wire racks to cool completely.

Yield: 2 loaves

Arlene Loman

DATE NUT BREAD

1 eight-ounce package pitted dates
2 cups flour
1 tsp. soda
1 cup sugar
1 egg

1 cup chopped nuts
1 Tb. butter or oleo
1 cup boiling water
1 tsp. vanilla
½ tsp. salt

Chop dates and sprinkle soda over dates. Pour boiling water over dates and soda. Add butter and sugar. Let cool. Add flour, egg, nuts and vanilla. Bake in buttered loaf pan at 325° for 30 minutes. Raise to 350° and bake until a wooden pick inserted in middle comes out clean.

Freezes well.

Frances Cox

BANANA TEA BREAD

½ cup butter
1⅓ cups sugar
2 eggs
¼ cup sour cream
2 Tb. milk
1 cup mashed banana
1½ cups chopped pecans

1 tsp. almond extract
2 cups flour
1½ tsp. baking powder
½ tsp. soda
¼ tsp. salt
Confectioners' sugar

Combine butter and sugar in a large mixing bowl. Cream until light and fluffy. Add eggs, sour cream, milk, almond extract and mix well. Combine flour, baking powder, soda and salt; add to creamed mixture, alternating with mashed bananas. Mix well. Stir in pecans. Pour batter into a greased 9¼ x 5¼ x 2¼-inch pan. Bake at 350° for 1 hour and 10 minutes or until done. If loaf gets too brown, cover with aluminum foil. Remove from pan and cool. Sprinkle with powdered sugar.

Dorothy Wilkinson
Gastonburg, Ala.

GLAZED ORANGE BREAD

¼ cup butter or margarine,
    softened
¾ cup sugar
2 eggs, beaten
2 tsp. grated orange rind
2 cups all-purpose flour

2½ tsp. baking powder
1 tsp. salt
¾ cup orange juice
¾ cup chopped pecans
2½ tsp. orange juice
½ cup sifted powdered sugar

Cream butter; gradually add ¾ cup sugar, beating well. Add the beaten eggs and grated orange rind. Mix well. Combine flour, baking powder and salt. Add to creamed mixture alternately with ¾ cup orange juice, beginning and ending with flour mixture. Mix well after each addition. Stir in pecans. Pour batter into a greased 9 x 5 x 3 inch loaf pan. Bake at 350° for 50-55 minutes or until a wooden pick in center comes out clean. Cool loaf in pan 10 minutes. Remove from pan and cool completely. Combine 2½ tsp. orange juice and powdered sugar; drizzle over loaf. Wrap and store overnight before serving.

Betty Pullam

Unsalted butter spoils easily; store it in the freezer.

PUMPKIN BREAD

3⅓ cups flour
3 cups sugar
2 tsp. soda
1½ tsp. salt
1 cup melted shortening or oil

4 eggs
⅔ cups water
2 cups canned pumpkin
1 tsp. cinnamon
1 tsp. nutmeg

Sift dry ingredients into a bowl and make a well. Add shortening, eggs, water, and pumpkin. Mix well and put into greased and floured loaf pan. Bake at 350° for 1 hour. If top seems too moist, return to oven.

Yield: 3 small loaves

Lindley Hodges

STRAWBERRY BREAD

3 cups flour
1 tsp. salt
1 tsp. soda
1 Tb. ground cinnamon
2 cups sugar
3 eggs, well-beaten

1¼ cups oil
2 ten-ounce packages frozen,
  sliced strawberries, thawed
  and drained
1¼ cups pecans, chopped
Red food coloring (optional)

Combine flour, salt, soda, cinnamon, and sugar. Make well in center of dry ingredients; add eggs and oil, stirring only until dry ingredients are moistened. Stir in strawberries and pecans. Blend in food coloring, if desired. Spoon batter into 2 greased 8 x 4 x 2 inch loaf pans. Bake at 350° for 1 hour or until toothpick inserted in bread comes out clean. Cool on wire rack. Let stand overnight before slicing.

Yield: 2 loaves

Becky Hight

CINNAMON FRUIT CRUNCHIES

1 ten-ounce can biscuits
½ cup sugar
½ tsp. cinnamon

¼ cup butter or margarine
10 tsp. favorite preserves

Preheat oven to 375°. Separate biscuit dough into 10 biscuits. Combine sugar and cinnamon. Dip both sides of biscuits in melted butter and then in sugar mixture. Made deep thumbprint in the center of each biscuit; fill with level teaspoon of preserves. Bake in ungreased 9 x 13 inch pan for 15 or 20 minutes. Serve warm or cool.

Serves 10

Byretta Fish
Star City, Arkansas

CORN SPOON BREAD

2 eggs, slightly beaten
1 8½-ounce package corn
  muffin mix
1 eight-ounce can cream-style corn
1 eight-ounce can whole kernel
  corn, drained

1 cup dairy sour cream
½ cup of butter or
  margarine, melted
½ cup (4 ounces) shredded
  processed Swiss cheese

Combine eggs, muffin mix, cream style and whole kernel corn, sour cream, and butter or margarine. Spread in 11 x 7 x 1¾ inch baking dish. Bake in 350° oven for 35 minutes. Sprinkle cheese on top; bake 10 to 15 minutes more or until knife comes out clean.

Serves 8   Evelyn Penick

INDIAN FRY BREAD

3 cups all-purpose flour
1½ cups milk (approximately)
¾ tsp. baking powder

1½ tsp. salt
1½ Tb. cooled, melted shortening

Sift together dry ingredients. Add shortening and milk. Mix well. Dough should be of biscuit dough consistency. If too dry, add a little milk. Heat 1 inch of shortening in electric skillet to 375° or use deep fat fryer. Let dough stand 20 minutes. Roll out to ¼-inch thickness. Cut into 3-inch diameter circles. Drop into hot fat and fry on each side until brown, turning only once. Bread will puff. Serve hot.

Very good with butter and honey.

Serves 9   Andrea Davenport

SAUSAGE BREAD

2 loaves frozen bread dough
1 pound Italian sausage (crumbled,
  cooked, and drained well)
8 ounces Mozarella cheese, shredded

Oregano
Basil
Salt
Pepper

Let dough rise and roll out each loaf thinly. Combine cooked, drained sausage with cheese and seasonings to taste. Spread over dough. Roll in jelly roll fashion. Place on cookie sheet, seam side down. Bake in 350° oven for 20-25 minutes. Slice into rounds.

Carolyn Waddington

YORKSHIRE PUDDING

2 eggs
1 cup evaporated milk

1 cup flour
1 tsp. beef drippings

Beat 2 eggs well (about 10 minutes). Add milk and beat for 10 more minutes. Add flour and beat for 15 minutes more. Place a teaspoonful of beef drippings in the bottom of muffin tins or pie pan. Turn batter into pans. (Fill about ⅔ full.) Bake at 425° for 25 minutes. Do not open oven during cooking!

This dish is to be served with a beef roast. Place the pudding on a plate and cover with beef gravy.

Serves 12-15

Vikki Koch

SHORTBREAD

2 sticks unsalted butter
¾ cup sugar
2 cups flour

½ tsp. salt
2 tsp. vanilla extract
Powdered sugar

Cream butter and sugar. Work in flour, salt and vanilla. Spread mixture on ungreased cookie sheets until approximately ¼-½ inch thickness. Sprinkle lightly with powdered sugar and bake at 350° for 20 minutes. Cut into squares while warm.

HERBED ROLLS

½ cup oleo
1½ tsp. parsley flakes
½ tsp. dillweed

1 tsp. onion flakes
2 tsp. Parmesan cheese
1 package buttermilk canned biscuits

Melt butter in 9-inch square pan. Mix herbs together and stir into butter. Let stand 30 minutes before swishing biscuits around in mixture, coating all sides with herb butter. Bake at 425° for 12-15 minutes. Cut biscuits in half for hot bread or in fourths for appetizers.

Mrs. Cecil Bailey

ROLLS À LA CANNED BISCUITS

Canned biscuits　　　　　　　**Grated Parmesan cheese**
Melted butter

Remove biscuits from package and separate, flattening with rolling pin. Dip each biscuit in melted butter and then in Parmesan cheese. Fold over each biscuit and place in greased pan. Bake at 400° until done. Brush liberally with melted butter when done.

Variations: Biscuits can also be rolled in corn flake crumbs instead of Parmesan cheese.

Gerrie Fletcher

QUICK BISCUITS

2 generous cups Bisquick　　　　**Scant ½ pint whipping cream**

Add whipping cream to Bisquick, substituting whipping cream for liquid. Cut out and bake as usual.

Delicious!

Charlotte Murray

SPEEDY CRESCENTS

1 three-ounce package chive　　　**2 packages Crescent dinner rolls**
**　cream cheese**　　　　　　　　　**　(8 to package)**
2 Tb. soft margarine　　　　　　　**3 Tb. parsley**
1 tsp. horseradish

Combine cream cheese, margarine, and horseradish. Separate rolls and spread with cheese mixture. Roll according to package directions. Place on baking sheet, sprinkle with parsley, and bake according to package directions.

When baking bread, always test the yeast before adding it to the recipe. Dissolve a package of dry yeast in ¼ cup of warm water. Stir in one tablespoon of sugar (or other sweetener used in recipe). Cover with towel and set aside for 20 minutes. If the mixture has not doubled its volume, throw it out and start over.

BISCUIT COFFEE CAKE

3 cans biscuits
8-ounces cream cheese
½ cup brown sugar, not liquid

½ cup granulated sugar
1 tsp. cinnamon
1 stick butter, melted

Flatten biscuits slightly. Cut cheese into 30 cubes. Put cheese inside each biscuit and roll into balls. Pinch shut. Roll each biscuit in butter and then in cinnamon-sugar mixture. Drop into Bundt pan. Bake at 350° for 40 minutes. Turn out and serve warm.

Very easy, but looks pretty and tastes scrumptious!

Pam Cupples

CRANBERRY COFFEE CAKE

¼ cup brown sugar
1 cup chopped pecans
¼ tsp. cinnamon
2 cups Bisquick
2 Tb. granulated sugar
1 egg

⅔ cup water or milk
⅔ cup whole cranberry sauce

Confectioners' Sugar Icing:
2 cups powdered sugar
1 tsp. vanilla
2 Tb. water

Heat oven to 400°. Grease 9-inch square pan. Mix brown sugar, nuts, and cinnamon. Combine Bisquick, granulated sugar, egg, and water; beat vigorously ½ minute. Spread in pan and sprinkle with nut mixture. Spoon cranberry sauce on top. Bake 20 to 25 minutes. While warm, spread with Confectioners' Sugar Icing.

Icing: Blend 2 cups powdered sugar, 1 teaspoon vanilla, and about 2 tablespoons water.

An attractive dessert for Thanksgiving or Christmas.

Serves 8-12

Mary Frances Beavers

QUICK CINNAMON COFFEE CAKE

3 ten-ounce cans refrigerated
  biscuits
1 cup sugar

½ cup chopped pecans
1½ sticks oleo
1½ Tb. cinnamon

Cut each biscuit in fourths. Combine sugar and cinnamon in a large cellophane bag. Place a few biscuit pieces at a time in bag and shake to coat biscuits. Layer coated biscuits in buttered Bundt pan. Sprinkle with chopped pecans. Melt oleo; add sugar mixture left in bag and mix well. Pour over biscuits and bake at 325° for 40-50 minutes.

Diane Hilburn

SOUR CREAM COFFEE CAKE

CAKE:

2 sticks butter or margarine
2 cups sugar
2 eggs
½ tsp. vanilla
¼ tsp. salt

2 cups cake flour
1 tsp. soda
1 tsp. baking powder
1 cup sour cream

TOPPING:

½ cup pecans
1 tsp. cinnamon

½ cup sugar

Cream butter, sugar, eggs and vanilla. Add dry ingredients and mix thoroughly. Stir in sour cream. Pour half of batter into a 13 x 9-inch greased and floured cake pan. Sprinkle with half of the topping mixture. Pour remaining batter, spread gently and then sprinkle with the remaining topping mixture. Bake at 350° for 60-70 minutes. Let stand for 10 minutes before cutting.

Lou Kelly

HUSH PUPPIES

½ cup sifted enriched flour
1½ cups white corn meal
2 tsp. baking powder
1 Tb. sugar

½ tsp. salt
1 egg, beaten
¾ cup milk
1 small onion, finely chopped

Sift together dry ingredients; add onion. Add beaten egg and milk to dry ingredients, stirring lightly. Drop by teaspoonfuls into hot fat, frying only a few at a time. Fry until golden brown. Drain on absorbent paper.

Makes about 20 hush puppies

Sherry Wright

MEXICAN CORNBREAD

1 cup cornmeal
2 eggs
1 onion, finely chopped
1 four-ounce can chopped
   green chilies
½ cup Wesson oil

1 cup milk
½ tsp. soda
¼ tsp. salt
1 small can cream corn
1 cup grated Cheddar cheese

Mix all ingredients well. Bake at 350° in a greased preheated iron skillet for one hour. Cool before removing from skillet.

Serves 8

Betty Rodgers

DONUTS

1 cup lukewarm water
¼ cup sugar
¼ cup oil
1 tsp. salt
1 egg, beaten

3½ cups flour
1 package yeast
1½ cups powdered sugar
2-4 tsp. milk

Dissolve yeast in ¼ cup lukewarm water. Heat remaining water, sugar, oil, and salt to lukewarm. Beat egg in separate bowl. Add 1 cup flour and yeast to egg. Add to sugar and oil mixture. Add 2 cups flour; let rise until double in size (2 hours). Knead in about ¼ - ½ cup flour (5 min). Roll out, cut with donut cutter and let rise. Fry in hot grease and drain. Glaze with sugar and milk mixture.

Glaze: Mix powdered sugar and milk in bowl. Dip fried donut in bowl to glaze it.

Dorothy Cornwell

FRENCH TOAST

1 loaf Texas toast slices
6 whole eggs
3 Tb. sugar

1 tsp. salt
1 tsp. cinnamon
1 cup milk

Beat together eggs, sugar, salt, and cinnamon. Add milk. Pour mixture into shallow pan, and lay bread slices individually in mixture. Let stand 30 minutes or overnight. Bake on heavily greased cookie sheet for 8 minutes on each side in oven preheated to 500°.

Wanda Reed

BEER MUFFINS

1½ cups Bisquick mix
6 ounces beer

2 Tb. brown sugar
1 tsp. granulated sugar

Combine all ingredients. Mix by hand until smooth. Fill greased muffin tins half full. Bake at 350° for 20-25 minutes, or until lightly browned.

Makes 8-10 muffins

Bobbie McKenzie

See no weevil! Put a bay leaf in your flour container to prevent weevils.

BRAN MUFFINS

3 cups sugar
1 heaping cup shortening
5 tsp. soda
1 tsp. salt
1 quart buttermilk

4 cups Kellogg's All-Bran
2 cups Nabisco 100% Bran
2 cups boiling water
4 eggs
5 cups flour

Pour boiling water over 100% Bran. Cover with cloth. Cream shortening, sugar, and eggs. Add milk, All-Bran, and other dry ingredients. Do not beat. Fold in 100% Bran. Do not stir. Spoon into greased muffin pans. Bake 15-20 minutes at 400°. Dough will keep in refrigerator 4 to 6 weeks. Bake as needed.

Marianne Gosser

FAVORITE APPLE MUFFINS

1 egg
½ cup milk
¼ cup salad oil
1 cup grated apple

1½ cups flour
2 tsp. baking powder
½ tsp. salt
½ cup sugar

TOPPING:

⅓ cup brown sugar, packed
½ tsp. cinnamon

⅓ cup broken walnuts

Preheat oven to 400°. Grease bottoms of 12 muffin cups. Beat egg. Stir in milk, oil, and apple. Mix in remaining ingredients until flour is just moistened. Batter should be lumpy. Fill muffin cups ⅔ full. Sprinkle with topping. Bake 25-30 minutes or until golden brown. Remove immediately from pan.

Yield: 12 muffins

Gayle Anderson

JORDAN MARSH BLUEBERRY MUFFINS

1½ cups butter
1½ cups sugar
2 eggs
2 cups flour
2 tsp. baking powder

½ tsp. salt
½ cup milk
2½ cups blueberries
Sugar

Cream butter and sugar. Add 2 eggs. Sift dry ingredients and add alternately with milk to butter, sugar, and eggs. Add blueberries. Fill non-stick muffin tins ¾ full. Sprinkle generously with sugar. Bake at 375° for 20-30 minutes.

Muffins freeze well.

Ann Chudy

SUPER EASY MUFFINS

2 cups Bisquick   **1 stick oleo, softened**
8 ounces sour cream

Blend ingredients until doughy. Fill paper muffin cups or greased tins ½ to ¾ full. Bake at 425° for 12-15 minutes.

A tasty treat!

Jananse Reding

BASIC CRÊPE BATTER

1½ cups flour   **1½ cups milk**
⅛ tsp. salt   **2 Tb. butter, melted**
3 eggs, slightly beaten

Sift dry ingredients into bowl. Beat eggs in separate bowl. Stir ingredients from both bowls together. Add milk and melted butter. Cover and set aside for at least 1 hour at room temperature or overnight in the refrigerator. To cook, brush a 6-inch skillet or crêpe pan with butter over moderately high heat. Add 2 Tb. of batter to pan; tip pan quickly so batter will run around pan thinly and completely over bottom. Turn heat down; let cook through. Crêpes need not be turned, but bottom should be golden. Stack crêpes; cover with towel; keep warm in a slow oven. If made in advance, place waxed paper between crêpes. They may be reheated or frozen.

Yield: 20

Cathy Simpson

BIG-MAMA'S APPLE PANCAKE

¼ cup sugar   **½ cup sifted flour**
1 teaspoon cinnamon   **¼ teaspoon salt**
1 large tart apple   **1 Tb. butter**
2 eggs   **¼ cup melted butter**
½ cup milk

Heat oven to 450°. Mix cinnamon and sugar. Peel and core apple. Slice thin and sprinkle with half of cinnamon mixture. Set aside. Mix eggs, milk, flour and salt. Beat with rotary beater for 2 minutes. Heat a heavy 10-inch skillet in oven until very hot. Put one tablespoon butter in skillet and pour batter into skillet. Place apple slices on top of batter, covering the bottom of the skillet. Bake uncovered for 15 minutes. As soon as batter puffs up in center, puncture with fork, repeating as often as necessary. Lower heat to 350° and bake for 10 minutes. Remove from oven, pour melted butter over pancake, and sprinkle with remaining cinnamon-sugar. Loosen from pan and serve immediately.

My German grandmother's special treat on cold mornings.

Serves 2

Carrie Carlton

WAFFLES

2 egg whites
2 egg yolks
1⅔ cups milk
¼ cup cooking oil

2 cups flour
1 Tb. sugar
½ tsp. salt
3 tsp. baking powder

Beat egg whites until stiff. Set aside. Beat egg yolks, milk, and oil. Sift dry ingredients and add to liquid mixture. Fold in egg whites. Use 1 cup batter for each waffle. Makes 4 waffles.

Jo Arnold

PIZZA SHELL

1½ cups flour
1 package yeast
¾ tsp. salt

2 tsp. olive oil
¾ cup water

Combine ingredients. For thin crust, prepare immediately. For thick crust, let rise about 15 minutes before preparing. Spread dough in oiled pizza pan.

Ann Cornwell

POPOVERS

1 cup all-purpose flour
2 cups milk
2 eggs, beaten

2 Tb. shortening, melted
¼ tsp. sugar
¼ tsp. salt

Mix and sift flour, salt, and sugar into a large mixing bowl. Combine 2 beaten eggs and 2 cups milk in a blender. Add egg mixture to flour mixture gradually, constantly beating at low speed. Add shortening while beating. Preheat well-greased muffin pan to sizzling hot, and fill cups about ½ full (no more than ¾ full) with popover mixture. The trick is a sizzling hot muffin pan. Bake at 450° for 20 minutes. Reduce to 350° for 20 minutes.

Variations: This recipe can be made more special with raisins, figs, etc., added. Drop fruit in after pouring mixture into sizzling muffin pan.

Serves 4

Hi Daniel

WORLD'S EASIEST BREAKFAST

Top a crispy toasted Eggo waffle with ⅓ to ½ cup of Dannon Vanilla yogurt. For a fancier variation, top with fresh, slightly sweetened strawberries or other fruit.

APRICOT SALAD

SALAD:

1 thirteen-ounce can pineapple tidbits
1 seventeen-ounce can apricots, diced
2 three-ounce packages orange gelatin

2 cups boiling water
½ cup apricot juice
½ cup pineapple juice

Drain pineapple tidbits and apricots, reserving juice. Dissolve gelatin in boiling water. Add ½ cup apricot and pineapple juices and then the fruit. Place in the refrigerator until firm.

TOPPING:

½ cup pineapple juice
½ cup apricot juice
2 Tb. butter
3 Tb. flour
½ cup sugar

1 egg, beaten
1 six and ¼-ounce package
    miniature marshmallows
½ pint Cool Whip

Cook juices, butter, flour, and sugar in saucepan. Add beaten egg and cook until thick. Add marshmallows to hot mixture. Let cool for fifteen minutes. Fold Cool Whip into mixture. Spread topping on salad and serve.

Grated cheese may be added to topping if desired.

Serves 12   Judy Wingfield

BAKED APRICOT CASSEROLE

2 twenty-nine-ounce cans pitted
    apricot halves
1 one-pound box dark brown sugar

1 twelve-ounce box Ritz
    cracker, crushed
½ pound butter

Grease baking dish with butter. Place a layer of apricots in baking dish. Sprinkle with half of the Ritz crackers and half of the brown sugar. Dot with half of the butter. Repeat. Bake at 300° for one hour.

This delightful casserole is good for a buffet; it is quick and easy.

Serves 10-12   Alice Lynn Overbey

To peel thin-skinned fruits such as tomatoes and peaches, submerge in boiling water 10 seconds and then plunge into cold water. The skins will peel off easily.

APRICOT SALAD

FILLING:

2 three-ounce packages apricot-
  flavored gelatin
4 cups hot water
1 cup miniature marshmallows

1 fourteen-ounce can
  crushed pineapple, drained
  (reserve juice)
2 large bananas, mashed

Dissolve gelatin in hot water and add marshmallows to mixture. Stir until dissolved. Let cool. Drain pineapple, reserving juice for custard. Add crushed pineapple and bananas. Pour mixture into 9 x 13 inch glass dish and refrigerate until salad congeals.

CUSTARD FOR TOP:

Reserved pineapple juice
½ cup sugar
2 Tb. flour
1 Tb. butter

1 eight-ounce package cream
  cheese, softened
1 four-ounce carton Cool Whip

In medium sauce pan combine pineapple juice, sugar, flour and butter. Cook until thick. Add cream cheese and let cool. Fold in Cool Whip and spread over top of congealed gelatin.

Serves 12

Becky Davidson
Judy Wilson

BING CHERRY SALAD

1 eight and ¼-ounce can crushed
  pineapple, drained (reserve liquid)
1 sixteen-ounce can dark pitted
  cherries, drained (reserve liquid)
2 three-ounce packages cherry-
  flavored gelatin
Juice from drained pineapple and
  cherries

Water to make two cups liquid
8 ounces Coca Cola
½ cup chopped pecans
Lettuce
Mayonnaise

Drain juice from pineapple and cherries and reserve. Add water to make two cups of juice. Heat juice-water mixture to boiling and pour over gelatin to dissolve. Cut cherries in half. Add Coca Cola, cherries and drained pineapple to gelatin mixture. Pour into 9 x 9-inch square pan. When mixture begins to thicken, add nuts. Refrigerate until firm. Cut into squares and serve on lettuce. Top each square with dollop of mayonnaise.

Serves 8-10

Judy Fletcher

BLUEBERRY SALAD

1 six-ounce package raspberry-
  flavored gelatin
2 cups boiling water
½ cup cold water
1 eight-ounce can crushed pineapple,
  drained

1 fifteen-ounce can blueberries, drained
1 eight-ounce package cream
  cheese softened
½ cup sugar
½ cup sour cream
½ cup pecans, chopped

Dissolve gelatin in boiling water. Drain pineapple juice into measuring cup, and add enough water to equal ½ cup. Mix in pineapple and drained blueberries. Pour gelatin and fruit mixture into 9 x 13-inch glass dish and congeal. Combine softened cream cheese, sugar, sour cream, and pecans and spread on top of gelatin.

Serves 16   Susan Eanes

CHRISTMAS CRANBERRY SALAD

1 thirteen and ½-ounce can
  crushed pineapple
Water
2 three-ounce packages strawberry
  gelatin

¾ cup cold water
1 sixteen-ounce can jellied
  cranberry sauce
⅓ cup chopped pecans
1 Tb. butter or margarine

TOPPING:

1 three-ounce package vanilla
  instant pudding mix
½ cup heavy cream

½ cup milk
1 three-ounce package cream cheese
  at room temperature

Drain pineapple juice into measuring cup; reserve pineapple. Add water to juice to make one cup. Bring to a boil. While liquid is boiling, remove from heat and stir in gelatin until dissolved. Add cold water and chill until it is like unbeaten egg whites. In medium-sized bowl, combine drained pineapple and cranberry sauce; stir into gelatin mixture. Pour into a 9″ square cake pan. Chill until firm.

Creamy Topping: Place pudding mix in small, deep bowl and prepare as directed on package, using one 1 cup of liquid. (½ cup heavy cream and ½ cup milk). When mixed, add cream cheese and blend well.

Meanwhile, heat oven to 350°. Place pecans and butter in shallow pan and bake for about eight minutes, stirring occasionally until pecans are toasted. Cool nuts. When gelatin mixture is firm, spread creamy topping over top. Sprinkle pecans over topping. Chill 2-3 hours until firm. Using wet knife, cut salad into nine squares. Decorate with salad greens.

Very attractive and good!

Serves 8-10   Rosemary Russell

CHRISTMAS RIBBON SALAD

1 three-ounce package strawberry
  gelatin
2 cups whole cranberry sauce
1 three-ounce package lemon gelatin
1 eight-ounce package cream
  cheese, softened
1 eight-ounce can crushed pineapple

¼ cup chopped pecans
1 three-ounce package lime gelatin
1 sixteen-ounce can pears, diced
½ cup juice (syrup) from pears
4¼ cups boiling water

CRANBERRY RIBBON: Dissolve strawberry gelatin in 1½ cups boiling water. Add cranberry sauce, mixing well. Chill until partially set. Pour into 8-cup ring mold or two loaf pans. Chill until almost firm. Top with Cheese Ribbon.

CHEESE RIBBON: Dissolve lemon gelatin in 1¼ cups boiling water; add cheese, beating smooth with electric beater. Add pineapple with juice. Chill until partially set. Stir in pecans and pour over cranberry layer in mold. Chill until almost firm. Top with Lime Ribbon.

LIME RIBBON: Dissolve lime gelatin in 1½ cups water. Add diced pears and ½ cup juice. Chill until partially set. Pour over cheese ribbon. Chill overnight. Unmold on serving tray to serve.

Serves 10-12

Margaret Wilkins

CURRIED HOT FRUIT

1 sixteen-ounce can sliced peaches
1 sixteen-ounce can sliced pears
1 sixteen-ounce can pineapple chunks
1 sixteen-ounce can apricot halves

1 cup brown sugar
2 tsp. curry powder
¾ stick margarine, sliced
½ cup chopped pecans

Drain fruit and mix together. Place one layer of fruit in 9 x 13-inch casserole. Mix curry powder and sugar. Sprinkle over first layer. Repeat layers. Put slices of margarine and pecans on top. Bake for 45 minutes at 350°. Serve hot.

Any size can of fruit may be used to increase or decrease volume, but all should be uniform.

Serves 8-10

Linda Bergquist

FROZEN FRUIT SALAD

2 cups sour cream
2 bananas, mashed
¼ cup chopped maraschino cherries
1 Tb. lemon juice

½ cup chopped pecans
¾ cup sugar
1 eight and ¼-ounce can crushed
  pineapple, strained and drained

Combine all ingredients and mix well. Pour in 9 x 5-inch glass dish and freeze. Cut into squares and serve on lettuce leaf. Can also be frozen in cupcake liners in muffin tin and then removed and stored in plastic bag for individual servings.

Serves 8

Mary Keeling
Diane Hilburn

FROZEN STRAWBERRY SALAD

1 eight-ounce package cream
  cheese, softened
¾ cup sugar
3 large bananas, sliced
½ cup chopped pecans

1 fourteen-ounce can pineapple
  chunks, drained
1 sixteen-ounce package frozen
  strawberries, thawed
1 eight-ounce carton Cool Whip

Cream together cream cheese and sugar. Add bananas, pecans, pineapple chunks, strawberries and Cool Whip. Mix well. Pour into a 9 x 13 inch dish. Freeze. Will keep for 4-6 weeks.

Serves 12

Wista Jones

HOT FRUIT CASSEROLE

1 sixteen-ounce can freestone
  peach halves, drained
1 sixteen-ounce can black
  cherries with juice
Juice and grated rind of 1 lemon

1 eight-ounce package dried apricots
Juice and grated rind of 1 orange
¾ cup brown sugar
Pinch of salt
1 eight-ounce carton sour cream

Combine first seven ingredients and pour into glass casserole. Bake at 350° for 1 hour. Serve warm with dollop of sour cream.

Serves 8

Dottie Hankins

LIME SALAD

1 three-ounce package lime-
  flavored gelatin
1 three-ounce package cream
  cheese, softened

1½ cups hot water
1 eight and ¼-ounce can
  crushed pineapple
½ cup chopped pecans

Cream together gelatin and cream cheese. Add hot water and stir until dissolved. Allow this to chill until partially congealed. Add pineapple and nuts. Pour into 9 x 9-inch casserole. Allow to chill several hours or overnight.

Serves 6

Nancy Harmon

OLIVE WREATH MOLD

1 fourteen-ounce can crushed
  pineapple
1 three-ounce package lime-
  flavored gelatin
½ cup grated American cheese
½ cup chopped pimiento

½ cup finely chopped celery
⅔ cup chopped walnuts
¼ tsp. salt
1 cup heavy cream, whipped
Stuffed olives

Drain pineapple, reserving syrup. Heat pineapple syrup and bring to boil. Add to gelatin and stir until dissolved. Cool. When gelatin begins to thicken, add all ingredients but whipped cream and olives. Fold in whipped cream. Place a row of stuffed, sliced olives in bottom of medium ring mold. Pour gelatin mixture on top and chill until firm. Unmold on lettuce or endive.

Serves 6

Mrs. Joe Carlton

ORANGE JELL-O SALAD

1 eight-ounce package cottage
  cheese, small curd
1 eleven-ounce can mandarin
  oranges, drained

1 fifteen and ¾-ounce can
  of crushed pineapple, drained
1 eight-ounce carton Cool Whip
1 three-ounce package orange Jell-O

Mix cottage cheese with drained fruit until oranges are broken up. Add Cool Whip and mix together. Sprinkle box of orange Jell-O over this mixture. Stir until thoroughly mixed.

Serves 8

Sheila Hammonds

ORANGE-MALLOW GELATIN

1 six-ounce package dry
  orange gelatin
1 eight-ounce carton sour cream

1 twelve-ounce carton Cool Whip
1 eleven-ounce can Mandarin oranges
1 cup miniature marshmallows

Mix dry gelatin with sour cream until dissolved. Add Cool Whip. Fold in drained Mandarin oranges and marshmallows. Chill in two quart container for approximately one hour.

Serves 8

Edwina Whalen

STRAWBERRY GELATIN SALAD

2 six-ounce packages strawberry
  gelatin
1½ cups boiling water
2 ten-ounce packages frozen
  strawberries, thawed

1 nine-ounce can crushed
  pineapple
½ cup chopped pecans
1 cup sour cream

Dissolve gelatin in water. Stir in thawed strawberries. Chill until slightly congealed. Add pineapple and pecans. Put ½ mixture in lightly oiled 9 x 13-inch pan. Chill slightly. Stir sour cream in remaining mixture. Pour over first layer. Chill until congealed.

Serves 10-12   Patty Lowe

STRAWBERRY JELL-O DELIGHT

1 six-ounce package of cherry Jell-O
1½ cups boiling water
1 eight-ounce can crushed pineapple
1 sixteen-ounce package frozen
  strawberries, thawed

1 eight-ounce container sour cream
½ cup finely chopped pecans
Lettuce leaves

Dissolve Jell-O in boiling water. Add crushed pineapple with juice. Add thawed strawberries. Pour one half of mixture into a 12 x 7-inch glass dish. Refrigerate until firm, about forty-five minutes. Spread sour cream over congealed mixture. Chop pecans and sprinkle over sour cream. Top with remaining Jell-O mixture. Congeal completely, approximately thirty to forty minutes more. Cut into squares and serve on individual lettuce leaves.

Serves 15-16   Darby Blair

WATERGATE SALAD

2 twelve-ounce cartons Cool Whip
2 three and ¾-ounce packages
  instant Pistachio pudding

1 cup miniature marshmallows
1 fifteen and ¼-ounce can crushed
  pineapple with juice

Mix all ingredients together. Pour into a 9 x 12-inch pan. Chill for about three hours.

Serves 8   Ann Cornwell

BROCCOLI CAULIFLOWER SALAD

1 cup sour cream
1 cup mayonnaise
Dash of lemon juice
1 package Ranch Style Dressing
1 bunch fresh broccoli, washed and
  chopped

1 bunch green onions, including tops,
  washed and chopped
1 head cauliflower, washed and
  chopped
1 ten-ounce package frozen English
  peas, half-thawed

Mix sour cream, mayonnaise, lemon juice, and Ranch Style Dressing. Pour over raw vegetables. Mix well. Cover. Refrigerate at least 24 hours before serving.

Cherry tomatoes create a more colorful dish.

Serves 8-10   Suzanne Best

CORN SALAD

2 twelve-ounce cans white or yellow
  whole kernel corn, drained
4 green onions, chopped

1 large tomato, chopped
2 Tb. mayonnaise
Salt and pepper

Drain corn. Chop onion and tomato and add to drained corn. Add mayonnaise and season to taste with salt and pepper.

Serves 8   Becky Davidson

FRITO SALAD

1 head lettuce
6 green onions
3 tomatoes
1 fifteen-ounce can kidney beans

¾ pound sharp Cheddar cheese, grated
1 eight-ounce package regular Fritos
Black pepper
Kraft Russian Salad Dressing

Shred lettuce. Chop green onions and tomatoes. Drain red kidney beans. Combine these ingredients in salad bowl. Add ¾ pound grated cheese, package of Fritos, Kraft Russian Salad Dressing and black pepper to taste. Toss well.

Serves 8   Vicki Lackie

WHITE SEEDLESS GRAPE SALAD

1 eight-ounce package Philadelphia
  cream cheese

5 Tb. half-and-half cream
3 pounds white seedless grapes

Mix cream cheese with half-and-half until the cheese is medium-thin. Stir grapes into mixture until all the mixture is used and all the grapes are covered with cheese. Refrigerate several hours or overnight before serving.

Great for a ladies' summer luncheon.

Serves 16

Donna Bartell

HOLIDAY SCALLOP

2 three and ½-ounce cans
  chopped mushrooms
2 large onions, thinly sliced
4 Tb. butter
1 pint small curd cottage cheese

1 pint sour cream
8 medium potatoes, cooked and sliced
2 tsp. each salt, pepper and thyme
2 cups grated Cheddar cheese

Sauté mushrooms and onion separately in butter. Combine cottage cheese and sour cream. Layer in two casseroles the potatoes, onions, mushrooms and cottage cheese mixture, sprinkling each layer lightly with seasonings and some of the grated cheese. Cover and bake 45 minutes at 350°. Uncover the last 15 minutes and continue to bake.

Suggestions: Dish may be prepared one or two days ahead of time and kept in refrigerator until ready to bake.

Serves 12

Judy Hale

LAYERED LETTUCE SALAD

6 hard-boiled eggs, sliced
1½ cups diced celery
1 red or white onion, diced
1½ cups diced green pepper
1½ pounds bacon, fried and crumbled
2 ten-ounce packages frozen peas

1 head lettuce
2½ cups mayonnaise
2 Tb. sugar
6 ounces Cheddar cheese, grated
Bacon bits and parsley for garnish

Boil eggs, cool and slice. Dice celery, onion, green peppers. Cook bacon until crisp; cool and crumble. Let peas come to room temperature. Tear lettuce into bite-size pieces. Put in 9 x 12-inch glass dish. Layer celery, eggs, peas, onion, green pepper and bacon in order given. Add sugar to mayonnaise and mix well. Spread mayonnaise mixture over salad. Top with grated cheese. Cover with clear plastic wrap, and refrigerate for twelve hours or overnight. Garnish with parsley and additional bacon.

Serves 12

Ann Cornwell

101

ORANGE-LETTUCE SALAD

1 head of lettuce
¼ cup chopped green onion
1 eleven-ounce can mandarin
  oranges
1 cup green grapes, halved

½ cup sliced almonds, toasted
⅔ cup salad oil
⅓ cup orange juice

DRESSING:

¼ cup sugar
3 Tb. vinegar
1 tsp. celery seed

2 Tb. chopped parsley
Dash of dry mustard
Salt to taste

Tear lettuce. Add green onion. Combine with drained oranges, grapes and almonds in large bowl. Combine remaining ingredients to make dressing and pour over salad.

Serves 6-8

Jean Edwards

SPINACH SALAD

SALAD:

1 pound fresh spinach
4-6 slices bacon
2 eggs, hard-boiled and sliced

1 eleven-ounce can mandarin
  oranges, drained
1 small red onion, thinly sliced

DRESSING:

½ cup sugar
½ cup vinegar
2 Tb. oil
1 Tb. chopped green onion
1 Tb. chopped parsley

1 Tb. chopped chives
1 tsp. Worcestershire sauce
¾ tsp. prepared mustard
Cracked black pepper
1 ice cube

SALAD: Tear spinach. Fry bacon until crisp; drain and crumble. Toss spinach, bacon, eggs, oranges and onion. Pour dressing over salad and toss well.

DRESSING: Mix sugar, vinegar, oil, chopped green onion, parsley, chives, Worcestershire sauce, mustard, pepper and ice cube in plastic container. Shake well and chill. The dressing keeps well in refrigerator for several days.

Variations: Substitute cherry tomatoes for oranges. Use a bottled dressing such as Good Seasons Old-Fashioned French.

Serves 4-6

Sue Dean
Darlene Martin

SPECIAL SPINACH SALAD

Fresh spinach
10 strips bacon
1 eight-ounce can water
  chestnuts, drained

1 fourteen-ounce can bean
  sprouts, drained
4 hard-boiled eggs, chopped

DRESSING:

1 cup Mazola oil
¾ cup sugar
⅓ cup catsup

¼ cup cider vinegar
1 Tb. Worcestershire sauce
1 medium onion, chopped

Wash and de-stem spinach; cut into small pieces. Fry bacon until crisp and crumble. Drain water chestnuts and bean sprouts. Mix spinach, water chestnuts, bean sprouts and eggs together.

Make dressing by blending oil, sugar, catsup, vinegar, Worcestershire sauce and onion in blender until creamy. Pour dressing over salad. Top with crumbled bacon.

Serves 6-8

MARINATED VEGETABLE SALAD

1 seventeen-ounce can white
  shoe peg corn, drained
1 fifteen and ½-ounce can French
  style green beans, drained

1 two-ounce jar diced pimiento, drained
½ cup diced celery
½ cup chopped onion
½ cup chopped green pepper

MARINADE:

1 cup sugar
½ tsp. pepper
1 tsp. salt

½ cup vegetable oil
¾ cup vinegar

Drain corn, beans, and pimiento. Combine drained vegetables with celery, onion, and green pepper in medium sized bowl or casserole dish. In small saucepan combine the sugar, pepper, salt, oil, and vinegar. Bring to boil over low heat, stirring occasionally. Pour hot mixture over vegetables, stirring gently to blend well. Cover and chill twenty-four hours.

Serves 10   Wista Jones

To prevent apples from turning brown while peeling, slice into a bowl of cold, slightly salted water.

POTATO SALAD

6 medium potatoes, cooked and diced
1 cup Italian dressing
1 onion, chopped
2 hard-boiled eggs, chopped
½ cup chopped celery

1 cup mayonnaise
2 tsp. mustard
½ tsp. celery seed
Salt and pepper to taste

Marinate cooked potatoes in Italian dressing for several hours in refrigerator. Add chopped onion, eggs, celery, mayonnaise, mustard, celery seed and salt and pepper to taste. Mix well.

Serves 6-8   Lou Kelly

NEW ORLEANS POTATO SALAD

8 medium potatoes, boiled in jackets
1½ cups mayonnaise
1 cup sour cream
1½ tsp. horseradish
1¼ tsp. celery seed

½ tsp. salt
2 medium sized onions, finely minced
1 cup chopped fresh parsley
   (do not omit or decrease)

Peel cooked potatoes and cut into ⅛-inch slices. Combine mayonnaise, sour cream, horseradish, celery seed and salt. Set aside. In another bowl mix parsley and onions. In large serving bowl arrange layer of potatoes. Salt lightly. Cover with a layer of mayonnaise-sour cream mixture, followed by a layer of the parsley-onion mixture. Continue layering, ending with parsley and onion mixture. Do not stir. Cover and refrigerate at least eight hours. May be prepared the day before serving.

Serves 10-12   Mrs. Dewey Whitfield

For easy removal of congealed salads from molds, first grease mold with salad oil or mayonnaise.

Remember when making a molded salad, these fruits float: fresh apples, bananas, fresh peaches or pears, raspberries and halved strawberries; and these fruits sink: canned apricots, Royal Ann cherries, canned peaches or pears, whole strawberries, prunes, plums, fresh orange sections and grapes.

GERMAN POTATO SALAD

6 cups potatoes, cooked and sliced
½ pound bacon
¼ cup bacon fat
½ cup onion
2 Tb. all-purpose flour
2 Tb. sugar
1½ tsp. salt

1 tsp. celery seed
Dash pepper
½ cup vinegar
1 cup water
2 hard-boiled eggs, sliced
1 Tb. parsley
1 Tb. pimiento

Cook potatoes. Cook bacon until crisp. Drain and crumble bacon, reserving ¼ cup fat. Cook onion in bacon fat until tender. Blend in flour, sugar, salt, celery seed and pepper. Add vinegar and one cup water. Cook and stir until thickened and bubbly. Add most of bacon and all of potatoes and eggs. Heat thoroughly, stirring constantly. Garnish with parsley, pimiento, and rest of bacon.

Serves 8-10   Pat Stanger

RICE SALAD

1 cup Minute Rice
1 Tb. lemon juice
1 cup mayonnaise
1 onion, finely chopped

1 small green pepper, finely chopped
1 stalk celery, sliced thin
8 radishes, sliced paper thin
Salt and pepper to taste

Cook 1 cup Minute Rice. Let cool. Add lemon juice to mayonnaise and combine all ingredients. Add salt and pepper to taste. Mix well and refrigerate for 6 hours or overnight.

Serves 6   Wista Jones

SOUR SWEET SLAW

1 medium cabbage, shredded
1 bell pepper, chopped
1 onion, chopped
1 cup sugar
1 cup cider vinegar

⅔ cup oil
1 tsp. salt
2 Tb. sugar
1 tsp. dry mustard

Place shredded cabbage, chopped bell pepper, and chopped onion in bowl. Pour sugar over mixture. Place other ingredients in saucepan and bring to a full boil. Pour over cabage mixture. Cover and refrigerate at once. Do not serve for several hours.

Serves 10-12   Dixie Smith
                                                                   Judy Fletcher

THREE BEAN SALAD

1 sixteen-ounce can string beans, drained
1 sixteen-ounce can kidney beans, drained

1 sixteen-ounce can wax beans, drained
1 small onion, sliced thin
½ cup chopped green pepper

DRESSING:
¾ cup sugar
⅔ cup vinegar
⅓ cup salad oil

1 tsp. salt
1 tsp. pepper

Mix vegetables. Combine sugar, vinegar, and oil. Pour over vegetables. Add salt and pepper. Toss lightly. Chill overnight. Before serving, toss to coat beans with marinade. Drain off excess marinade.

Serves 6-8

VEGETABLES IN MARINADE

1 sixteen-ounce can LeSeur peas, undrained
1 sixteen-ounce can French-style beans, undrained
1 sixteen-ounce can Chinese vegetables, undrained
2 eight-ounce cans mushrooms, drained

2 8-ounce cans water chestnuts, drained and sliced
1 two-ounce jar pimientos with liquid
2 Tb. olive oil
½ cup sugar
⅔ cup vinegar
⅓ cup vinegar with tarragon

Mix first seven ingredients in large bowl. Bring sugar and vinegars to a boil in a saucepan. Pour over vegetables. Marinate in refrigerator overnight. Stir several times before serving.

Serves 16-18   Janice Davies

WINTER SALAD

1 head lettuce, shredded
1 onion, sliced thin
1 pound bacon, browned and crumbled, or 1½ cups bacon bits
1 head cauliflower, broken in pieces

Salt and pepper
2 Tb. sugar
1 cup Parmesan cheese
1½ cups mayonnaise
2 Tb. lemon juice

Layer lettuce, onion, bacon, cauliflower, salt, pepper and sugar in large bowl. Mix Parmesan cheese, mayonnaise and lemon juice. Spread over top of vegetable layers. Cover bowl with clear plastic wrap and store in refrigerator for twenty-four hours. Toss just before serving.

Serves 8-10   Marilyn Hamm

HOT CHICKEN SALAD

2 Tb. finely chopped onion
2 cups diced celery
½ cup toasted almonds
2 Tb. lemon juice
½ tsp. salt

2 cups cooked, diced chicken
¾ cup mayonnaise
Potato chips, crushed
1 cup grated Cheddar cheese

Mix first seven ingredients. Place in 9 x 9-inch baking dish. Top with potato chips and Cheddar cheese. Bake for 20 minutes at 350°.

Serves 6   Thelma Powell

POLYNESIAN CHICKEN SALAD

2 cups diced, cooked chicken
1 cup pineapple chunks, drained
¼ cup chopped, toasted almonds

¼ cup flaked coconut
1 cup mayonnaise
1 cup diced celery

Combine all ingredients, mixing well. Toss lightly and chill. If desired, serve in pineapple boats.

Serves 6   Mrs. M. E. Argo

JAMBALAYA SALAD

JAMBALAYA DRESSING:

1 envelope onion-mushroom
  soup mix
2 cups sour cream
½ cup chili sauce

2 Tb. lemon juice
½ tsp. garlic powder
Hot pepper sauce to taste

SALAD:

1½ pounds or 5 cups chopped
  cooked ham, chicken, shrimp,
  or combination of all three
1 cup sliced celery

1 medium green pepper,
  cut into chunks
4 cups cooked rice, chilled
2 medium tomatoes, cut into wedges

Jambalaya dressing: In medium bowl, blend onion-mushroom soup mix and sour cream. Add chili sauce, lemon juice, garlic powder, hot pepper sauce and chill in refrigerator.

Salad: In large bowl mix first three ingredients. Arrange rice in a ring on large platter, and top with tomatoes. Fill center with salad mixture and serve with chilled dressing.

Serves 6   Ann Cornwell

107

CRAB-STUFFED AVOCADO

2 ripe avocados
Lemon juice
Salt

Salad greens
1½ cups cooked or canned
crabmeat, chilled

DRESSING:

2 tsp. lemon juice
Dash tabasco
⅛ tsp. Worcestershire sauce

½ cup mayonnaise
½ cup minced celery
¼ cup minced pimiento

Halve avocados lengthwise. Remove pits and peel. Sprinkle with lemon juice and salt. Arrange each half on bed of crisp greens. Fill halves with crabmeat. Combine ingredients for dressing. Top each serving with dressing.

Serves 4   Muriel McCord

SHRIMP AND RICE SALAD

½ cup uncooked, long grain rice
12 ounces shrimp, cooked
    and deveined
Salt and pepper to taste
Wishbone Italian Salad Dressing

1 Tb. minced onion
3 Tb. stuffed olives, sliced
½ cup chopped green pepper
1 cup chopped cauliflower
2 tsp. capers

Cook rice according to package directions. Cool. Marinate in small amount of Wishbone Italian Salad Dressing overnight. Marinate shrimp in small amount of the dressing overnight, too. Drain the shrimp, but not the rice. Combine onion, pepper and olives. Put all ingredients together and toss with a little more dressing just before serving.

Serves 8   Dorothy Priddy

SHRIMP MOLD

1 ten and ½-ounce can tomato soup
1 eight-ounce package cream cheese
2 envelopes gelatin
½ cup cold water
1 cup mayonnaise

1 pound cooked shrimp, chopped
1 cup minced celery
½ cup minced green peppers
1 small onion, grated

Heat tomato soup. Add cream cheese and stir until well blended. Soften gelatin in cold water. Add to soup mixture. Let it cool. Combine mayonnaise, shrimp, celery, green pepper and onion. Add to soup mixture. Pour into one quart mold. Chill overnight. Serve on lettuce with mayonnaise garnish.

Serves 8   Maxine Boyd

BANANA NUT DRESSING

½ cup mayonnaise
1 banana, mashed
2 cups chopped pecans

3 Tb. heavy cream
1 Tb. lemon juice

Blend mayonnaise, banana, pecans, heavy cream and lemon juice. Mixture may be put into bowl with tight lid and refrigerated for several days. This is good for fresh fruit salads.

Servings 6

Bernice Hanchey

BLEU CHEESE DRESSING

1 quart mayonnaise
8 ounces bleu cheese, crumbled
2 cloves garlic, finely chopped

1 cup buttermilk
1 cup half-and-half cream
Salt and pepper to taste

Mix all ingredients. Refrigerate for 24 hours.

Yield: 1 quart

Linda Elliott

CATALINA SALAD DRESSING

¼ tsp. black pepper
¼ cup vinegar
½ cup catsup
1 small onion, minced

½ tsp. salt
½ cup sugar
1 cup salad oil

Using a blender, mix all ingredients, except oil, in order given. Gradually add oil while blending. Refrigerate.

Yield: 1 pint

Karen Bryant

Bury avocados in a bowl of flour to ripen them.

Frosted Grapes: Combine slightly beaten egg white with a little water. Brush over cluster of white grapes and sprinkle with granulated sugar. Place on rack until sugar is dry.

POPPY SEED DRESSING

1½ cups sugar
2 tsp. dry mustard
1 tsp. salt

⅔ cup cider vinegar
2 cups oil
3 Tb. poppy seeds

Mix sugar, mustard, salt, and vinegar in blender. Slowly add oil, blending until thick. Stir in poppy seeds. Dressing keeps in refrigerator for weeks.

It is great over melon balls or fruit salad.

Serves 10-12   Carol Ann Allison

ROQUEFORT DRESSING

1 cup sour cream
¼ cup olive or salad oil
2 or 3 Tb. lemon juice
¼ tsp. onion powder

¼ tsp. garlic powder
½ tsp. salt
½ tsp. sugar
½ cup Roquefort or Bleu cheese,
**   crumbled**

Slowly add oil to sour cream. When blended, add lemon juice and seasonings. Stir in crumbled Roquefort cheese. Dressing can be thinned with cream if too thick. Cover and chill at least one hour before serving.

Serves 12   Susan Plunkett

THOUSAND ISLAND DRESSING

2 hard-boiled eggs, chopped
1 four-ounce bottle stuffed
**   olives, chopped**

1½ cups chili sauce
2 cups mayonnaise

Chop eggs and olives. Mix chili sauce and mayonnaise. Add eggs and olives to chili sauce and mayonnaise. Thin with olive juice, if desired.

Linda Johnson

Lemons yield twice as much juice if dropped into hot water before squeezing.

Store whole lemons in a tightly sealed jar of water in the refrigerator. They will yield much more juice than when first purchased.

Soups & Sandwiches

CHEESE SOUP

2 cups boiling water
1½ tsp. salt
¼ tsp. pepper
1 chicken bouillon cube
2 cups chopped potatoes
½ cup sliced carrots
½ cup chopped celery

¼ cup chopped onion
¼ cup butter
¼ cup flour
2 cups whole milk (or 1 cup milk and
    1 cup half and half)
8 ounces sharp Cheddar cheese
1 cup chopped ham (optional)

Add salt, pepper and bouillon cube to boiling water. Cook vegetables in boiling water until crisp and tender. Melt butter over medium heat. Add flour. When mixture bubbles, add milk slowly. Stir until thick. Add cheese to milk mixture, stirring constantly until cheese is melted. Add vegetables, stock, and ham to cheese sauce.

Serves 4-6   Suzie Thompson

CHILI

3 pounds ground beef
1 onion, chopped
2 ten and ¾-ounce cans tomato soup
2 tsp. salt
6 shakes garlic salt

2 Tb. cumin
3 Tb. chili powder
1 tsp. pepper
4 soup cans water
2 fifteen-ounce cans pinto beans,
    drained

Brown hamburger and onion; drain. Add remaining ingredients except beans. Simmer for 1½ to 3 hours. Add beans right before serving.

Serves 10   Nedra Dumas Wood

COLD AVOCADO SOUP

3 fully ripe avocados
1½ cups chicken broth
1 tsp. salt
¼ tsp. onion salt

Pinch of white pepper
1 tsp. lemon juice
1¼ cups light cream
Lemon slices as garnish

Halve avocados lengthwise, remove seeds, and peel. Blend with chicken broth in electric blender until smooth. Add seasonings and lemon juice and blend until mixed well. Add cream and mix by hand. (If blender is used to mix cream, use lowest speed for short time so that cream will not whip.) Pour into glass container and refrigerate overnight. Garnish with lemon slices, and serve chilled in glass cups. If soup becomes too thick, stir in more cream.

Serves 6   Jephrey Hubener

BEAN SOUP

2 pounds dried Navy beans
1 tsp. salt
1½ pounds smoked ham hock
1 large onion, chopped
2 Tb. margarine

¼ tsp. salt
¼ tsp. dillweed
¼ tsp. dry mustard
¼ tsp. tarragon leaves
¼ tsp. coarsely ground pepper

Wash beans. Place in heavy soup pot and cover with water. Add salt. Cover beans and soak overnight. Add enough water to kettle to make 4 quarts of liquid. Add ham hock and bring to a boil. Saute onion in margarine until soft and add to beans. Stir in remaining ingredients; reduce heat and simmer for 4 hours or until beans are tender, sirring occasionally. Remove ham hock from soup, separate meat from bone, and return meat to soup.

Serves 10-12   Becky Hight

HELEN'S CHILI

2 pounds lean ground beef
1 medium onion, finely chopped
1 eight-ounce can tomato sauce
1 package Williams Chili Seasoning
2 whole bay leaves

1 Tb. chili powder
¼ tsp. powdered cloves
2 sixteen-ounce cans pinto beans
Salt and pepper

Brown meat and onion. Drain off any excess liquid or fat. Add all other ingredients, except beans. Simmer 1½-2 hours. Add beans, if desired. Simmer additional fifteen minutes longer. Remove bay leaves. Salt and pepper to taste before serving.

This is better if made a day before and refrigerated over night. However, it can be eaten the same day. If hotter chili is desired, add one can Rotel chilies and tomatoes. For thinner chili, add one cup tomato juice.

Serves 6-8   Colleen Wallace

Keep a "soup pot" in the freezer. In a large plastic container put liquids from canned vegetables, left-over vegetables and broths from beef or chicken. When you are ready to make soup, you will have a good start with the ingredients from your soup pot.

CORN CHOWDER

5 medium potatoes, peeled and diced
1 seventeen-ounce can cream style
  corn
1 ten and ¾-ounce can cream of
  mushroom soup
2 medium onions, diced
1 medium green pepper, diced

2 Tb. butter
1 pint cream
2 cups milk
8 strips bacon
1 two-ounce can mushrooms
1 package oyster crackers

Boil potatoes until tender. Drain and add corn and mushroom soup. Stir. Sauté onions and peppers in butter until tender, but not brown. When they are done, add to potato mixture. Add cream and milk and stir. Fry bacon until crisp and crumble. Add bacon and mushrooms to mixture. Heat until almost boiling, but *do not boil.* Ladle into bowls and add oyster crackers.

This is an authentic New England chowder recipe and is perfect with a salad for a winter supper.

Serves 6-8   Shirley Hale

CREAM OF ARTICHOKE SOUP

3 Tb. butter
½ cup chopped green onions
1 stalk celery, chopped
1 bay leaf
1 carrot, chopped

Pinch of thyme
1 quart chicken consommé
1 cup sliced artichoke hearts, cooked
1 cup heavy cream
2 egg yolks

Sauté green onions, celery, carrots, bay leaf and thyme in butter. Add consommé. Simmer 10-15 minutes. Remove from heat. Add beaten yolks and cream. Add artichoke hearts. Season with salt and pepper to taste and serve.

Serves 4   Mrs. John J. Truemper, Jr.

When adding dried herbs to a recipe, first rub them in the palm of your hand to bring out the flavor.

CREAM OF CARROT SOUP

2 Tb. butter or margarine
¾ cup chopped onion
8 to 10 carrots, peeled and chopped
3 to 5 potatoes, peeled and chopped
6 cups rich chicken broth
½ tsp. dried thyme
1 small bay leaf

1 clove garlic, halved
⅛ tsp. Tabasco sauce
½ tsp. sugar
½ tsp. salt
1 cup milk
1 Tb. butter or margarine

Heat 2 Tb. butter or margarine in a soup kettle and add onion. Cook for 5 minutes, stirring. Add the carrots and potatoes and toss for 2 minutes. Add the chicken broth and the rest of the ingredients with the exception of the milk and the 1 Tb. butter or margarine. Bring to a boil and simmer for 50 minutes. Put the mixture through a food mill or blender, ⅓ at a time. Return to heat and bring to a boil. Add milk and heat thoroughly; correct seasoning. Remove from heat and stir in the remaining 1 Tb. butter or margarine.

Serves 8

Pam Gustavus

CREAM OF LETTUCE SOUP

1 head unblemished Boston lettuce
5 cups chicken stock
1 large onion, minced
⅛ tsp. minced garlic
1 stalk celery, finely chopped

¼ cup butter
2 Tb. flour
½ cup heavy whipping cream
Salt and pepper

Wash and core lettuce and finely shred. Boil in 1 cup of stock for 5 minutes. Remove from heat and reserve. Sauté onion, garlic and celery in butter until soft, but not browned. Dissolve flour in a small amount of stock. Add remaining stock to vegetables. Add flour mixture to stock and vegetables. Bring to boil and cook for 15 minutes, uncovered. Add lettuce and stock in which it was cooked. Reheat. Add cream, salt and pepper to taste, and serve.

E.G. Finch

DIETER'S SPECIAL SOUP

1 head of cabbage
6 large onions
1 bunch celery
1 large green pepper

Any leftover roast or steak
Forty-six-ounce can V-8 juice
12 beef bouillon cubes
1 package onion soup mix

Cut all vegetables and meat into medium bite-size pieces. Place all ingredients in large soup pot. Cover and boil for 10 minutes. Lower heat on stove and cook for 2½ hours.

Rosemary Glover
Anne Glover

Serves 10-12

EASY GAZPACHO

1 thirteen and ½-ounce can beef
  bouillon
2½ forty-six ounce cans tomato juice
¼ cup lemon juice
¼ cup finely chopped onion
1 clove garlic, split and speared on
  toothpicks

Salt and pepper to taste
⅓ cup finely chopped cucumber
⅓ cup finely chopped bell pepper
⅓ cup finely chopped celery

Mix first five ingredients well; add salt and pepper. Chill for 2 hours. Add chopped vegetables. Chill 1 more hour. Remove speared galic and serve in chilled mugs.

If a hotter soup is desired, the juice may be a mixture of half Snap-E-Tom and half tomato juice.

Serves 6   Betsy Davies

EGG SOUP (NORTHERN ITALIAN CUISINE)

⅓ cup olive oil (never vegetable oil)
2 medium cloves garlic, finely
  chopped
3 thirteen and ½-ounce cans
  Swanson's broth plus enough
  water to equal 3½ quarts liquid
4 eggs, well beaten

½ cup grated Parmesan cheese
½ cup fresh parsley, finely
  chopped
Egg noodles
Salt
Pepper

In a 5-quart saucepan gently sauté and lightly brown the garlic in olive oil. To this pan, add the chicken broth and water, and bring to a full boil. To the beaten eggs, add cheese and parsley and mix. Slowly pour the egg-cheese mixture into the boiling liquid, stirring constantly. Return liquid to a boil. Add enough egg noodles to obtain a soup of desired consistency. Add salt and pepper to taste.

Serves 12   Andrea Davenport

FISH CHOWDER

1 medium potato, peeled and diced
1 onion, chopped
2 slices bacon, chopped
1 pound fish fillets, cut in bite-size
  pieces
1½ cup chopped celery

2½ cups water
1½ tsp. salt
¼ tsp. pepper
4 Tb. oleo
¼ cup flour
2 cups evaporated milk

Cook potato in water until tender. Add onion and bacon and cook. Stir in fish, celery, water, salt, and pepper. Simmer covered 25 minutes. Melt butter in another pan. Add flour and then milk. Cook until mixture thickens. Stir flour mixture into fish mixture and heat through.

Serves 8   Gerrie Fletcher
                                                                      Pine Bluff

FRENCH ONION SOUP

4 large onions, thinly sliced
1 clove garlic, mashed
3 Tb. bacon drippings
2 Tb. flour
1 quart chicken broth
Sprig of parsley
Pinch of thyme

1 cup dry white wine or vermouth
½ tsp. salt
White pepper
1 Tb. cognac
Toasted French bread
Grated Swiss cheese

Sauté onions and garlic in bacon drippings until soft. Add flour and cook until brown. Add chicken broth, parsley, thyme, salt, pepper and wine. Simmer at least 2-3 hours. Add cognac. Soup is best if made early in the day and let stand. Pour soup in oven-proof bowls. Float a slice of French bread on soup and cover with cheese. Put under broiler until bubbly and lightly browned.

Serves 6-8

ICED CUCUMBER VICHYSSOISE

1 medium onion, finely chopped
4 leeks or 1 bunch green onions,
   white part only, finely sliced
4 medium cucumbers, peeled and
   chopped
¼ pound butter or margarine
2 large potatoes, peeled and chopped

2 quarts chicken stock or canned
   chicken broth
Salt and white pepper to taste
4 cups light cream (half & half) or more
   to desired consistency
8 sprigs parsley, to decorate

Sauté onion, leeks (or green onions), and cucumbers in butter until soft. Drain butter. Add potatoes and chicken stock, salt, and pepper. Bring to a boil and simmer until potatoes are soft, approximately 20 minutes. Run through blender or fine sieve. Adjust seasoning; and cool. Add cream. Chill thoroughly. Serve in cream soup bowls or mugs, well-chilled. Drop a sprig of parsley on top.

Serves 8   Myrtle McCord

To cut the odor of cabbage while cooking, add a little vinegar to the pot.

Remember: White pepper is stronger than black pepper.

POTATO SOUP

½ cup oleo
2 cups chopped onion
¼ cup chopped scallions
1 quart chicken broth (or 2 cans
   Swanson or Sweet Sue broth)

4 medium potatoes, thin sliced
⅛ tsp. pepper
1½ tsp. salt
1 cup light cream
1 Tb. chopped parsley

Melt oleo in saucepan. Add chopped onions. Cook until tender, but not brown, with the chopped scallions, reserving 1 Tb. Add potatoes. Add chicken broth, salt and pepper. Simmer until vegetables are tender, about 10-15 minutes. Add 1 cup light cream, chopped parsley, and 1 Tb. scallions. Reheat.

Variation: Sauté 2 cups chopped onion in one stick oleo. Cook potatoes in the quart of chicken broth. When onions are done, combine with cooked potatoes and broth. Process in blender until smooth.

Delicious served with a gelatin salad and hot corn bread.

Serves 3-4   Ruth Jackson

ROSEMARY'S BORSCHT

2 chicken bouillon cubes
1 small onion, finely chopped
2 large carrots, finely chopped
1 cup finely chopped cabbage
1 bay leaf
1½ cups water
1 eight-ounce can tomato sauce

1 heaping Tb. margarine
2 Tb. vinegar
1 heaping Tb. sugar
Black pepper to taste
1 twenty-ounce can beets, finely
   chopped (save liquid)
Sour cream

Boil together first six ingredients for 10 minutes. Remove bay leaf. Add tomato sauce, margarine, vinegar, sugar and pepper. At last minute add beets and liquid. Do not boil over 3 minutes or color will fade. Serve with dollop of sour cream on top.

Substitution: Chicken stock may be sutstituted for 1½ cups water and 2 bouillon cubes.

Serves 6   Janice Davies

Freeze soup in milk cartons. The pint size is convenient for small amounts of leftovers and just right to take to a sick friend.

119

SEAFOOD OKRA GUMBO

2 pounds shrimp
½ dozen crabs or one-pound can
  crabmeat
½ pound ham (optional)
⅓ cup shortening
1 large onion, chopped
1 clove garlic, chopped
4-6 cups boiling water
2 pounds okra

1½ dozen oysters (optional)
1 green pepper
1 fifteen-ounce can tomato sauce
1 Tb. Worcestershire sauce
1 bay leaf
1 sprig thyme
1 stalk celery
1 Tb. chopped parsley

Clean and wash shrimp and crabs. Cut ham into small pieces. Fry shrimp, crabs, and ham in skillet with half of shortening. When brown, put into large covered saucepan with boiling water. Add remaining shortening to skillet; brown onion and garlic slightly. Add okra and green pepper. Stir okra 20 minutes until it is brown and is no longer ropy or slimy. To avoid scorching okra, keep okra constantly moving in the skillet. When fresh okra is not available, chopped frozen okra may be used. Frozen okra will not require as long to brown as fresh. Add tomato sauce and rest of seasonings. Add to shrimp, crabs and ham in saucepan; simmer for 2 hours. Add oysters 10 minutes before serving. If canned crab meat is used, add it near the end of cooking time. Serve over rice in soup plates.

Ann Chudy

ROSEMARY'S SHRIMP GUMBO

1 cup chopped celery
½ cup chopped green pepper
½ cup chopped onion
2 cloves garlic, finely chopped
⅓ cup cooking oil
4 beef bouillon cubes
4 cups boiling water
1 sixteen-ounce can stewed
  tomatoes

2 ten-ounce packages frozen okra,
  chopped
4 tsp. salt
½ tsp. pepper
½ tsp. thyme
2 whole bay leaves, crushed
1 sixteen-ounce can V-8 juice
2 Tb. rice
6 cup cocktail shrimp, fresh or frozen

Cook celery, green pepper, onion and garlic in oil until tender. Dissolve bouillon cubes in water. Add bouillon, tomatoes, okra, seasonings, V-8 juice, and rice. Cover and simmer for 30 minutes. Add shrimp. Cover and simmer another 20 minutes.

May be frozen.

Yield 1½ gallons

Rosemary Russell

SHRIMP GUMBO

¼ green pepper, chopped
2 cups celery, chopped
1 cup onion, chopped
1 clove garlic, minced, or ¼ tsp. garlic
   powder
2 Tb. Worcestershire sauce
Dash of hot sauce

1 four and ¼-ounce can small shrimp
½ tsp. oregano
1 package frozen cut okra
2 eight-ounce cans tomato sauce
2 cans water
1 tsp. salt
¼ tsp. pepper

Sauté all chopped vegetables in bacon drippings until onions are clear. Add other ingredients in order listed and simmer about 1½ hours. Add water if needed. Serve over rice.

Variation: Crabmeat may be added to make a seafood gumbo.

Serves 6

Alice Kepner

DELICIOUS BEEF STEW

4 slices bacon, cut into small pieces
2 medium onions, quartered
1 pound lean stew beef (or use
   leftover roast beef)
1 can beef bouillon
⅓ cup soy sauce

1 Tb. Worcestershire sauce
2 tsp. oregano
Garlic powder to taste
Salt and pepper to taste
6 medium potatoes, quartered

Sauté onion and bacon together until onion is tender. Add stew meat and brown well. Add remaining ingredients, except potatoes, and simmer over low heat for 2 hours. Add water as needed. About 45 minutes before stew is done, add potatoes and continue cooking until potatoes are tender.

For variety, other vegetables such as mushrooms or carrots may be added.

Serves 4

Suzie Thompson

GROUND BEEF SOUP

1 pound ground beef
6 pieces celery, chopped
1 medium onion, chopped
Salt and pepper
1 sixteen-ounce can tomatoes

4 cups tomato juice
1 envelope onion soup mix
2 fifteen-ounce cans mixed vegetables
2 cups water or liquid from vegetables

Brown ground beef, celery and onion. Drain. Season to taste with salt and pepper. Add tomatoes, tomato juice and onion soup mix. Simmer 1 hour. Add vegetables with liquid or drained vegetables and water. Simmer 30 minutes.

Freezes well.

Serves 10-12

Robin Dean

121

HAMBURGER VEGETABLE SOUP

1 pound ground beef
½ cup chopped onions
6 cups water (more if desired)
1½ cups chopped carrots
1½ cups chopped celery
1½ cups chopped potatoes
2 tsp. salt
¼ tsp. pepper

1 tsp. Kitchen Bouquet
1 bay leaf
1 twelve-ounce can corn
½ of an eight-ounce can okra (optional)
2 sixteen-ounce cans Tomato Sauce
  Special
20 pieces spaghetti, broken into 2-inch
  lengths

Brown meat and onion; drain. Add all other ingredients except corn, okra, tomato sauce and spaghetti. Heat to boiling. Reduce heat and simmer 40 minutes. Add corn, okra, tomato sauce and broken spaghetti. Simmer 40 minutes longer or until vegetables are tender.

Variation: 2 tsp. chili powder may be added for a spicier taste.

Serves 8   Beverly Russell

HEARTY VEGETABLE SOUP

3 quarts boiling water
1 small arm roast or two-pounds soup
  meat
2 packages onion soup mix
1 one-pound can tomato sauce
1 one-pound can tomatoes
1 eight-ounce can Snap-E-Tom
1½ tsp. marjoram

1½ tsp. basil
1 Tb. Worcestershire sauce
1½ tsp. pepper
1 tsp. garlic powder
1 Tb. salt
2 bay leaves
1½ tsp. parsley
1 large package frozen vegetables

Cook first 3 ingredients 20-25 minutes. Add remaining ingredients, except frozen vegetables and cook 15 minutes. Add frozen vegetables and simmer 2-2½ hours.

Alix Matthews

MAGIC MENNEFEE STEW

2 pounds stew meat
1 ten and ¾-ounce can cream of
  mushroom soup
1 medium onion, chopped

3 potatoes, peeled and chopped
½ soup can of water or wine
4 carrots, cleaned and chopped
1 sixteen-ounce can English peas

Combine meat, soup, onion and potatoes in covered casserole or pot. Add water or wine. Stir. Cover and cook for 5 hours in 250° oven. Add carrots and peas and cook for 30 minutes more. Serve with corn bread or noodles.

Serves 4-6   Louise Harper

BAKED CHEESE SANDWICHES

8 slices buttered, decrusted bread
6 slices sharp Cheddar cheese
3 eggs
2 cups milk

1 tsp. salt
¼ tsp. black pepper
1 tsp. dry mustard
2 shakes Worcestershire

Fit bread snugly into a 7x11-inch buttered dish. Layer cheese on top. Beat eggs, milk, salt, pepper, mustard and Worcestershire and pour over sandwiches. Cover and leave in refrigerator overnight. Place baking dish in a larger dish (11x14) of boiling water and bake in 350° oven for one hour. Trim with parsley, bacon curls and/or mushrooms. Cut into squares to serve.

Variation: Add sliced olives to sandwiches.

Serves 8

Susan Eanes

BAKED CHICKEN SANDWICHES

1½ cups cooked, chopped chicken
1 ten and ¾-ounce can cream of
   mushroom soup
1 seven-ounce can chicken gravy

2 Tb. chopped pimiento
2 Tb. chopped onion
1 cup sliced water chestnuts
20 slices bread

AFTER FREEZING:

4 eggs, beaten
2 Tb. milk

Crushed potato chips

Mix chicken, soup, gravy, pimiento, onion and water chestnuts. Cut crusts from bread. Spread mixture on bread. Wrap and freeze sandwiches. Dip frozen sandwiches in mixture of beaten eggs and milk. Coat with crushed potato chips and place on buttered cookie sheet. Bake at 300° for one hour.

Serves 10

Helen McLean

CHICKEN ALMOND PITA SANDWICHES

3 cups cubed cooked chicken
½ cup plain yogurt
½ cup chopped toasted almonds
2 Tb. lemon juice
½ tsp. salt

¼ tsp. pepper
⅛ tsp. dried dillweed
4 six-inch pocket bread rounds
2 cups shredded lettuce
1 cup alfalfa sprouts

Combine first seven ingredients, mixing well; set aside. Cut pita rounds in half; fill each half with lettuce and alfalfa sprouts. Spoon in chicken mixture. Chill one hour before serving.

Yield: 8 sandwiches

Ann Ouellette

123

CREAMY CRAB SANDWICH

1 eight-ounce package cream cheese,
   softened
¼ tsp. butter or margarine
1 tsp. Worcestershire sauce
1 tsp. chopped onion
1 tsp. prepared mustard
1 tsp. lemon juice

1 six-ounce frozen crab meat, thawed
   and drained
4 English muffins, split
8 tomato slices
8 slices bacon, cooked and halved
8 slices American cheese

Cook first six ingredients; beat until fluffy. Fold in crab meat. Spread mixture on muffin halves. Top each with a tomato slice, cheese slice and 2 pieces of bacon. Bake at 350° for 8-10 minutes.

Serves 4   Dixie Smith

FROZEN HAM SANDWICHES

1 stick butter
1 Tb. chopped onion
1 Tb. poppy seeds
¼ cup prepared mustard

6 sesame seed hamburger buns
12 slices baby Swiss cheese
6 slices ham

Melt butter; add onion, poppy seeds and mustard. Brush on sesame seed hamburger buns. Add layer of cheese, boiled ham and more cheese. Wrap in heavy-duty aluminum foil and freeze. Thaw 20 minutes; heat 30 minutes in a 300° oven, still wrapped in foil. Serve hot.

These are convenient to keep in the freezer for unexpected company or for times when there isn't time to fix supper. Delicious!

Serves 6   Shirley Hale

OLIVE NUT SANDWICHES

1 six-ounce package cream cheese,
   softened
½ cup mayonnaise
1¼ cup sliced salad olives

½ cup chopped nuts
2 Tb. juice from the olives

Mix all ingredients well and let sit in refrigerator 24 hours to thicken. Serve on thin toast or bread.

Yield: 1 pint   Gerrie Fletcher

REUBEN SANDWICH

1 twelve-ounce can corned beef	Sauerkraut, drained
Rye bread	Swiss cheese
Mayonnaise	

Spread slices of rye bread with mayonnaise. Spread corned beef over one side of bread. Place one slice of Swiss cheese over beef; spread kraut over cheese. Cover with other slice of bread. Wrap in foil and place in oven (slow to warm). Serve with chips and pickles.

Serves 6   Eloise Evans

STACKED SANDWICH

1 large piece light rye bread	1 slice Swiss cheese
1 slice turkey	1 slice tomato
1 slice ham	2 slices bacon, cooked

Stack above ingredients in order given. Top with sauce.

SAUCE

½ cup mayonnaise	1 boiled egg, grated
½ cup catsup	

Mix together. Makes one cup. Use 3 Tb. per sandwich.

Yield: 4 sandwiches   Nancy Harmon

TUNA CHEESE BUNS

¼ pound cubed sharp American cheese	¾ tsp. salt
2 boiled eggs, chopped	3 tsp. chopped stuffed olives
1 cup chunk style tuna	2 tsp. pickle relish
1 tsp. minced green pepper	½ cup mayonnaise
2 tsp. minced onion	6 hamburger buns, buttered

Combine all ingredients and mix. Spoon between split buns. Wrap each bun in foil. Refrigerate. To serve, bake in foil at 350° for 20 minutes.

Yield: 6 sandwiches   Ann Cornwell

TWENTY-FOUR HOUR TUNA SANDWICH

2 six-and-½-ounce cans tuna
½ four-ounce can ripe olives, chopped
4 hard-boiled eggs, chopped
⅔ cup mayonnaise
1 Tb. chopped onion

20 slices bread, trimmed
3 jars Kraft Sharp Old English cheese
1 cup butter, softened
3 eggs, separated

Mix tuna, olives, boiled eggs, mayonnaise and onion. Spread on bread to make 10 sandwiches. Place on cookie sheet. Beat egg yolks and whites separately. Mix cheese, butter and beaten yolks. Fold in beaten egg whites. Use this mixture to ice sandwiches. Cover completely. Refrigerate for 24 hours or freeze. Bake 10 minutes at 450° if unfrozen, or 15 minutes at 425° if frozen.

Serves 10

Linda Elliott

When making stock, don't salt the water. It will concentrate as it cooks and be too salty. Wait until you have finished, and then season to taste.

Start vegetables that grow above the ground in boiling water; start vegetables that grow under the ground in cold water.

Burned the vegetables again? Set the pan in a pan of cold water and let it stand 15-30 minutes. Don't scrape the bottom of the pan.

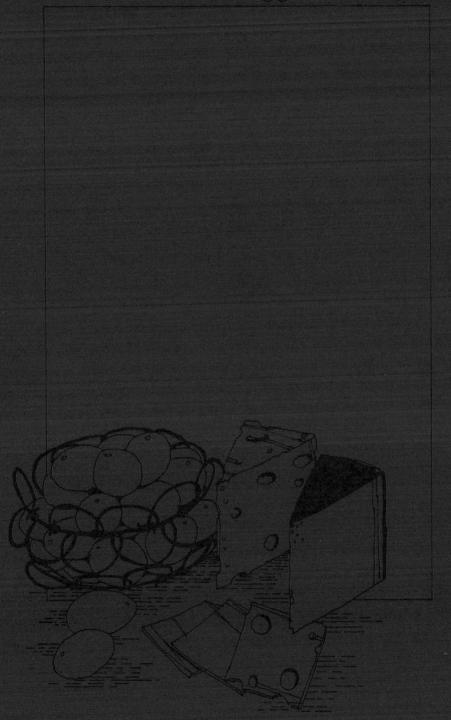

ARKANSAS OMELETTE

1 large egg per omelette
1 tsp. water per egg

Salt and pepper to taste
1 Tb. butter per omelette

SAUCE (Enough for 4-6 omelettes)

1 sixteen-ounce can stewed tomatoes
½ onion, chopped
½ cup grated Kraft Jalapeño cheese

1 Tb. cumin
2 Tb. Tabasco sauce

Beat eggs with water, salt and pepper until blended. Melt butter in a small skillet. When butter is hot and evenly covering pan, pour enough egg mixture into pan to cover bottom thinly. When eggs have begun to bubble around edges, add ¼ cup sauce mixture. When eggs are lightly browned on bottom, fold them over like a sandwich to cover sauce. Continue to cook until sauce is well heated. Be careful not to burn the bottom of the egg mixture.

Pat Carlton

GOOD MORNING CASSEROLE

6 eggs, beaten slightly
1 tsp. salt
1 tsp. dry mustard
2 cups milk
1 pound bulk sausage, browned and drained

6 slices bread, cubed in one-inch pieces or 1 English muffin (2 halves), torn into small pieces
1 cup shredded Cheddar cheese
3 Tb. chopped green onions (optional)

Mix eggs, spices and milk. Add meat and stir. Set aside. In greased casserole, layer ½ bread cubes, meat and egg and milk mixture, ending with remaining bread cubes. Cover with grated cheese. Refrigerate overnight, or at least 6-8 hours. Bake at 350° for 40-50 minutes.

For a full breakfast, serve with a glass of orange juice.

Variation: For a less fat dish, use Rich's Turkey sausage.

Serves 6-8

Sharon Ferguson
Marion Grant

To avoid confusing cooked with uncooked eggs in the refrigerator, place the outer skins of brown onions in the pot as eggs are cooking to color the shells.

EGGS BENEDICT

2 English muffins (halved and buttered)   Canadian bacon
4 poached eggs   Hollandaise sauce

Place Canadian bacon on buttered muffins. Top with eggs and cover with Hollandaise sauce.

HOLLANDAISE SAUCE:

3 egg yolks
2 Tb. lemon juice
½ cup butter

½ tsp. salt
Dash cayenne pepper

Beat egg yolks in top of double boiler. Gradually add lemon juice to egg yolks, stirring constantly. Add one third of butter to egg mixture. Cook over hot (not boiling) water, stirring constantly, until butter melts. Add another third of butter, stirring constantly. As sauce thickens, stir in remaining butter. Stir in salt and cayenne pepper. Cook until thickened.

Serves 2

Judi Dietz

EGG BRUNCH

SAUCE:

4 slices bacon, diced
½ pound chipped beef, coursely
   shredded
½ cup flour
1-2 four-ounce cans sliced mushrooms,
   well drained

¼ cup butter or oleo
1 quart milk
Pepper to taste

Sauté bacon. Remove pan from heat. Add chipped beef and flour. Mix well. Add ¾ of the mushrooms and butter, reserving remaining mushrooms for garnish. Mix well. Gradually stir in milk. Cook until sauce is thickened and smooth, stirring constantly. Add pepper to taste. Set aside.

SCRAMBLED EGGS:

18 eggs
¼ tsp. salt
1 cup evaporated milk

¼ cup butter or oleo, melted
Reserved mushrooms

Combine eggs with salt and milk and scramble in butter in a large skillet. Alternate layers of eggs and sauce, ending with sauce. Garnish with reserved mushrooms. Cover and bake at 275° for 1 hour. May be prepared the day before and refrigerated.

Serves 12

Mrs. Jack Hattan

EGG CASSEROLE

24-36 eggs
1½ tsp. salt
½ cup milk
1 pound sharp Cheddar cheese, grated
1 ten and ¾-ounce can cream of
  mushroom soup

1 cup sliced mushrooms
½ cup sherry (optional)
½ cup Parmesan cheese
1 tsp. paprika

Scramble eggs lightly over medium heat with salt and milk until soft. Add cheese. Put into greased oblong baking dish; refrigerate overnight. The next day, mix together soup, mushrooms and sherry. Pour mixture over eggs. Sprinkle with Parmesan cheese and paprika. Bake at 325° for 25 minutes.

Serves 20-25   Terri Caple

CHILI EGG PUFF

10 eggs
½ cup flour
1 tsp. baking powder
1 tsp. salt

1 pint small curd cottage cheese
1 pound Monterey Jack cheese, grated
½ cup melted butter
½ four-ounce can green chilies

In large bowl, beat eggs until light colored. Add flour, baking powder, salt, cottage cheese, cheese and butter. Blend until smooth. Add chilies. Pour into greased 9 x 13-inch pan; bake 35-40 minutes at 300° until brown.

Serves 10-12   Sherry Wright

MUSHROOM SCRAMBLE

1 six-ounce package frozen
  mushrooms
16 eggs
1 cup milk
1 Tb. chives
¾ tsp. Worcestershire sauce

½ tsp. salt
¼ tsp. pepper
2 Tb. butter
8 slices Canadian bacon

In a large skillet prepare mushrooms according to package directions. Combine eggs, milk, chives, Worcestershire, salt and pepper in mixing bowl, and stir. Melt butter in skillet with mushrooms; pour in eggs. Cook over medium heat until eggs are thickened. Heat bacon and place around sides of large dish or chafing dish. Fill with egg mixture. Garnish with chives.

Serves 8   Mrs. Bill Brady

DARBY'S DEVILED EGGS

6 hard-boiled eggs, cooled and shelled
2 Tb. mayonnaise
1 tsp. vinegar

1 tsp. French's mustard
Salt and pepper to taste
Paprika

Halve hard-boiled eggs lengthwise. Remove yolks and mash well with fork. Yolks will look finely crumbled. Add all ingredients except paprika; mix well. If mixture is not creamy enough, add about 1 tsp. more mayonnaise. Fill egg whites with yolk mixture, a little more than full. Lightly sprinkle paprika over stuffed eggs. Serve on a bed of lettuce or an egg plate.

Serves 12   Darby Blair

CHEESY SOUR CREAM ENCHILADAS

1 eight-ounce carton sour cream
2 ten and ¾-ounce cans cream of
  mushroom soup
1 four-ounce can chopped green chilies
¼ tsp. salt
¼ tsp. pepper

½ tsp. garlic powder
2 cups grated Cheddar cheese
1 cup chopped green onion
1 eight-ounce package corn tortillas

Combine sour cream, soup, green chilies, salt, pepper and garlic powder in medium saucepan. Mix well. Cook over medium heat until hot, stirring often. Combine cheese and onion; mix well. Cook each tortilla in hot oil for a few minutes until soft. Drain on a paper towel. Immediately spoon 1½ Tb. cheese mixture and 2 Tb. soup mixture onto the center of each tortilla. Roll up tightly and place in a greased 9 x 13-inch baking dish. Spoon remaining soup mixture over top of enchiladas and sprinkle with remaining cheese mixture. Bake at 350° for 20-30 minutes.

Serves 6   Sherri Phelps

FETTUCCINE

¼ pound stick of butter, softened
2½ cups heavy cream (add more if too
  thick)
2-3 cups grated Parmesan cheese
4-6 quarts water

Dash of salt
1 pound fettuccine, homemade or
  commercial
Additional Parmesan cheese

Sauce for Fettuccine: Melt butter over low heat. Add cream to butter and stir. Add Parmesan cheese and mix.

Fettuccine: Bring water to boil and cook fettuccine according to package directions. Add dash of salt. Serve fettuccine covered with sauce. Top with Parmesan cheese.

Serves 6-8   Mary Beth Vowell

CHEESE PETA

½ stick butter or margarine
3 Tb. flour
1 eight-ounce package Old English
  cheese slices
3 eggs

1 ten-ounce package frozen chopped
  spinach, drained
1 sixteen-ounce carton small curd
  cottage cheese

Melt butter and mix with flour. Tear cheese slices into small pieces. Beat eggs well. Add cheese and drained spinach. Stir in flour and butter mixture, along with cottage cheese. Pour into buttered casserole and bake 1 hour at 350° (325° in glass dish). Let stand 10 minutes before serving.

This is a delicious lucheon dish served with sliced tomatoes.

Serves 8   Betty Croom

CHEESE SOUFFLÉ

4 Tb. butter
4 Tb. flour
½ tsp. salt
1½ cups milk
2 cups grated sharp cheese

5 eggs, separated
White pepper to taste
¼ tsp. cream of tartar
Paprika

Melt butter. Blend in flour, salt and milk, stirring constantly. Cook until thick. Stir in cheese and cook until melted. Remove from heat; stir in well-beaten egg yolks and a dash of white pepper. Add cream of tartar to egg whites and beat until stiff. Carefully fold into cheese mixture. Pour into buttered 2-quart casserole. Sprinkle paprika over top. Bake at 325° uncovered for 50-60 minutes. Serve immediately.

Serves 6   Nancy Barrow

MANICOTTI WITH SPINACH

1 pound ricotta cheese or cottage
  cheese
½ cup Parmesan cheese
½ pound mozzarella cheese, grated
2 eggs
1 ten-ounce box frozen spinach,
  thawed

Salt and pepper to taste
1 tsp. garlic
1 box manicotti shells
1 thirty-two-ounce jar spaghetti sauce
¼ cup Parmesan cheese

Mix cheeses and eggs with spinach, salt, pepper and garlic until well blended. Cook manicotti shells according to package directions. Rinse and drain. Fill shells. Place shells on the bottom of a 9 x 13-inch glass dish and cover with spaghetti sauce. Sprinkle additional Parmesan cheese over top and bake 25-30 minutes at 350°.

Pam Gustavus

133

QUICHE

1 deep-dish pie shell
1 three-ounce can fried onion rings
3 eggs
1 cup milk
6 ounces Cheddar cheese, grated
½ tsp. salt

Dash of red pepper
1 four-ounce can sliced mushrooms
2 chicken breasts, cooked and chopped
4 slices bacon, cooked crisp and chopped
2 green onions, chopped

Cook pie shell at 400° for 20 minutes. Fill bottom of shell with ½ can of fried onion rings. Beat eggs. Slightly blend in milk, ½ of Cheddar cheese, salt, pepper and mushrooms. Add bacon, chicken, onions and pour into pie shell. Put remaining cheese on top; bake at 325° for 45 minutes. After 45 minutes top with remaining onion rings. Bake 5-10 minutes longer. Let cool for 10 minutes before cutting.

Serves 6

Gus Arrington

ASPARAGUS QUICHE

9-inch pie crust
1 fourteen and ½-ounce can asparagus, drained
4 eggs
1 eight-ounce carton whipping cream

1 tsp. salt
¼ tsp. nutmeg
¼ cup Parmesan Cheese
1 Tb. minced onion
4 to 5 slices bacon

Make a crust slightly thicker than usual pie crust and pre-bake at 400° for five minutes. Mix next 7 ingredients in blender until smooth. Fry 4-5 slices of bacon until crisp. Drain and crumble into crust. Add asparagus mixture. Sprinkle lightly with black pepper. Bake 30 minutes at 375°. Cool 10 minutes before cutting. This makes a 9-inch quiche. If made in a pie plate, use a 10-inch plate.

Serves 6-8

Nell Steenburgen

Out of copper polish? Try rubbing copper pots with Worcestershire sauce or catsup.

Separate eggs directly from the refrigerator. They will break cleanly, and the yolk of a cold egg is less likely to shatter than one at room temperature.

EGGS & CHEESE

QUICHE CRÊPES

CRÊPE BATTER MIX:

1 cup all-purpose flour
1⅓ cups milk
3 eggs

2 Tb. sugar
2 Tb. melted butter
⅛ tsp. salt

QUICHE LORRAINE FILLING:

4 eggs
¾ tsp. salt
⅛ tsp. cayenne pepper
2 cups half and half

¼ tsp. sugar
1 cup shredded Swiss cheese
8 slices bacon, fried and crumbled
⅓ cup minced onion

Crêpes: In bowl combine flour, milk, eggs, sugar, butter and salt; beat with a rotary beater until blended. Heat a lightly greased (with butter) 6-inch skillet. Remove from heat. Dip ¼ cup of batter and pour into skillet. Lift and tilt skillet to spread batter evenly. Return to heat; lightly brown on one side. An inverted crêpe pan may also be used. Repeat to make enough to fill muffin tins, greasing skillet each time.

Filling: Mix eggs, salt, and cayenne with wire whisk until blended. Add half and half and sugar. Stir until smooth. Add cheese, bacon, and onion. Grease muffin tins with butter; tuck crêpe into each, pressing down and leaving sides fluted. Fill with quiche mixture and bake 20 minutes at 375°.

Serves 8   Pat Carlton

Store cottage cheese cartons upside down. Cheese will keep twice as long.

If you break an egg on the floor, spinkle it heavily with salt. After 5-10 minutes sweep up the dried egg into a dust pan.

Remove eggs stuck to the carton by wetting the box. The eggs will come out without cracking.

WHIPPED BUTTER

½ pound butter
½ pound margarine

¼ cup sour cream

Mix butter and margarine with electric mixer at medium speed until well-blended. Beat in sour cream one tablespoon at a time until smooth and fluffy.

Margaret Tester

BECHAMEL SAUCE

6 Tb. butter
4 Tb. flour
1 tsp. salt
Milled pepper

1½ cups milk, warmed
1 cup heavy cream
Pinch of grated nutmeg

Melt butter, adding flour as it melts. Stir until smooth, sprinkling in salt and milled pepper. When mixture is smooth, slowly stir in milk. Stirring constantly until thick and smooth. Add salt, pepper and nutmeg.

Serves 6-8   Mrs. John Truemper, Jr.

RAISIN SAUCE

¾ cup seedless raisins
1¾ cups water
1 Tb. cornstarch
1 tsp. dry mustard
⅓ cup brown sugar

½ tsp. salt
⅛ tsp. pepper
3 Tb. white vinegar
1 Tb. butter

Simmer raisins in water about 10 minutes. Combine cornstarch, mustard, sugar, salt, pepper and vinegar. Add to cooked raisins and water. Cook 3 minutes longer, stirring constantly. Add butter. Serve warm with baked ham.

Yield: 2 cups   Maxine Boyd

To keep horseradish fresh, turn upside down in refrigerator between uses.

To sterilize jars for canning, put washed jars in a cold oven. Heat to 250°. Heat jars 30 minutes. Turn off heat and leave in oven until ready to use.

139

BUBBA'S FAVORITE HOT SAUCE

2 cups tomatoes, peeled and sliced
1 large bell pepper, chopped
1 large onion, chopped
1 cup sugar
3 hot (red or green) peppers, chopped

½ cup cider vinegar
½ tsp. salt
½ tsp. black pepper
Dash Tabasco

Using an aluminum saucepan, stir tomatoes, bell pepper, onion and hot peppers with sugar and vinegar over low heat with a wooden spoon. When mixture begins to bubble, removed from heat and pack into a hot, sterilized jar.

Delicious served atop cheese and crackers with cocktails!

Yield: 1 pint

Ann Carruth Logan

JEZEBEL

1 eighteen-ounce jar apple jelly
1 eighteen-ounce jar pineapple preserves

1 five-ounce jar horseradish
3 Tb. dry mustard
1 Tb. coarse black pepper

Mix all ingredients and refrigerate.

This sauce keeps forever. It can be used on cream cheese, meats or crackers.

SALSA

1 twenty-eight-ounce can whole tomatoes
1 four-ounce can chopped green chilies
1 or 2 jalapeno peppers

2 cloves garlic, finely chopped
2 fresh green onions, finely chopped
½ tsp. salt
1 tsp. sugar

Combine all ingredients in blender by pressing "chop" button about three times. Pour mixture into jar and chill 24 hours.

Use as dip with chips or add to cheese dips.

Mrs. Clarence Laughter

JALAPEÑO PEPPER JELLY

¾ cup ground sweet peppers
½ cup ground hot peppers
1½ cup vinegar

6 cups sugar
Green or red food coloring
1 six-ounce bottle Certo

Wash and remove stems from peppers. Combine all ingredients except Certo, and bring to boil. Cook 5 minutes, remove from heat, add Certo. Pour into clean jars and seal with lids or paraffin.

Yield: 2 pints   Bobbie Phelps

PICKLED SQUASH

1 gallon sliced squash
Water
¼ cup salt
5 cups sugar

5 cups vinegar
2 tsp. tumeric
8 medium onions, sliced
3 medium bell peppers, sliced

Cover squash in water to which ¼ cup salt has been added. Soak 3 hours and drain. Combine remaining ingredients and bring to boil. Pour over squash. Reheat and put into sterilized pint jars. Seal.

Yield: 4-6 pints   Charlotte Lloyd

BREAD & BUTTER PICKLES

2 quarts thinly sliced
  cucumbers (about 4 large)
2 cups thinly sliced onion
  (1 large)
¼ cup salt

2 cups white wine vinegar
1½ cups sugar
2 tsp. celery seed
2 tsp. mustard seed
1½ tsp. nutmeg

Combine first three ingredients and let stand overnight. Combine remaining ingredients and add to cucumber mixture. Boil for three minutes. Seal while hot.

Yield: 4 pints   Florine Tyler

SUPER EASY PICKLER

1 gallon sour or dill
   pickles (sliced or whole)
5 pounds sugar

½ two-ounce bottle Tabasco
4-5 garlic buttons, chopped

Drain pickles completely. If whole pickles are used, slice to desired thickness. Return pickles to original jar in five layers in the following order: pickles, sugar, Tabasco, chopped garlic. Pack firmly into jar. Close lid tightly. Let stand at room temperature for six days, turning jar once a day (Alternate, turning upside down to rightside up). Remove from gallon jar and place into containers of desired size. Store in refrigerator.

Becky Witcher

SLANG-JANG

4 large tomatoes, chopped
2 green bell peppers, chopped

3 medium onions, chopped

DRESSING:

½ cup vinegar
¼ cup water
3 Tb. sugar (or less to taste)

½ tsp. salt
¼ tsp. pepper

Dressing: Mix vinegar, water and sugar. Add salt and pepper.

Toss chopped vegetables with the dressing and chill. Serve over black-eyed peas.

Patsy Searcy
Hot Springs, Arkansas

COLD MEAT SAUCE

⅓ cup prepared mustard
1 cup mayonnaise
⅓ cup sour cream
⅓ cup chili sauce

1 Tb. finely grated onion
1 Tb. horseradish
1 tsp. oregano
¼ tsp. cayenne pepper

Mix all ingredients well and refrigerate.

This dressing will keep for several weeks and is especially good accompanying a tray of turkey, chicken, ham or other cold cuts. It is good on sandwiches, too!

Betty Croom

DEBBIE'S MARINADE FOR SHISKABOB

Good Seasons Italian Dressing Mix　　**6 ounces vinegar**
12 ounces cooking oil　　**¼ cup Burgundy**

Mix ingredients together. Pour over meat, bell pepper, Bermuda onion sections, fresh mushrooms, and cherry tomatoes in large bowl with tight lid. Let stand for 24 hours before cooking, stirring occasionally (shake bowl upside down). Skewer meat and vegetables and cook on grill.

Really adds good flavor!　　　　　　　　　　Deborah Dorsa Carman

JIFFY BARBECUE SAUCE

¾ cup chopped onion　　　　**3 Tb. sugar**
½ cup Wesson oil　　　　　**3 Tb. Worcestershire sauce**
¾ cup catsup　　　　　　　**2 Tb. prepared mustard**
¾ cup water　　　　　　　　**2 tsp. salt**
⅓ cup lemon juice　　　　　**1½ tsp. black pepper**

Cook onion in hot oil until soft. Add remaining ingredients and simmer for 15 minutes. Makes enough sauce for basting and serving with two chickens.

　　　　　　　　　　　　　　　　　　　Margaret Kennedy

SHRIMP COCKTAIL SAUCE

1 cup chili sauce　　　　　**1 Tb. Worcestershire sauce**
1 cup catsup　　　　　　　**2 Tb. lemon juice**
3 Tb. horseradish　　　　　**Hot sauce to taste**
2 Tb. vinegar

Combine all ingredients, mixing well. Chill at least half an hour before serving.

Yield: 2 cups　　　　　　　　　　　　　　Becky Hight

That catsup may be "slow" good, but you're tired of waiting. Push a straw to the bottom of a new bottle and the catsup will flow faster.

HOT MUSTARD

4 eggs
6 Tb. sugar
1 can Coleman's dry mustard
1 cup cider vinegar

1 tsp. salt
2 tsp. cayenne pepper
1 stick butter

Mix all ingredients in top of double boiler. Cook about 10 minutes over low heat, using a wire whisk or an electric mixer to blend. Cool and store in refrigerator in covered container. Will keep indefinitely.

Good served with ham or turkey.

Yield: 2 cups

Mary Ann Schnipper
Hot Springs, Arkansas

SWEET AND SOUR MUSTARD

4 ounces dry mustard
1 cup cider vinegar

1 cup sugar
2 beaten eggs

Mix mustard and vinegar together and let sit overnight. Add sugar and eggs. Cook over low heat, stirring constantly, until thick. Will keep for weeks in refrigerator.

Great on sandwiches, eggs rolls and weiners.

Carol Ann Allison

Quick Thousand Island dressing: Mix a little catsup with sweet pickle relish and mayonnaise.

Quick tartar sauce: Mix sweet pickle relish with mayonnaise.

Before opening a package of bacon, roll it into a tube. The slices will be easier to separate.

CANDIED WILD DUCK

2 or 3 wild ducks
1 quartered apple per duck
1 six-ounce can frozen orange
  juice, thawed

1 six-ounce can apple juice
½ cup chopped pecans

Cover ducks with water in a large pot. Add apples and simmer 2 to 3 hours until tender. Water will look very messy. Pour off water and throw away apples. Skin and bone ducks. Cut or tear into bite-sized pieces. Place meat in buttered casserole. Spoon 2 Tbs. orange concentrate per duck over meat. Add apple juice and sprinkle pecans on top. Bake in 350° oven for about 30 minutes or until well-heated.

Serves 6-8

Doris Miller

DUCK CASSEROLE

2 ducks
1 onion, sliced
2 ribs celery, chopped
½ cup butter
½ cup chopped onion
¼ cup flour
1 six-ounce can sliced mushrooms

1½ cups milk
1 Tb. chopped parsley
1½ tsp. pepper
1 six and ¾-ounce box long grain
  and wild rice
1 three and ½-ounce package
  slivered almonds

Boil ducks 2 hours with sliced onion and celery. Cook rice according to directions on box. In deep skillet, melt butter; sauté chopped onion, and stir in flour. Add mushrooms and their liquid. Add milk, parsley, salt and pepper. Add rice. Bone ducks and add chunks to the other ingredients. Place in greased 2 quart casserole, sprinkle with almonds and bake at 350° for 25 minutes.

Serves 8-10

DUCKS IN SHERRY

4-6 ducks
Salt
2 - 3 onions, chopped
10 stalks celery, chopped
1 stick butter

1 ten and ¾-ounce can beef consommé
½ soup can of water
1 Tb. Worcestershire sauce
½ cup sherry

Rub washed ducks heavily, inside and out, with salt. Brown onion and celery in butter. Place onion and celery inside ducks. Add all other ingredients to the onion and celery pan-drippings. Pour over ducks. Cook covered for 3 hours at 350°. Baste every 20 minutes.

Serves 6-8

Vikki Koch

GRILLED MARINATED DUCK BREASTS

6 boned duck breasts
2 Tb. salt
2 cups Italian dressing

1 Tb. Worcestershire sauce
6 slices bacon

Cover duck breasts with water. Add 2 Tb. salt and let soak for 30 minutes. Drain. Cover duck breasts with 2 cups Italian dressing added to 1 Tb. Worcestershire sauce. Marinate for 1½ hours or longer if desired, turning several times. Wrap each breast with bacon and secure with toothpicks. Grill over medium coals until bacon is done.

Serves 6   Patty Brady

MALLARD WITH RICE DRESSING

1 six-and-¾-ounce box long grain
   and wild rice
3 mallards
2 tsp. salt
4 Tb. minced onion
4 Tb. minced green pepper

4 Tb. minced celery
4 ounce can mushrooms,
   drained and chopped
½ tsp. pepper
¼ pound butter, melted
3 cups orange juice

Mallards should be aged overnight in refrigerator, wrapped in a damp dish towel. The next day, prepare rice according to package. To the cooked rice add onion, pepper, celery, mushrooms, salt, pepper and the melted butter. Stuff the mallards with this dressing and roast in 350° oven for 2 hours or until a fork inserted into breast produces a clear juice. Baste ducks frequently with the orange juice mixed with equal parts of water. Use a baking pan that has a rack on top and a pan to catch grease on the bottom.

Serves 6-8   Mary Frances Beavers

POPCORN DUCK

Ducks (breasts only)
1 cup soy sauce
1 cup Worcestershire sauce

Garlic salt to taste
Flour
Shortening

Cut duck breasts into half-inch cubes. Mix soy sauce and Worcestershire sauce, half and half. The amount depends on the number of ducks used. Add a little garlic salt to taste. Pour marinade over ducks. Marinate for 4 to 24 hours. Roll cubes in flour and deep-fry. Drain. Serve with hot mustard, sweet and sour sauce, or sauce of your choice.

Serves 2 persons per duck as main course
Serves 4 persons per duck as appetizer   Larry M. Jones

ONION SOUP DUCK

1 wild duck, cleaned   **1 package Lipton's onion soup mix**

Place duck in large piece of aluminum foil. Sprinkle dry soup mix over top of duck. Wrap foil tightly and place in covered pan. Bake 3½ hours at 250°.

Serves 2   Ginny Matthews

ROAST DUCK BITES

Roast duck, cut into bite-sized   **1 egg, beaten**
** pieces**   **1 Tb. vodka**
Bacon, cut into pieces   **Bread crumbs**

Roast duck. Cut into bite-sized pieces. Wrap with bacon and secure with toothpicks. Dip in beaten egg mixed with vodka; roll in bread crumbs. Fry in deep fat until bacon is crisp.

May be served with orange or cherry sauce.

Serves 6-8   Betty Ketzcher

PHEASANT

2 pheasants, cup-up   **Salt**
2 ten-and ¾-ounce cans cream   **Pepper**
** of mushroom soup**   **Flour**
1 thirteen-ounce can condensed milk

Salt, pepper and flour cut-up pheasant. Brown on both sides in hot grease or oil. Mix two cans mushroom soup and one can of milk. Pour over pheasant; cover and cook on low heat (simmer) for about one hour.

Variation: Pour one can of condensed milk over cut-up pheasant and let sit overnight. Drain and cook.

Serves 4-6   Pat Fisher

A metal colander upside down over the skillet will allow steam to escape, but keeps fat from spattering.

VENISON STEW

2 pounds venison, cubed
1¼ cups red wine
1 carrot, sliced
1 onion, sliced
2 cloves garlic, minced
3 Tb. olive oil

Salt and pepper
Bouquet Garni*
2 Tb. butter
1 cup bacon, diced
3 Tb. flour
1 bay leaf

Place meat in shallow dish. Mix wine, carrot, onion, garlic, oil, Bouquet Garni and seasonings. Pour over meat and marinate for 12 hours. Dry meat and reserve marinade. Heat butter. Sauté bacon and onions. Remove from heat. Add meat and brown over high heat; sprinkle with flour. Mix well and cook 1 minute. Strain marinade liquid (discard vegetables) over meat, adding just enough water to cover. Bring to a boil, stirring constantly. Lower the heat. Add bacon and onions and bay leaf. Season. Cover and cook 1½ hours to 2 hours. Remove bay leaf.

*Bouquet Garni can be bought or made from tying the following in cheese cloth: ½ tsp. dried parsley, ¼ tsp. of thyme and marjoram, pinch of bay leaf and ½ tsp. of dried celery.

Betsy Davies

VENISON MEAT LOAF

1½ pounds ground venison
Juice of ½ lemon
2 Tb. margarine
1 cup cracker crumbs
1 tsp. salt
½ tsp. pepper

1 small finely chopped onion
1 beaten egg
¼ cup milk
Small celery stalk with a few leaves
1 eight-ounce can tomato soup
   or sauce

Mix all except soup and put into a buttered loaf pan. Pour ½ cup water into pan. Pour soup or sauce over loaf. Bake uncovered for 1½ hours in 325° oven. Add more water if necessary.

Serves 6-8

Mary Ann Schnipper

BAKED FISH

1 pound fish fillets
2 onions, quartered
6 carrots, sliced
1 green pepper, sliced

1 fourteen and ½-ounce can
   tomatoes
1 tsp. sugar
1 stick of butter, sliced

Place fish in a baking dish. Parboil onions, carrots and green pepper. Lay on top of fish. Pour tomatoes over fish. Sprinkle with sugar and top with butter. Bake 45 minutes uncovered in a 350° oven.

Serves 4

Mrs. M. E. Argo

BROILED LEMON FISH FILLET

Fish fillets
Black pepper
Sweet basil

Juice of 1 lemon
Cooking oil

Sprinkle each fish fillet with pepper, basil and lemon juice. Marinate for 1 hour. Lay fish in a shallow tray and coat lightly with oil. Broil 5 minutes.

Anne Harris

CURRIED TUNA SPAGHETTI

3 ten and ¾-ounce cans cream
** of chicken soup**
2 ten and ¾-ounce cans cream
** of mushroom soup**
1 cup milk
½ cup water
4 tsp. curry powder dissolved in
** ¼ cup warm water**

½ tsp. dried thyme
¼ tsp. basil
¼ tsp. oregano
1 tsp. chopped onion
1 six-ounce can mushrooms and
** liquid**
2 six and ½-ounce cans tuna
1 pound thin spaghetti, cooked

Combine first 4 ingredients. Stir well and simmer 10 minutes. Add next six ingredients. Cook 10 minutes. Add tuna; toss in cooked spaghetti. Put into a four-quart casserole. Heat in 325° oven 10-15 minutes.

Serves 12

Jo Arnold

QUICK AND EASY SALMON PATTIES

1 fifteen-ounce can pink salmon
1 egg
⅓ cup minced onion
½ cup flour

1½ tsp. baking powder
Salt and pepper to taste
1¼ cup shortening

Drain salmon and set aside 2 Tb. of the juice. In medium mixing bowl, mix salmon, egg and onion until sticky. Stir in flour. Add baking powder to salmon juice; stir into salmon mixture. Form into small patties and fry in hot shortening until golden brown. Serve with tartar sauce or Caesar salad dressing.

Serves 4-5

CRABMEAT REMICK

¼ pound lump crabmeat per person

SAUCE:

3 pints mayonnaise
1 bottle chili sauce
4 tsp. Tabasco or to taste

½ cup prepared mustard
¼ cup Worcestershire sauce

GARNISHES:

Bacon, crisp crumbled
Parsley

Chives

Sauté crabmeat in small amout of butter and place on plate. In separate bowl mix together ingredients for sauce. Top crabmeat with Remick sauce and bacon and broil for 2-3 minutes. Sprinkle a little fresh chopped parsley or chives on top.

Yield: Approximately ½ gallon sauce

Carol Ann Penick

SCALLOPED OYSTERS

1½ cups coarse cracker crumbs
8 Tb. melted butter
1 pint of oysters in liquid
½ tsp. salt

⅛ tsp. pepper
Dash nutmeg
2 Tb. milk

Combine cracker crumbs and butter. Set aside. Combine oysters, salt, pepper and nutmeg. Heat over medium heat until oysters curl. Add milk. Put thin layer of crumbs in bottom of 8 x 8-inch baking dish; alternate 2 layers each of crumbs and oysters. Pour remaining liquid over all; top with crumbs. Bake at 450° for 30 minutes.

Serves 8

Francille Turbyfill

Clams and oysters will be simple to open if washed with cold water, and then placed in a plastic bag in the freezer for an hour.

SEAFOOD CASSEROLE

3 Tb. flour
1 heaping Tb. butter or margarine
2½ cups milk (or part cream for
   richer taste)
Dry mustard to taste
Salt to taste
Accent
Cayenne pepper to taste
Chopped parsley
4 eggs, hard boiled

1 pound shrimp, cooked in seasoned
   water; deveined, halved or left whole
2 lobster tails, cooked 20 minutes
   in seasoned water; cubed
1 six-ounce package frozen or
   canned crab
White wine or sherry (optional)
Buttered bread crumbs (Pour melted
   butter over bread crumbs.)

In double boiler, mix flour with butter. When blended, add milk and seasonings to taste. When sauce is thick, remove from heat and cool. Add egg yolks, mashed to a paste. Add egg whites, slivered; add seafood. Stir in white wine or sherry to taste. Pour into 2-quart casserole. Top with buttered bread crumbs. Bake at 350° for 30 minutes in preheated oven. Serve in chafing dish, over muffins or crisp toast.

Serves 6

Peggy Bevans

BARBECUED SHRIMP

1 cup butter
1 cup vegetable oil
2 tsp. minced garlic
4 whole bay leaves, crushed fine
2 tsp. dried rosemary, crushed
½ tsp. dried basil
½ tsp. oregano

½ tsp. salt
½ tsp. cayenne
1 Tb. paprika
¾ tsp. fresh black pepper
1 tsp. lemon juice
2 pounds large whole fresh shrimp
   in the shell, rinsed

Melt butter in a heavy saucepan. Add oil and mix well. Add remaining ingredients except shrimp. Cook over medium heat, stirring constantly until mixture begins to boil. Reduce heat; simmer 7-8 minutes, stirring often. Remove from heat; let stand uncovered at least 30 minutes at room temperature. Add shrimp in shell to mixture. Cook 6-8 minutes or until shrimp turns pink. Preheat oven to 450°. Put shrimp in over-proof 8 x 8-inch dish; bake 10 minutes. Serve each portion with about ½ cup sauce.

Serves 4

Carol Long

For that "fresh-caught" flavor, thaw fish in milk.

DEEP DELTA SHRIMP

¼ cup butter or margarine
¼ cup flour
2 medium onions, thinly sliced
1 medium green pepper, sliced
½ cup chopped celery
1 clove of garlic, minced
1 bay leaf
¼ tsp. oregano

¼ tsp. liquid hot pepper
1 tsp. chili powder
1 tsp. Worcestershire sauce
1 Tb. salt
1 six-ounce can tomato soup
3 cups water
1 pound cooked and peeled shrimp

Cook flour in butter until golden. Stir in onions, green pepper, celery and garlic. Sauté until tender. Add all seasonings, tomato paste and water. Cook, stirring until thickened. Cover and simmer for 30 minutes. Add shrimp and simmer 5 minutes. Serve over cooked rice.

Refrigerate. When ready to serve, add shrimp and heat for about 15 minutes.

This is better if the sauce is made a day or two before using.

Serves 8

Mrs. Watson E. Shepard

SHRIMP RING

2 four and ½-ounce cans shrimp
¾ cup green onions, chopped
1 ten and ¾-ounce can tomato soup
1 eight-ounce package cream cheese, softened

1½ Tb. unflavored gelatin
1 cup mayonnaise
¾ cup celery, chopped
Salt and pepper to taste

Mix all ingredients together and put into a ring mold. Refrigerate.

This is better made up to a day ahead of serving.

Serves 12

Serve lemon butter balls with fish: 1 tablespoon lemon juice, 1 tablespoon chopped parsley, 2 tablespoons butter. Mix, roll into balls and chill.

SHRIMP CURRY

2 medium onions, chopped
2 apples, sliced
1 stick butter
2 Tb. curry powder
2 tsp. cinnamon

1 tsp. salt
½ cup flour
2 ten and ½-ounce cans beef
  consommé
5 pounds shrimp, cleaned
3 cups half and half

Sauté onions and apples in butter until onions are clear. Add curry powder, cinnamon, salt and flour. Add consommé. Cook about 5 minutes. Add shrimp and cream. Cook until shrimp is done (about 10 minutes). Serve over rice.

CONDIMENTS: Serve at least 4 to make curry interesting.

Chutney
Shredded coconut
Bacon
Green onions

Boiled egg
Peanuts
Pineapple chunks
Avocado

Serves 8-10   Wanda Blodgett

SHRIMP CREOLE

¾ cup sliced onions
½ cup diced celery
1 clove garlic, minced
3 Tb. butter or margarine
1 Tb. flour
1 tsp. salt

1 tsp. granulated sugar
2 to 3 tsp. chili powder
1 cup water
2 cups canned tomatoes
2 cups cleaned, cooked,
  deveined shrimp
1 cup raw rice, cooked

Cook first 4 ingredients until tender in a large skillet over medium heat, about 10 minutes. Add combined flour, salt, sugar and chili powder, mixed with ¼ cup water. Add ¾ cup water. Simmer uncovered 15 minutes. Meanwhile, cook rice according to package directions, and keep hot. When onion mixture has cooked 15 minutes, add tomatoes and shrimp. Serve over rice.

Serves 6   Muriel McCord

Something fishy going on? To remove the odor of shrimp while cooking, drop fresh celery leaves in the pot.

PARTY SHRIMP AND ASPARAGUS CASSEROLE

2 cups cooked rice
1 one pound-three ounce can
    asparagus spears, drained
8 ounces cleaned and cooked
    shrimp
⅛ tsp. black pepper

1 ten and ¾-ounce can cream of
    mushroom soup
¾ cup milk
1 Tb. chopped pimiento
1 cup grated American cheese

Put rice in a greased shallow baking dish (10-inch square). Cut asparagus spears in half. Place them over rice and top with shrimp. Mix together pepper, soup, milk and pimiento. Pour over shrimp. Sprinkle with cheese. Bake in a 400° oven about 30 minutes or until hot and the cheese begins to bubble and brown. Add milk if the mixture cooks dry.

Serves 6

Mrs. Steve Kavanaugh

SHRIMP AND NOODLE CASSEROLE

1 ten and ¾-ounce can cream
    of mushroom soup
2 Tb. sherry
1 pound cooked shrimp
¼ cup chopped pecans
¼ cup chopped onions

½ cup chopped celery
½ cup sliced water chestnuts
½ tsp. Worcestershire sauce
2 Tb. melted butter
2 cups chow mein noodles,
    reserve ¼ cup

Combine all ingredients, reserving ¼ cup of chow mein noodles for topping. Pour into a greased 9 x 13-inch Pyrex dish. Crush remaining noodles and sprinkle over top. Bake at 350° for 30 minutes.

Serves 6

Vicki Lackie

BEEF ROLL-UPS

6 thinly sliced sandwich steaks
1½ cups herb stuffing mix
½ cup chopped celery
½ cup chopped onion
3 Tb. margarine

1 ten and ¾-ounce can mushroom
    soup
1 soup can of water
1 tsp. Kitchen Bouquet
2 Tb. bottled steak sauce

Salt and pepper steaks. Sauté celery and onion in margarine and mix with stuffing mix. Place a portion of stuffing mixture on each steak. Roll up meat, tucking ends in and securing with toothpicks. Brown roll-ups in a little oil in skillet. Remove steaks to crockpot. Skim fat in skillet; add soup, water, Kitchen Bouquet and steak sauce. Bring to a boil, stirring constantly. Pour over steaks in crockpot. Set crockpot on low and cook 6-8 hours.

Serves 6

Darla Graham

BEEF STROGANOFF I

2 pounds beef, cut in one-inch
  bite-size pieces
2 Tb. flour
2 Tb. butter
1 ten and ½-ounce can beef
  consommé

1 ten and ½-ounce can cream
  of mushroom soup
1 cup sour cream
2 cloves garlic, minced
1 two and ½-ounce jar sliced
  mushrooms

Brown beef in a little shortening. Remove from skillet and keep hot. Make gravy of 2 Tb. flour, 2 Tb. butter, one can beef consommé and 1 can mushroom soup. Add sour cream, garlic and jar of mushrooms. Heat and stir. Add beef and bake covered for 1 hour at 350°. Serve over rice or noodles.

Serves 6

BEEF STROGANOFF II

1½ pounds fillet of beef
6 Tb. butter
Olive oil
2 Tb. green onions, chopped
¼ cup white wine or vermouth

A-1 Sauce or Worcestershire sauce
1½ cups sour cream
Salt
Pepper
Chopped parsley

Ask the butcher to cut the meat into very thin slices. Melt 4 Tb. of the butter in a deep skillet and heat. Add a small amount of olive oil to the butter to keep it from turning brown. Sauté the beef slices in the hot fat until they are delicately browned on both sides and remove them to a hot platter. Add the remaining butter and chopped green onions and cook for 1 minute. Add white wine or vermouth, a dash or two of A-1 Sauce or Worcestershire sauce and sour cream. Stir well and heat through, but do not boil or the sour cream will curdle. Salt to taste and pour sauce over beef. Top with a sprinkling of freshly ground black pepper and chopped parsley. Serve with rice or noodles.

Serves 4-6   Joyce Holsted

When using glass baking dishes, reduce oven temperature by 25 degrees.

CHUCK WAGON PEPPER STEAK

1 three-pound round bone arm
   chuck roast or boneless round
   roast, 2 inches thick
2 tsp. meat tenderizer
2 Tb. instant minced onion
2 tsp. thyme
1 tsp. marjoram

1 bay leaf, crushed
1 cup wine vinegar
½ cup olive oil or salad oil
3 Tb. lemon juice
¼ cup peppercorns, coarsely
   crushed, or 2 Tb. cracked pepper

Sprinkle meat evenly on both sides with tenderizer (no salt). Pierce deeply all over with a fork. Place in shallow pan. Mix onion, thyme, marjoram, bay leaf, vinegar, oil and lemon juice. Pour over meat and let stand at room temperature 1 to 2 hours, turning to marinate well. Remove meat from marinade and pound half the pepper into each side. Grill 6 inches above coals — 15 minutes per side for a rare steak. Placed on carving board and cut diagonally into ½ inch thick slices.

Serves 6

Roberta K. Herlocker

GRECIAN BEEF WITH CHEESE NOODLES

1½ pounds round steak
¼ cup salad oil
2 medium onions, sliced
3 Tb. flour
1 ten and ¾-ounce can condensed
   tomato soup, undiluted
1 cup water

2 Tb. lemon juice
⅛ tsp. cloves
¼ tsp. cinnamon
½ tsp. salt
¼ tsp. pepper
3 cups uncooked noodles
½ cup grated Parmesan cheese

Cut steak into thin bite-size pieces, about 1½ x ¼-inches. Brown meat strips in hot oil and remove. Sauté onion slices until golden brown. Stir in flour, tomato soup and water. Return meat to skillet. Add lemon juice, cloves, cinnamon, salt and pepper. Simmer covered about 45 minutes until fork tender. Just before meat is done, cook noodles as directed on package. Mix in grated Parmesan cheese. Serve meat over noodles on a heated platter.

Serves 6

Pat Pennebaker

To make tough cuts of meat more tender, add a little vinegar to the water in which it is cooked.

GRILLED ORIENTAL FLANK STEAK

¾ cup oil
¼ cup soy sauce
¼ cup honey
2 Tb. vinegar
1½ tsp. ground ginger

3 Tb. minced green onion
including tops
Garlic powder to taste
1 to 1½ pound flank steak

Combine first six ingredients for marinade. Sprinkle steak with garlic powder and place in marinade for 3 to 4 hours, turning occasionally. Broil meat over hot coals, basting with marinade. Cook 5 minutes on each side for medium steak. Slice across the grain to serve. Marinade may be saved and used again.

Serves 4   Suzie Thompson

KOREAN SPICED BEEF

1½ pounds sirloin steak,
1½ inches thick
2 Tb. oil
½ cup soy sauce

1 Tb. sherry
1 Tb. minced fresh ginger root
1 Tb. sugar
1 tsp. minced garlic (optional)

Broil steak 2 inches from flame 7½ minutes on each side for a total of 15 minutes. Mix marinade in a shallow glass baking dish which will accommodate the steak. Add broiled steak and leave overnight. Turn once if not covered by liquid. To serve: drain and slice very thin. Arrange on platter, garnish and serve cold. Strain the marinade to serve separately if desired.

Very good on a hot day.

Serves 6   Mrs. Fred Henker

Polish silver without elbow grease! Line sink with aluminum foil, add ½ cup Tide detergent and fill with warm water. Stir until Tide dissolves. Then simply wash silver as you would dishes. For stubborn tarnish, soak in solution a few minutes. Soaking will not remove ornamental oxidation unless the piece soaks for a long time.

CHILI BEEFSTEAK

1 clove garlic	2 six or eight-ounce filets mignon
2 Tb. chili powder	Butter
2 Tb. wine vinegar	Salt

Crush garlic and mix with chili powder and vinegar to make a paste. Rub steaks with the paste (chili adobo), and let them stand three or four hours. Fry steak in butter. The steak is not salted until time to serve.

This dish is always served with plenty of country-fried potatoes.

Serves 2   Carrie Carlton

LONDON BROIL MARINADE

¼ cup dry sherry	1 small clove garlic, minced
¼ cup salad oil	(or equivalent)
Juice of one lemon (2 Tb.)	¼ cup soy sauce

Mix all ingredients. Pour over meat and refrigerate overnight. Turn meat several times. Before broiling let stand at room temperature at least one hour.

Adequate for 3 pounds of meat. Good on flank, steaks, pot roast, shish kabobs and even dove, quail and venison.

Kathy Contreras

PEPPERED EYE OF BEEF

5 to 6 pounds boneless rib eye	½ tsp. garlic powder
of beef or eye of round	1 tsp. paprika
⅓ cup coarsely ground pepper	1 cup soy sauce
½ tsp. ground cardamom seed	¾ cup vinegar
1 Tb. tomato sauce	

On the day before cooking, marinate meat as follows: combine pepper and cardamom and rub all over beef, pressing in with heel of palm. Place in shallow pan. Combine tomato paste, garlic powder, paprika, soy sauce and vinegar. Carefully pour over roast. Marinate in refrigerator overnight, spooning marinade over meat several times.

When ready to cook: remove meat from marinade and let stand at room temperature for 1 hour. Wrap the meat in foil, place in shallow pan and roast in 300° oven for 2 hours for medium rare. Open foil, reserve meat drippings and serve warm as a sauce.

Serves 8-10   Frances Lance

POOH'S SHISH KABOBS

Extra thick sirloin
1½ cups salad oil
¾ cup soy sauce
¼ cup Worcestershire sauce
2 Tb. dry mustard
1½ tsp. parsley flakes
2½ tsp. salt
1 Tb. pepper

½ cup wine vinegar
⅓ cup lemon juice
1 clove garlic, crushed
bell peppers
onions
pineapple (optional)
fresh mushrooms
cherry tomatoes

Cut sirloin into chunks. Mix next ten ingredients. Place meat in the sauce and let marinate at least six hours or overnight. Cut into quarters: bell peppers, onions and pineapple (optional). Alternate meat and vegetables on skewers. Cook on grill until done.

Serves 4   Harriet Waddington

SAVORY BEEF

3 large onions, sliced
3 Tb. fat
2 pounds beef: shank, plate,
   rump or round
3 Tb. flour
1 tsp. salt

¼ tsp. black pepper
¼ tsp. ground cloves and thyme
1 pint brown stock or boiling
   water and meat extract
2 Tb. vinegar
1 Tb. catsup

Brown onions slowly in fat. Cut meat into serving pieces; add to onions and brown. Mix flour and dry seasonings. Sprinkle over meat. Add stock, vinegar and catsup. Cover closely. Simmer until meat is tender, allowing 2 hours for shank or plate and 1½ hours for rump or round.

Serves 6   Charlotte Steen

Tired of scrubbing burned pots? Sprinkle them liberally with baking soda and add just enough water to moisten. Let stand several hours. Burned portions should lift right out.

SAVORY PEPPER STEAK

1½ pounds round steak,
   ½ inch thick
¼ cup flour
½ tsp. salt
⅛ tsp. pepper
¼ cup oil
1 eight-ounce can tomatoes

1¾ cups water
½ cup chopped onion
1 small clove garlic, minced
1 Tb. beef flavored gravy base
1½ tsp. Worcestershire sauce
2 large green peppers,
   cut into strips

Cut steak into strips. Combine flour, salt and pepper. Coat meat strips in flour mixture. Cook meat in hot oil until browned. Drain tomatoes, reserving liquid. Add tomato liquid, water, onion, garlic and gravy base to meat in skillet. Cover and simmer about 1½ hours or until tender. Uncover and stir in Worcestershire sauce. Add green pepper strips. Cover and simmer 5 minutes. If necessary, thicken the gravy. Add drained tomatoes. Cook about 5 minutes more. Serve over hot rice.

Serves 6

Judi Dietz

SWISS STEAK

1 round steak
Flour
Salt
Pepper
Oil

1 medium onion
1 eight-ounce can tomato sauce
1 four-ounce can mushrooms, drained,
   or four ounces fresh mushrooms
   sliced

Cut the round steak into pieces and dust with seasoned flour. Heat oil in a heavy skillet and brown steak pieces. Place in a dutch oven or large pot. Slice onions over the meat. Pour hot water over meat to cover. Add the tomato sauce and mushrooms; simmer slowly over low heat for 2 to 3 hours. Gravy may be thickened with flour.

Serves 4

Deeana Montgomery

ORIENTAL ROAST AND VEGETABLES

1 five-pound sirloin tip
   roast
½ cup soy sauce
½ tsp. crushed garlic
1 bay leaf
½ cup oil
½ cup lemon juice

Butter and soy sauce for sautéing
1 large bell pepper, sliced
1 large white onion, sliced
½ to 1 pound fresh mushrooms,
   sliced
Cooked rice

Cut five-pound sirloin roast into strips (approximately ½ x 2 inches), cutting off fat. Mix soy sauce, garlic, bay leaf, oil and lemon juice. Put in large flat dish. Place meat strips in mixture and marinate 4-10 hours. Sauté vegetables in a little butter and soy sauce (should be firm, not soggy). Remove vegetables from pan and sauté meat until done. Mix vegetables and meat together. Cook rice according to package directions. Pour meat and vegetables over rice and serve.

Serves 4-6   Mary Beth Clark

VEAL WITH ARTICHOKE HEARTS

⅓-½ pound veal slices per
   person (two slices)
Flour
Salt and pepper
2-6 Tb. butter or margarine
1-2 Tb. olive oil
½ cup boiling water
1 tsp. chicken bouillon granules

½ cup white wine
Juice of 1 medium lemon
2 Tb. chopped parsley
1-1½ Tb. flour (optional)
¼-½ cup water (optional)
1 eight and ½-ounce can
   Spanish artichoke hearts, drained

Place veal slices between 2 sheets of waxed paper and pound to ⅛ to ¼-inch thickness. Lightly flour pounded veal and season with salt and pepper. Sauté veal in butter and olive oil, one minute on each side. (If cooking for 4 or more, add more butter and olive oil as needed.) Remove veal from pan and keep warm on serving platter. Dissolve chicken bouillon granules in boiling water. Add wine, lemon juice and parsley to bouillon. Cook for one minute. If thicker sauce is desired, make a medium paste of flour and water. Add gradually to sauce mixture, stirring constantly. Add drained artichoke hearts and heat until warm. Serve over veal.

Colleen Wallace

BAR-B-Q BRISKET

Rolled brisket
1 cup Worcestershire sauce
½ cup liquid smoke

1 cup barbecue sauce
(Old Hickory)

Marinate brisket overnight in Worcestershire sauce and liquid smoke. Cook, covered, 1 hour per pound at 250°. During the last 45 minutes of cooking time, pour off all liquid except 1 cup. Add 1 cup barbecue sauce to this and pour over brisket. Cook 30-45 minutes longer.

This is great made a day ahead and reheated. The flavor improves!

Colleen Wallace

COMPANY-IS-COMING BRISKET ROAST

5 to 6 pound brisket, trimmed
    of fat
3 tsp. meat tenderizer
Garlic powder
Celery salt

Onion salt
Salt and pepper to taste
¼ cup Worcestershire sauce
½ bottle Liquid Smoke

Sprinkle approximately 1½ tsp. meat tenderizer on each side of meat. Prick with a fork. Place meat on heavy duty foil (enough to make a tent for meat) on cookie sheet. Sprinkle both sides with garlic powder, celery salt and onion salt. Rub ¼ cup Worcestershire sauce and ½ bottle Liquid Smoke into meat. Wrap foil to form a tent over meat. Leave overnight in refrigerator. Cook in 250° oven 5 hours. Slice to desired thickness. Freezes well.

Serves 12-15

Margaret Ilwain

NEW YORK ROAST

Eye of round roast
1 Tb. oil
½ tsp. garlic powder
1 tsp. salt

½ tsp. paprika
½ tsp. pepper
1 tsp. oregano

Rub roast with oil. Mix other ingredients and rub into roast. Bake covered in 350° oven 20 minutes per pound. Slice thinly and serve warm.

Will make lots of sandwiches! Delicious on second day sliced thin and served cold on rye or white bread.

Terry Stanger

PARTY POT ROAST

3½ to 4 pound chuck roast
2 Tb. oil
¼ cup water
¼ cup red wine or beef broth
1 medium onion, sliced

2 bay leaves
1 tsp. thyme
¾ ounce envelope brown gravy mix
1 three or four-ounce can sliced
mushrooms

Brown meat in oil in heavy pan. Add water, wine or broth, onion, bay leaves and thyme. Cook covered at 350° for 2 hours or until tender. Remove meat from pan and keep warm in oven. Discard bay leaves and drain fat, if any. Add gravy mix to pan liquids. Add mushrooms and liquid from can. Bring to a boil, stirring until thickened. Slice meat and spoon some of the sauce over the meat. Remaining sauce may be served as a side dish.

Serves 6-8   Carol Long

BEEF AND BACON FILLETS

1 pound hamburger
1 tsp. salt
⅛ tsp. pepper
½ tsp. oregano
⅛ tsp. garlic powder
⅛ tsp. poultry seasoning
1 Tb. chopped parsley

½ cup fine dry bread crumbs
  or ½ cup Bisquick
2 Tb. water
1 egg
4 slices bacon
2 Tb. barbecue sauce

Combine all ingredients except bacon and barbecue sauce. Form into four fillets. Wrap one strip of bacon around each fillet and secure with toothpick. Place in 2½-quart baking dish and bake at 400° for 25-30 minutes. Brush tops with barbecue sauce.

Serves 4   Edwina Whalen

Garlic cloves can be stored in the freezer. When ready to use, peel and chop before thawing.

BAKED BEANS

1 pound sausage or hamburger
1 onion, chopped
1 bell pepper, chopped
2 sixteen-ounce cans pork and
   beans
½ cup light brown sugar

¼ cup Grandma's molasses
1 tsp. dry mustard
2 tsp. Worcestershire sauce
½ cup catsup
Black pepper to taste

Brown meat and break into bite-sized pieces; remove from skillet. Brown onion and bell pepper in meat drippings. Drain meat, onion and pepper well. Stir together pork and beans, brown sugar, molasses, mustard, Worcestershire, catsup and black pepper. Mix in meat, onions and bell pepper. Pour into lightly greased casserole. Bake at 325° for about 1 hour or until slightly thickened and meat is done.

Serves 6-8

Keeta McClure
Mary Beth Clark

CABBAGE ROLLS

1½ pounds ground chuck
Salt and pepper to season
1 medium onion, finely chopped
½ cup Progresso bread crumbs
1 egg

1 ten-ounce can fried rice
1 eight-ounce can shrimp
2 ten and ¾-ounce cans Campbell's
   tomato soup
1 head cabbage, core removed

Scald the cabbage in boiling water. Remove scalded leaves and cut out the vein on the back of each leaf. Mix meat, seasonings, onion, bread crumbs, egg, rice, shrimp and 1 can of tomato soup diluted with ½ can of water. Place a generous portion of meat mixture on each cabbage leaf. Roll to center and tuck in sides. Remaining cabbage may be cut up in chunks and placed in the bottom of Dutch oven or roaster. Place remaining meat over the cut-up cabbage. Arrange cabbage rolls on top. Pour remaining can of tomato soup over the rolls. Cover and bake at 350° for 1-1½ hours.

Variation: People who do not care for seafood might prefer to omit the can of shrimp. Also, sprinkling the recipe with grated Parmesan cheese might add to appearance and flavor.

Serves 6-8

Rid hands of onion or garlic odor by rubbing them with salt.

CHALUPAS

1 pound ground beef
1 package taco seasoning
Salt and pepper to taste
1 sixteen-ounce can Mexican
  refried beans
Tortillas — flat (frozen and fried
  crisp or store-bought and
  pre-fried)

Lettuce, shredded
Onion, chopped
Tomatoes, chopped
Mexican hot relish
Guacamole (optional)
Cheddar cheese, grated

Brown ground beef; drain excess fat. Add taco seasoning and water and cook 20 minutes according to package directions. Add salt, pepper and refried beans. Cook until heated thoroughly. Heat flat tortillas in oven. Serve meat mixture on top of tortillas. Top with shredded lettuce, onions, tomatoes, cheese, hot relish and guacamole.

Serves 6-8   Pat Stanger

STUFFED TOMATO CUPS

4 large tomatoes
Salt
Dried basil leaves, crushed
½ pound ground beef
¼ cup chopped onion

1 cup cheese croutons
  (maybe a little more)
1 tsp. Worcestershire sauce
4 tsp. grated Parmesan cheese

Cut tops off tomatoes; remove pulp. Chop tops and pulp; drain. Cut sawtooth edges around tomato shells; drain. Sprinkle inside with salt and basil. In skillet, brown beef and onion; drain. Stir in pulp, part of croutons, salt and Worcestershire sauce; stuff shells. Sprinkle tomatoes with cheese. Put croutons on top. Place in shallow baking dish; fill dish with ½ inch water. Bake at 375° for 25-30 minutes. Garnish with parsley if desired.

Serves 4   Cheri Kennedy

MEAT LOAF

1½ pounds ground chuck
1 cup Progresso bread crumbs
2 beaten eggs
1 eight-ounce can tomato sauce
½ cup chopped onions
2 tsp. pepper

1½ tsp. salt
1 bay leaf
Dash of marjoram
1 cup grated Cheddar cheese
Chili sauce

Combine all ingredients but the chili sauce. Shape and put in loaf pan. Score top of loaf and cover with chili sauce. Bake at 350° for 1½ hours.

This can also be cooked in the microwave. Assemble as above and cook for 20 minutes.

Serves 6-8   Marilyn Hamm

DEEP DISH PIZZA

1 pound bulk sausage
(or hamburger meat)
1 eight-ounce can crescent rolls
1½ cups (six ounces) shredded
mozzarella cheese
1 four-ounce can mushrooms,
drained

¼ cup chopped green peppers
¼ cup catsup
½ tsp. basil leaves
½ tsp. fennel seed
½ tsp. oregano
Parmesan cheese

Preheat oven to 325°. Brown meat in skillet while preparing crust. Separate crescent dough in eight triangles. Place triangles in ungreased 9-inch pie pan; press over bottom and up sides to form crust. Drain meat. Stir in 1 cup mozzarella cheese (reserve ½ cup for topping), mushrooms, green pepper, catsup and herbs. Spoon into crust, top with remaining cheese and sprinkle with Parmesan cheese. Bake at 325° for 30-35 minutes until crust is golden brown. For easier serving, let stand 5 minutes before cutting into wedges.

Serves 4-6   Madeline Johnson

HAMBURGER GOULASH

1 pound ground beef
1 medium onion, chopped
1 ten and ¾-ounce can tomato
soup
1 tsp. salt.
½ cup chopped celery

½ cup chopped green peppers
1 fifteen-ounce can Ranch-style
beans
1 cup grated processed cheese

Brown meat and onion; drain. Mix in soup, salt, celery, peppers and beans. Pour in lightly greased 1½-quart casserole. Top with grated cheese. Bake at 350° for 30 minutes.

Serves 4   Becky Hight

HAMBURGER PIE

1 pound ground beef
½ cup onion, chopped
⅓ cup bell pepper, chopped
1 eight-ounce can tomato soup
2 Tb. catsup

Salt and pepper to taste
½ tsp. garlic powder
½ tsp. chili powder
Pinch of parsley
1 box Jiffy Corn Muffin Mix

Brown meat, add onion and bell pepper; cook about 10 minutes. Add tomato sauce, catsup and stir. Add seasonings. Simmer meat mixture while mixing cornbread. Prepare Jiffy Corn Muffin Mix as directed on package. Pour over top of meat mixture in skillet and bake at 350° for about 30 minutes, or until cornbread is done. To serve, turn upside down onto plate so cornbread is on bottom.

Serves 5-6   Pat Johnson

CHISM SPECIAL

2-3 pounds ground beef
2 Tb. oil
1 medium onion, diced
3 pods garlic, minced
2 bell peppers, chopped
Salt and pepper to taste
1 ten and ¾-ounce can tomato soup

6 Tb. chili powder
1 Tb. Worcestershire sauce
Catsup (optional)
1 twelve-ounce package spaghetti, cooked and drained
Grated Cheddar cheese (optional)

Heat oil in heavy Dutch oven. Add meat and brown with onion, garlic, bell pepper, salt and pepper. Cook over medium-low heat for 30 to 40 minutes. Add soup, chili powder, and Worcestershire sauce. Let simmer at least one hour. If too thick, add catsup. Serve over cooked spaghetti. Top with grated Cheddar cheese.

This is great served with a tossed salad and garlic bread. It can be frozen.

Serves 6-8   Colleen Wallace

LASAGNE

½ cup chopped onion
1 pound ground beef
¾ tsp. salt
Dash pepper
1 tsp. oregano
⅛ tsp. garlic powder
1 ten and ¾-ounce can tomato soup
1 sixteen-ounce can stewed tomatoes
6 ounces lasagne noodles

3 cups cottage cheese
½ cup Parmesan cheese
2 eggs, beaten
2 tsp. salt
½ tsp. pepper
2 Tb. parsley
2 six-ounce packages sliced cheese
1 Tb. oil

In large skillet brown ground beef and onion; drain well. Add salt, pepper, oregano, garlic powder, tomato soup and tomatoes. Cook slowly until thickened (approximately 30 minutes). Cook lasagne noodles according to package directions. (Add a small amount of oil so noodles won't stick.) Drain noodles well. Lay on paper towels to dry. Mix cottage cheese, Parmesan cheese, eggs, salt, pepper and parsley. Lightly grease the bottom of a 9 x 13 x 2 inch baking dish. Make one layer of noodles. Over this spread one-half the cottage cheese mixture, one package of mozzarella cheese, and one-half meat mixture. Make a second layer of noodles, cottage cheese, mozzarella cheese and meat. Be certain that the meat sauce ends up on top so the lasagne will not dry out as it bakes. Bake at 375° for 40 minutes. Let stand 15 minutes before cutting.

This can be made ahead of time and frozen. Also can be made in two 8 x 8 inch pans and frozen for two later meals.

Serves 6   Betsy Davies

MANICOTTI

SAUCE:

2 pounds ground beef
1 to 2 stalks celery, chopped
1 clove garlic, minced
1 small onion, chopped
1 sixteen-ounce can tomatoes
1 sixteen-ounce can tomato sauce

½ to 1 tsp. chili powder
½ to 1 tsp. Italian seasoning
1 tsp. salt
1 four-ounce jar sliced
mushrooms, drained (optional)

FILLING:

¾ to 1 pound mozzarella
cheese, shredded
½ cup Parmesan cheese
1 large carton Ricotta cheese

2 eggs, slightly beaten
1 tsp. parsley
Salt and pepper to taste
1 package manicotti noodles, cooked

SAUCE DIRECTIONS: Brown meat with garlic, celery and onions. Add remaining sauce ingredients and simmer about 2 hours. During the last 30 minutes of cooking time, add mushrooms.

FILLING DIRECTIONS: Mix all filling ingredients together well and stuff the cooked manicotti noodles.

ASSEMBLY: Grease a 9 x 13 inch baking dish. Put a small amount of sauce in bottom of dish. Lay stuffed noodles on top of sauce. Spoon generous amount of sauce down the center of noodles (on top). Bake covered at 350° for 25-30 minutes. Sprinkle Parmesan cheese on top (optional).

Serves 6-8   Sue Moore

QUICK MANICOTTI

8 manicotti shells
1 pound ground beef
1 clove garlic, crushed
1 cup cottage cheese
1 cup mozzarella cheese,
shredded

½ tsp. salt
¼ cup mayonnaise
1 fifteen and ½-ounce jar
spaghetti sauce
½ tsp. whole oregano
⅓ cup grated Parmesan cheese

Cook manicotti shells according to package directions; drain. Rinse in cold water; drain and set aside. Saute' ground beef and garlic until beef is no longer pink. Drain off pan drippings. Add cottage cheese, mozzarella cheese, salt and mayonnaise to skillet; stir well. Stuff manicotti shells with meat mixture. Arrange stuffed shells in a lightly greased 9 x 13 x 2 inch baking dish. Combine spaghetti sauce and oregano; pour over manicotti. Sprinkle with Parmesan cheese. Cover and bake at 350° 15 minutes. Uncover and bake an additional 10 minutes.

Serves 8   Jenny Gosser

MEATBALLS

MEATBALLS:

1½ pounds ground beef
¾ cup oatmeal
¼ tsp. oregano
1 egg

¼ cup chopped onion
1½ tsp. salt
¼ tsp. black pepper
½ cup milk

SAUCE:

½ cup chopped onions
⅓ cup chopped green pepper
1 sixteen-ounce can tomatoes
1 eight-ounce can tomatoes
Dash cayenne pepper

½ tsp. salt
¼ tsp. garlic powder
¼ tsp. oregano
1 bay leaf

Meatballs: Combine all meatball ingredients. Shape into balls and brown in electric skillet in 4 tablespoons oil. Remove meatballs.

Sauce: Sauté onions and peppers. Add remaining sauce ingredients. Simmer for 20 minutes. Add meatballs and simmer 30 minutes more. Remove bay leaf and serve.

Serves 6   Marianne Gosser

ITALIAN MEAT SAUCE FOR SPAGHETTI

2 Tb. oil
½ cup minced onion
1 pound gound chuck
2 cloves garlic or ¼ tsp.
   garlic powder
1½ tsp. salt.

¼ tsp. black pepper
Italian seasoning to taste
1 sixteen-ounce can tomatoes
1 eight-ounce can tomato sauce
½ cup Parmesan cheese

Sauté onions in hot oil in skillet. Add ground chuck and cook until red color disappears. Slice garlic and mash with salt (or use garlic powder and salt) and add to meat. Add pepper, Italian seasoning, tomatoes and tomato sauce. Simmer covered for 45 minutes. Add Parmesan cheese the last 12 minutes. Serve over spaghetti.

This will freeze very well. Leave out Parmesan cheese when freezing and add while reheating. The flavor is enhanced when it is refrigerated for 24 hours before serving.

Serves 4-6   Donna Bosley

MOTHER'S SPAGHETTI

10 ounces shell macaroni
2 Tb. salt
2 Tb. salad oil
5 medium onions, chopped
2 pounds ground beef
1 pound Cracker Barrel Sharp
   cheese, grated

2 three-ounce cans mushrooms,
   sliced or stems and pieces
2 fifteen-ounce cans tomato sauce
½ cup Burgundy (optional)

Cook macaroni with 2 Tb. salt in water until tender. Sauté onions in oil until soft. Add meat and cook until browned. Add cheese and mix well until well melted into meat; add mushrooms. Add cooked macaroni to mixture and stir in tomato sauce. Add burgundy if desired. Serve immediately or refrigerate and warm in 350° oven for 20 minutes.

This freezes well.

Serves 6-8   Nancy Harmon

SUSAN'S SPAGHETTI SAUCE

1 pound ground beef
1 small onion, chopped
½ green pepper, chopped
1 four-ounce can mushrooms
3 tsp. garlic powder
1 tsp. oregano
Pepper to taste

¼ tsp. anise seed
¾ tsp. sweet basil
1 one-pound can whole tomatoes
   mashed
1 eight-ounce can tomato sauce
1 cup water
¼ cup red wine

Brown meat in Dutch oven. Add onion and green pepper; sauté. Drain well. Add all other ingredients except wine. Simmer uncovered over low heat for at least 2 hours (the longer the better). More water may be added if drying occurs. About 20 minutes before serving add wine and simmer. Serve over spaghetti sprinkled with Parmesan cheese.

Variation: If tomato paste is used instead of tomato sauce, increase water.

This is a good make-ahead dish. Tastes great when left in the refrigerator overnight and reheated.

Serves 4-6   Susan Langley

SPAGHETTI SAUCE

¼ cup butter
1½ pounds ground chuck
½ cup chopped green pepper
1 large onion, chopped
½ pound mushrooms, chopped
6 cloves garlic, crushed
1½ six-ounce cans tomato paste
1 twenty-eight-ounce can tomatoes

½ Tb. Worcestershire sauce
½ Tb. Angostura Bitters
½ Tb. sugar
½ cup dry red wine
½ tsp. celery salt
2 bay leaves
Salt and pepper

Cook meat, peppers, onion, mushrooms and garlic in butter. When meat is done, drain and place in a large pot. Add remaining ingredients. Salt and pepper to taste. Cook over low heat 2 hours. Serve over spaghetti.

Serves 6

Virginia Phelps

ZESTY ITALIAN CRESCENT CASSEROLE

1½ pounds ground beef
¼ cup chopped onion
1 envelope spaghetti sauce mix
1 eight-ounce can tomato sauce
1½ cups (6 to 8 ounces) mozzarella
   or Monterey Jack cheese, shredded

1 cup sour cream
1 eight-ounce can Pillsbury
   Crescent Dinner Rolls
⅔ cup Parmesan cheese
4 Tb. melted margarine

Preheat oven to 375°. Brown ground beef and onion; drain. Stir in sauce mix and tomato sauce. Heat until bubbly. Pour hot meat mixture into ungreased 7 x 12-inch or 9 x 13 x 2-inch pan. Combine cheese and sour cream; spoon over meat. Separate dough into two rectangles. Place over cheese and sour cream. Combine Parmesan cheese and margarine. Spread evenly over dough. Bake at 375° for 18-25 minutes.

Serves 8

Renetta Ketcher

Butter or oil added to the cooking water will prevent rice, noodles, or spaghetti from boiling over.

HAM LOAF

¾ pound cured ham, fat free
¼ pound fresh pork, fat free
1 egg, well beaten
½ cup bread crumbs
½ cup milk

Pepper to taste
½ cup vinegar
½ cup brown sugar
½ cup water

Chop meat. Thoroughly mix together ham, pork, egg, bread crumbs, milk and pepper. Shape into loaf and bake in shallow roasting pan 45 minutes at 350°. Baste often with vinegar, brown sugar and water mixture.

This recipe is excellent when reheated, sliced and used for sandwiches.

Serves 4   Colleen Wallace

POTATO, HAM AND CHEESE CASSEROLE

¾ pound thinly sliced ham
1 minced onion
4 to 6 thinly sliced potatoes
3 Tb. flour
½ tsp. salt

¼ tsp. black pepper
1 cup grated American cheese
1 cup milk
2 Tb. margarine

Preheat oven to 350°. Arrange ham slices in a greased 1½ or 2-quart casserole. Top with half of the minced onion and half of the potatoes. Sprinkle with half of the flour, salt, pepper and cheese. Repeat in same order with remaining half of ingredients. Heat milk with butter and pour over all. Bake, covered, for 40 minutes; remove cover and bake 30 minutes longer.

Serves 6   Sharon Ferguson

PORK CHOPS

6 pork chops
2 sixteen-ounce cans sauerkraut

2 sixteen-ounce cans applesauce

Pour layer of sauerkraut over bottom of a 9 x 12-inch casserole. Top with layer of applesauce and then repeat layers. Lay pork chop on top and bake at 400° for 45 minutes to 1 hour.

Serves 4-6   Lois Stevenson
                                                                      Columbia, South Carolina

CHEESE STUFFED PORK

4 butterfly pork chops
1 cup grated Cheddar cheese
   or Swiss cheese
1 four-ounce can chopped
   mushrooms, drained

2 Tb. parsley
Salt
Toothpicks

Have butcher cut pocket in both sides of pork chops. Mix cheese, mushrooms, parsley and salt. Stuff sides of chops with mixture. Secure with toothpicks in a lacing effect. Cook on grill over medium coals for ten minutes per side or until done.

Serves 4

Betsy Davies

PORK CHOPS AND CHEESE BISCUITS

CHEESE BISCUITS:

2 cups Bisquick
½ cup cold water

½ cup shredded Cheddar
   cheese (two ounces)

Heat oven to 450°. Mix 2 cups Bisquick, cold water and shredded cheese until soft dough forms. Beat vigorously 20 strokes. Gently smooth dough into a ball on floured cloth-covered board. Knead 5 times. Roll dough ½ inch thick. Cut with floured two-inch biscuit cutter. Place on ungreased cookie sheet and bake until golden brown, 8-10 minutes.

4 pork loin chops, ¾ inch
   thick (about one pound)
½ cup Bisquick
¼ cup shortening
¼ cup all-purpose flour

1½ cups water
2 tsp. beef-flavored instant
   bouillon, or 2 beef bouillon cubes
⅓ cup milk

Coat pork chops with Bisquick. Heat shortening in ten-inch skillet over medium heat until melted. Cook pork until brown on both sides; remove from skillet. Stir flour into skillet, stirring constantly until mixture is smooth and bubbly. Stir in water and bouillon. Heat to boiling, stirring constantly until bouillon is dissolved. Boil and stir one minute. Add pork and reduce heat. Cover and simmer 20 minutes. Remove pork chops. Stir milk into mixture gradually and thoroughly. Serve biscuits with pork and gravy.

Serves 4

Sheila Hammonds

DIXIE PORK CHOPS

8 pork chops
½ tsp. salt
½ tsp. sage
4 Taft apples, cored and sliced
¼ cup brown sugar

2 Tb. flour
1 cup hot water
1 Tb. vinegar
½ cup seedless raisins

Brown pork chops in small amount of oil in skillet. Sprinkle with salt and sage. Place in baking dish and top with apple rings. Sprinkle with brown sugar. Add the flour to fat in skillet and blend. Add the water and vinegar. Cook until thick, stirring constantly. Add the raisins and pour over chops. Bake at 350° for 1 hour.

Serves 4-6   Kaye Stroud

EASY ORANGE PORK CHOPS

6 pork chops, ¾-inch thick
2 Tb. oil
Salt and pepper to taste
2 cups minute rice, pre-cooked

2 cups orange juice
1 10-ounce can chicken with
   rice soup

In skillet, brown pork chops on both sides in oil. Season with salt and pepper. Pour rice into 9 x 13-inch baking dish. Cover with orange juice. Arrange pork chops on top of rice. Pour chicken soup over all. Cover and bake at 350° for 45 minutes. Uncover and bake 10 minutes.

Serves 4-6

PINEAPPLE PORK CHOPS

6 porkchops
Oil
Salt and pepper
1 thirteen-ounce can pineapple
   chunks, (reserve juice)
½ green pepper, cut in strips
½ onion, chopped

1 cup chopped celery
1 sixteen-ounce can water
   chestnuts
1 can pea pods (optional)
Cornstarch
Rice

Brown pork chops on both sides in a little oil. Season with salt and pepper. Drain off excess fat. Cover chops with pineapple juice. Add ½ cup water. Add onion, green peppers, water chestnuts and pineapple chunks. Cover and simmer 20-30 minutes. Add celery and pea pods and cook 10-15 minutes or until celery is crisp-tender and pork is done. Thicken juices with cornstarch that has been dissloved in a little water. Serve over cooked rice.

Serves 6   Kathy King

SWEET AND SOUR PORK CHOPS

8 pork chops
1 Tb. oil
1 beef bouillon cube
1 cup water
¼ cup vinegar
2 Tb. soy sauce
¼ cup sugar

1 eight and ¾-ounce can
 pineapple chunks
6 green pepper rings,
 cut into quarters
¼ cup chopped onion
2 Tb. cornstarch
2 Tb. water

Brown chops in oil. Add bouillon cube, water, vinegar, soy sauce, sugar, pineapple (including juice), green pepper and onion. Cover and simmer for 1 hour. Remove chops to heated platter. Combine cornstarch and water; stir into cooking liquid and cook for about 5 minutes, stirring constantly. Pour over chops. Serve with rice.

Serves 6-8   Pat Stanger

POT PORK CHOP SUPPER

4 pork chops, 1½ inches thick
1 ten and ¾-ounce can
 tomato soup
½ cup water
1 tsp. Worcestershire
½ tsp. salt

½ tsp. caraway seeds
6-8 small potatoes,
 quartered
4 small carrots, split
 lengthwise and cut in
 2-inch pieces

Salt and pepper pork chops. In a skillet, brown the chops and pour off fat. Add rest of ingredients. Cover and simmer 45 minutes or until tender. It is best to delay putting in the potatoes until the last 30 minutes to avoid overcooking.

Serves 4   Marilyn Brown

PORK CHOPS WITH RICE AND WINE

4 pork chops
2 Tb. oil
Salt and pepper to taste
½ tsp. poultry seasoning
4 thick onion slices

4 green pepper rings
½ cup uncooked brown rice
1 fifteen-ounce can tomato sauce
¾ cup dry white wine
½ cup water

Slowly brown chops on both sides in hot oil. Place in dish. Sprinkle with salt, pepper and poultry seasoning. Place onion and pepper on each chop. Sprinkle rice around chops. Combine tomato sauce, wine and water. Pour over chops. Bake covered at 350° for 1 hour or until chops are tender.

Serves 4   Leah Cloud

STUFFED PORK CHOPS

6 pork chops, 1 inch thick

STUFFING

1 cup dry stuffing mix	**¼ tsp. salt**
¼ cup water	**¼ tsp. onion salt**
2 Tb. butter or margarine	

SAUCE

1 sixteen-ounce can	**¼ tsp. onion salt**
applesauce	**1 clove garlic, crushed**
¼ cup water	**Pinch each of thyme, marjoram**
¼ tsp. salt	**and oregano**

GARNISH

Stuffed green olives	**Parsley**

Cut pockets in pork chops. Mix stuffing ingredients together and fill pockets. Brown pork chops in 5 Tb. butter or margarine. Place chops in shallow casserole and cover with sauce mixture. Bake covered 1½ hours in 350° oven. Uncover and baste. Continue baking uncovered for 20 minutes or until tender. Garnish with olives and parsley.

Holds well in oven for delayed dinner.

Serves 6

Mrs. M. E. Argo

HONOLULU SPARERIBS

2-3 pounds spareribs,	**1 tsp. salt**
cut in pieces	**¼ tsp. pepper**

HONEYFRUIT SAUCE

2 Tb. cornstarch	**2 small green peppers,**
½ cup tomato juice	**chopped**
¼ cup lemon juice	**1 twenty-ounce can pineapple**
½ cup honey	**chunks in heavy syrup**

Salt and pepper spareribs. Bake in 9 x 12-inch baking dish at 400° for 40 minutes. Drain off all excess grease. Moisten cornstarch with small amount of tomato juice. Add bulk of juices, including honey. Blend well. Add pineapple and green pepper. Pour mixture over partly cooked ribs and lower oven temperature to 350°. Bake the ribs until tender (1½ hours). Baste several times with sauce mixture. Heat remaining sauce before ribs are done and pour over when ready to serve.

Serves 6-8

Martha C. Haguewood

PORK ROAST AND DUMPLINGS WITH SAUERKRAUT

Pork roast, 5 to 7 pounds
Garlic powder to taste

Pepper to taste

Generously rub roast with garlic and pepper. Place in roasting pan and roast uncovered (or if you prefer, with a loose tent of foil) at 325° for 3½-5 hours or until meat thermometer reads 170°.

HILDA'S DUMPLINGS WITH GRAVY

1½ loaves bread
  (day-old white)
1 large onion, chopped and
  sautéed with bacon
6 strips bacon, fried
  and diced

1-2 cups flour
1-2 cups milk
3 eggs, beaten lightly
1-2 Tb. parsley
Salt to taste

GRAVY

1 ten and ¾-ounce can
  cream of mushroom soup

Roast drippings
Flour or constarch

Cube bread about one inch square. Place in roasting pan and brown lightly on all sides. Combine bread cubes in large mixing bowl with diced bacon and onions. Add parsley, salt and eggs. Mix well. The mixture will be gooey. Add milk and mix until mixture is soft. Let stand 30 minutes. Fill a large Dutch oven half full of water and 2 Tb. salt. Bring water to boil. Add flour to bread mixture. Mix well. It will be dry and sticky. Wet hands and form balls. Drop into boiling salt water. Cook 20-25 minutes. Remove to warm pan. Cut into fourths. Serve with roast gravy made from roast drippings combined with one can cream of mushroom soup and thickened to desired consistency.

SAUERKRAUT

1 large can sauerkraut,
  washed and drained
2-3 tsp. caraway seeds

½-1 tsp. garlic salt
Water
Cornstarch

Combine and heat. Thicken with water and cornstarch mixture. Serve with roast and dumplings.

Serves 4-6

Hilda Fitch

After frying fish or onions, remove the odor from the oil by frying a slice of potato.

PORK TENDERLOIN

2 pork tenderloins
4 strips lean bacon
½ cup soy sauce
3 Tb. grated onion

2 Tb. cider vinegar
¼ tsp. pepper
3 Tb. sugar
3 cloves garlic, minced

Place tenderloins side by side in large roasting pan. Wrap bacon across both, tucking ends under tenderloins. Combine soy sauce, onion, vinegar, pepper, sugar and garlic; pour over top. Bake at 300° for 1¾-2 hours. Baste often with juices during cooking. Can be marinated several hours or cooked immediately.

Serves 4-6

Sidney Nesbit

CHICKEN WITH CHIPPED BEEF

1 two and ½-ounce jar
    chipped beef
6 chicken breasts, boned
6 slices bacon
Pepper to taste
1 ten and ¾-ounce can
    cream of chicken soup

1 pint sour cream
1 three-ounce package
    cream cheese
1 four and ½-ounce can
    sliced button mushrooms
¼ cup dry sauterne

Place chipped beef, crumbled, in bottom of 9 x 13-inch baking dish. Wrap bacon around the chicken breasts and sprinkle with pepper only. Combine soup, sour cream and cream cheese in blender or electric mixer. Add mushrooms with spoon and pour mixture over chicken breasts in casserole. Cover with foil. Bake in 300° oven for 2 hours. Remove foil and add sauterne. Cook uncovered for 1 more hour. Rice is an excellent accompaniment.

Serves 6

Mrs. Todd S. Bender

CHICKEN BREAST PIQUANT

1 cup rice
8 chicken breasts
¼ cup soy sauce
¼ cup oil
¾ cup white wine

¾ cup water
1 clove garlic
1 tsp. ginger
¼ tsp. oregano
1 Tb. brown sugar

Place one cup raw rice (brown, white or wild) in casserole. Lay chicken breasts on top of rice. Mix together all other ingredients. Pour combined mixture over chicken and rice. Cover. Bake at 325° for 2½ to 3 hours.

Serves 8

Barbara Hoffman

AUNT MARY'S CHICKEN-RICE CASSEROLE

1 whole chicken, cooked
  and boned, or 4-5 breasts
½ cup cooking oil
1 cup chopped celery
½ cup chopped onion
½ cup chopped green pepper

1 cup minute rice
1 ten and ¾-ounce can
  cream of celery soup
1 ten and ¾-ounce can
  cream of mushroom soup
2 Tb. chili powder

Sauté celery, onion and pepper in cooking oil until tender. Place cooked chicken in 8 x 12-inch casserole. Stir in rice, soups, chili powder and sautéed vegetables. Bake covered at 350° for 35-45 minutes.

Serves 8   Jo Cobb

BISCUITS ON CREAMY CHICKEN

1 seventeen-ounce can
  LeSeur peas
1 sixteen-ounce can sliced
  carrots
1 ten and ¾-ounce can cream
  of chicken soup

½ cup sour cream
2 cups cooked chicken, diced
1¼ cups Cheddar cheese,
  grated
Rolled biscuits (Bisquick)

Heat oven to 425°. Rinse peas and carrots. Mix together peas, carrots, soup , sour cream and chicken. Pour into 6½ x 10-inch glass dish. Top with cheese. Prepare biscuits according to directions on Bisquick package, using the rolled biscuit recipe. Place on top of cheese. Bake 20 minutes.

This is really great for a busy day. It may be prepared ahead of time, but not frozen. If made early and refrigerated, remove 30-45 minutes before cooking in order for the dish to get hot.

Serves 6-8   Patti Pyron

BROCCOLI AND CHICKEN CASSEROLE

2 ten-ounce packages frozen
  chopped broccoli
3 cups cooked chicken, diced
¾-1 cup mayonnaise
¼ tsp. curry powder

½ tsp. lemon juice
2 ten and ¾-ounce cans
  cream of chicken soup
½ cup grated sharp cheese

Cook broccoli half as long as directed on package. Layer broccoli, chicken, and mayonnaise in 9 x 13-inch casserole dish. Mix lemon juice, chicken soup and curry powder and add as a layer to casserole. Top with cheese. Bake at 350° for 30 minutes.

Serves 8   Mickey Vestal

CHICKEN BREASTS IN WINE

Flour
Salt and pepper to taste
8-10 small chicken breasts
1 stick butter or oleo
6 Tb. finely chopped onion

1 cup dry white wine
1 ten and ¾-ounce can cream
  of chicken soup
1 package chicken gravy mix
1¼ cups water

Skin chicken breasts. Salt and pepper breasts; dredge in flour. Sauté breasts in butter until lightly browned. Add onions and wine. Cook gently for about 1 hour or until chicken is tender. Remove breasts from pan; place in oven to keep warm. Add chicken soup, gravy mix and water to drippings in pan. Cook about 5 minutes. Serve chicken breasts arranged on top of large platter of rice. Serve gravy in a bowl.

Serves 8

Bobbie McKenzie

CHICKEN-SAUSAGE CASSEROLE

3 packages dry chicken
  noodle soup mix
9 cups boiling water
2 cups rice, uncooked
2 pounds seasoned bulk
  sausage, crumbled

3 cups diced chicken
1 bunch celery, chopped
2 large onions, chopped
2 green peppers, chopped
½ cup blanched almonds

Stir soup mix into 9 cups water; bring to boiling point for 9 minutes. Add rice and boil 9 minutes more. Brown sausage, reserving fat. Mix sausage and chicken. Sauté celery, onions, peppers and almonds in reserved fat. Place layer of rice mixture, layer of chicken-sausage mixture and layer of celery mixture in casserole. Cover and bake 1 hour at 350°.

Serves 20-24

Florine Tyler

CHICKEN SHERLEN

3 cups cooked chicken
1 six-ounce package Uncle Ben's
  Wild Rice, cooked
1 ten and ¾-ounce can cream
  of mushroom soup
1 cup mayonnaise
1 sixteen-ounce can French
  cut green beans, drained

1 small onion, chopped
1 eight-ounce can water
  chestnuts, drained
1 two-ounce jar pimiento, sliced
1 three-ounce can sliced
  mushrooms
Salt and pepper to taste

Mix all ingredients and bake at 350° for 15 minutes.

Serves 8

Jane Ann Benafield

182

CHICKEN WITH DUMPLINGS

4 whole chicken breasts
3 onions, quartered
4 carrots, pared and cut
2 stalks celery, cut
4 potatoes, quartered
1 ten and ¾-ounce can
  condensed chicken broth
2½ tsp. salt
2 small bay leaves

⅛ tsp. pepper
¼ tsp. thyme
2 Tb. lemon juice
3 cups water
6 Tb. flour
½ cup water
1 cup Pioneer Biscuit Mix
⅓ cup milk

Split chicken breasts, skin and put in a six-quart Dutch oven. Add onions, carrots, celery, potatoes, undiluted chicken broth, salt, bay leaves, pepper, thyme, lemon juice and 3 cups water. Bring to a boil. Reduce heat and cover. Simmer for 45 minutes or until chicken and vegetables are tender. With slotted spoon, remove chicken and vegetables to platter. In small bowl blend flour and ½ cup water until smooth. Pour mixture into boiling broth, stirring constantly until broth thickens. Return chicken and vegetables to Dutch oven. Prepare biscuit mix with milk and drop by rounded tablespoonfuls into boiling chicken and vegetables. Cook uncovered for 10 minutes. Cover and cook another 10 minutes or until dumplings are puffed and a toothpick inserted comes out clean.

Serves 6   Sandra Cook

CHICKEN AND GREEN CHILI PEPPER CASSEROLE

Doritos
1 fryer, cooked, boned and
  chopped into large pieces
½ pound Velveeta cheese, grated
1 ten and ¾-ounce can cream
  of mushroom soup
1 four-ounce can green chili
  peppers, chopped

1 ten and ¾-ounce can cream
  of chicken soup
1 cup Cheddar cheese, grated
1 five and ⅓-ounce can
  evaporated milk

In a 2-quart greased casserole, place layers of Doritos, chicken, Velveeta cheese, cream of mushroom soup, green chili peppers, cream of chicken soup and Cheddar cheese. Pour evaporated milk over top of casserole and bake at 350° for 45 minutes.

Serves 6-8   Becky Hight

CHICKEN ROMANO

⅓ cup flour
½ tsp. salt
¼ tsp. pepper
3 whole chicken breasts,
    split and skinned
2 Tb. melted shortening or
    vegetable oil
¼ cup minced onion
2 cups tomato juice
2 Tb. grated Romano or
    Parmesan cheese
1 Tb. sugar

½ tsp. salt
½ tsp. garlic salt
½ tsp. whole oregano
¼ tsp. basil leaves
1 tsp. vinegar
1 four-ounce can sliced
    mushrooms, drained
1 Tb. minced parsley
½ cup grated Romano or
    Parmesan cheese
Hot cooked spaghetti

Combine flour, salt and pepper. Dredge chicken in flour mixture and brown in hot shortening. Drain chicken on paper towels. Pour off all but 1 Tb. of pan drippings. Sauté onion in reserved drippings until tender. Add next ten ingredients, stirring well. Return chicken to skillet with sauce; cover and simmer 45 minutes or until tender. At serving time, sprinkle chicken with ½ cup Romano or Parmesan cheese. Serve over spaghetti.

Serves 6

CHICKEN BREASTS- ST. LOUIS

3 to 5 large chicken breasts
¼ cup flour

Salt and pepper to taste
Paprika

SAUCE:

6 green onions including
    tops, chopped
1 pound fresh mushrooms,
    sliced
½ stick butter

2 ten and ¾-ounce cans
    cream of mushroom soup
1 cup sour cream
¼ cup sherry
½ cup sliced almonds

Coat chicken with flour and brown on both sides in shortening. Season with salt and pepper. Sprinkle with paprika. Bake uncovered in 350° oven for 45 minutes.

SAUCE: Sauté onions and mushrooms in butter; blend in soup and sour cream. Add sherry and heat. Do not boil. Pour over chicken and scatter almonds over top. Return to oven and bake until almonds are crisp but not brown.

Serves 4

Sidney Nesbit

CHICKEN HÉLENE

1 2½-3-pound chicken, cut-up
Flour seasoned with salt and
  pepper
6 Tb. butter
2 Tb. flour
¾ cup chicken broth
½ cup dry white wine

¼ cup thinly sliced green
  onions including tops
½ cup sliced fresh mushrooms
  sautéed in butter
1 nine-ounce package frozen
  artichoke hearts, cooked
  and drained

Dust chicken with seasoned flour. Melt 4 Tb. butter in shallow baking pan. Place chicken in pan, skin side down; bake uncovered in preheated 350° oven for 45 minutes. Meanwhile, melt remaining butter in saucepan; stir in flour. Add broth and wine; cook, stirring constantly, until thickened and smooth. Remove chicken from oven. Turn pieces over; sprinkle with onions, mushrooms and artichokes. Pour sauce over top. Return to oven; reduce heat to 325° and bake 25-30 minutes longer.

May be prepared ahead of time and refrigerated. If refrigerated, adjust baking time.

Serves 4   Frances Lance

CHICKEN KIEV

1 stick butter, softened
Juice of ½ lemon
1 Tb. parsley

4 whole chicken breasts,
  halved and boned

COATING

1 egg
2 Tb. water

Bread crumbs
Flour

Mix butter, lemon juice and parsley. Roll into 1-inch stick; place in freezer for 30-45 minutes. Pound chicken breast to ¼-inch thick; roll butter inside chicken tucking in ends. Salt and pepper and roll in flour. Mix 1 egg and 2 Tb. water in a bowl. Dip floured chicken in egg mixture; roll in bread crumbs. Chill one hour. Fry in deep hot fat 7-10 minutes.

Serves 4   Carole Hoofman

Chicken rolled in powdered milk instead of flour will fry to a golden brown.

185

CHICKEN AND STUFFING SCALLOP

1 eight-ounce package herb
  seasoned stuffing (cornbread)
3 cups chopped cooked chicken
½ cup butter or oleo
½ cup flour

¼ tsp. salt
Dash of pepper
4 cups chicken broth
6 slightly beaten eggs
1 recipe pimiento mushroom sauce

PIMIENTO-MUSHROOM SAUCE

1 ten and ¾-ounce can cream of
  mushroom soup
¼ cup milk

1 cup sour cream
¼ cup chopped pimientos

Place stuffing as directed on package. Scatter stuffing in 3-quart buttered, rectangular casserole; add chicken. Melt butter in large saucepan. Blend in flour and seasonings. Add cool broth. Cook and stir until thickened. Stir small amount of hot mixture into eggs and return eggs to broth mixture. Pour over chicken and stuffing. Bake in slow oven at 325° 40-45 minutes, or until knife inserted halfway into center comes out clean. Let stand 5 minutes. Cut into squares. Serve pimiento mushroom sauce over squares.

Serves 12   Linda Bergquist

CHICKEN AND WILD RICE CASSEROLE

2-3 pound whole broiler/fryer
1 cup water
1 cup dry sherry
½ tsp. curry powder
1½ tsp. salt
1 medium onion, sliced
½ cup celery

1 pound fresh mushrooms
¼ cup butter
2 six-ounce packages long grain
  and wild rice with seasonings
1 cup sour cream
1 ten and ¾-ounce can
  cream of mushroom soup

Place chicken, water, sherry, curry powder, salt, onion and celery in pan. Cover and bring to a boil. Reduce heat. Cook 1 hour. Remove from heat and strain broth. Refrigerate and cool. Remove chicken from bone and cut into pieces. Wash, slice and sauté mushrooms in butter. Reserve caps for top of casserole. Measure chicken broth and use as part of liquid for rice. Cook rice; combine chicken, mushrooms and rice in a 3-quart casserole. Blend in sour cream and mushroom soup. Mix with rice. Arrange mushrooms caps on top. Cover and refrigerate overnight. Bake uncovered at 350° for 1 hour.

Serves 8-10   Mrs. George Penick

CHICKEN WITH ZUCCHINI AND CORN

1 fryer, cut up
1 Tb. oil
½ onion, chopped
2 Tb. flour
1½ tsp. cumin
3-3½ cups sliced zucchini

3 cups water
1 twelve-ounce can corn
Dash of pepper
Dash of garlic powder
Salt to taste

Boil chicken until very tender. Let cool and remove bones. Heat oil in a skillet. Add chicken meat and sprinkle with the flour. Add the rest of the ingredients and bring to a boil. Reduce heat. Simmer, covered for 30 minutes.

Variations: Substitute 4 pork chops for chicken.

Serves 8   Paulette Mercer

COUNTRY CHICKEN

8 chicken breasts
Flour
Salt and pepper to taste
½ cup Mazola oil
2 onions, chopped
2 green peppers, chopped
1 cup chopped celery
1 clove garlic, minced

½ stick butter
2 tsp. oregano
1 sixteen-ounce can whole
   tomatoes
4 tsp. curry powder
1 tsp. salt
2 tsp. thyme
¼ chopped parsley

Skin chicken. Roll chicken in flour, salt and pepper; brown in Mazola. Keep chicken warm. Sauté onions, green peppers, celery and clove garlic in ½ stick butter until tender. Add tomatoes, curry powder, salt, oregano, thyme and parsley. Add this mixture to heated chicken breasts. Cover and bake 1½ hours at 325°. Serve over rice with toasted almonds. Garnish with fresh parsley.

Serves 6-8   Janice Harris

CHICKEN ROLL-UPS

6-8 chicken breasts, boned
   and tenderized
¼ pound Cheddar cheese, sliced
1 egg, beaten
2 cups bread crumbs
Vegetable oil
1 cup mushrooms

½ cup chopped green pepper
½ cup chopped onion
2 cups chicken broth, or
   2 bouillon cubes dissolved
   in 2 cups water
2 Tb. flour

Wrap chicken breast around a slice of Cheddar cheese and roll up. Dip chicken breasts in beaten eggs; roll in bread crumbs. Use enough oil to almost cover chicken. Fry until done. Mix mushrooms, green pepper, onions, broth and flour. Pour the sauce into a 9 x 11-inch baking dish. Lay chicken breasts on top. Cover with foil and bake 30 minutes at 325°. Serve over rice.

Serves 6-8   Madeline Johnson

CORN-CRISP CHICKEN

6 pieces of chicken
Salt and pepper

1 four and ¾-ounce can
   evaporated milk
Kellogg's corn flake crumbs

Wash chicken pieces and sprinkle with salt and pepper. Dip pieces in evaporated milk (do not use regular milk). Roll thoroughly in crumbs and place in baking dish. Bake 1-1¼ hours at 350°. Serve hot.

Serves 6

CORNISH GAME HENS WITH RICE STUFFING

6 one-pound (or larger) Cornish
   game hens
Salt to taste
Pepper to taste
6 Tb. sliced almonds
6 Tb. chopped onion
1 cup uncooked long-grain rice

9 Tb. butter or margarine
3 cups water
3 chicken bouillon cubes
3 tsp. lemon juice
1½ tsp. salt
3 three-ounce cans chopped
   mushrooms, drained

Season game hens inside and out with salt and pepper. In saucepan, cook almonds, onion and rice in butter for 5-10 minutes, stirring frequently. Add water, bouillon cubes, lemon juice and salt. Bring mixture to a boil, stirring to dissolve bouillon cubes. Reduce heat; cover and cook slowly about 20-25 minutes or until liquid is absorbed and rice is fluffy. Stir in mushrooms. Lightly stuff birds with rice mixture. Place birds breast-side up in a 9 x 13-inch pan. Brush birds with melted butter or margarine. Roast covered at 400° for 30 minutes. Uncover and roast 1 hour longer or until drumstick can be twisted easily in socket. Brush birds with melted butter during last 15 minutes.

Serves 6   Betsy Davies

CREAMED CHICKEN IN AVOCADO SHELL

3 Tb. margarine, melted
3 Tb. all-purpose flour
1 cup milk
½ tsp. salt

1½ cups diced cooked chicken
1 two-ounce can mushrooms,
   drained
3 avocados

Combine margarine and flour; blend well. Add milk and salt. Cook and stir until mixture boils and is thick. Blend in chicken and mushrooms and heat thoroughly. Keep hot in double boiler. Preheat oven to 300°. Cut each avocado in half. Place in shallow pan and pour one-fourth inch warm water in bottom of pan. Heat for 10-15 minutes. Remove avocado to serving plate and fill with hot chicken mixture. Serve at once.

Serves 6   Cheri Kennedy

CRESCENT CHICKEN ROLL-UPS

⅓ cup crushed corn flakes
¼ cup chopped pecans
1 three-ounce package cream
  cheese
1½ tsp. chopped chives
2 Tb. butter

1 cup cooked, cubed chicken
½ cup mushrooms
Crescent roll dough (See
  recipe for rolls or use
  canned crescent rolls.)
3 Tb. melted butter

In small bowl, combine ⅓ cup crushed corn flakes and nuts; set aside. Mix cream cheese, chives and 2 Tb. butter and mix well. Stir in chicken and mushrooms. Spread about ¼ cup chicken mixture on each triangle roll up, starting at short edge. Tuck sides and end under to seal. Roll in melted butter and then in nut mixture. Place on ungreased cookie sheet. Bake at 375° for 15-20 minutes until golden. Serve with chicken gravy.

Serves 8　　　　　　　　　　　　　　　　　　　　　　　　　　Terri Caple

CRESCENT CHICKEN SQUARES

1 eight-ounce cream cheese,
  softened
4 Tb. margarine, melted
4 cups cubed chicken
¼ cup milk
½ tsp. salt

¼ tsp. pepper
2 cans crescent rolls
Seasoned bread crumbs
1 ten and ¾-ounce can chicken
  mushroom soup
⅓ soup can milk

Combine cream cheese, margarine, chicken, milk, salt and pepper. Mix well. Separate 2 cans of crescent rolls into 8 rectangles. Press perforations to seal. Spoon ½ cup chicken mixture into each rectangle. Pull 4 corners to the top of filling and twist firmly. Seal the corners. Place on 2 ungreased cookie sheets and brush with melted butter. Sprinkle with seasoned bread crumbs. Bake 20-30 minutes at 350° until a golden brown. Combine soup and milk to make a sauce which is poured over the squares when served.

Serves 8

DEVILED CHICKEN

2 cups diced, cooked chicken
1 small onion, chopped
1 cup cooked rice
1 ten and ¾-ounce can
  mushroom soup
1 tsp. lemon juice

3 hard-boiled eggs, chopped
¾ cup diced celery
½ cup mayonnaise
¼ cup sliced almonds
2-3 cups crushed potato chips

Mix together chicken, onion, rice, mushroom soup, lemon juice, hard boiled eggs, chopped celery, mayonnaise and almonds. Place in buttered 9 x 9-inch casserole. Top with crushed potato chips. Bake at 370° for 40 minutes.

Serves 8　　　　　　　　　　　　　　　　　　　　　　　　Bernice Hanchey

DORA'S CHICKEN POT PIE

1 potato
1 carrot
1 Tb. salt
1 Tb. diced onion
Dash pepper
1 ten and ¾-ounce can cream
  of celery soup

½ thirteen-ounce can milk
2 five-ounce cans Swanson's
  boned chicken
1 eight and ½-ounce can
  peas
Pie crust for a two-crust pie

Peel and dice potato and carrot. Cook in sufficient water (about ¾ cup) with 1 Tb. salt, 1 Tb. dried onion and dash of pepper. Heat cream of celery soup with ½ can of milk. When potato mixture is done, drain and combine with soup. Add 2 cans of Swanson's boned chicken and 1 small can peas, drained. (Leftover peas may be used.) Preheat oven to 400°. Make pie crust for double crust. Roll bottom crust to 13-inch diameter. Place in a 1½-quart round glass dish, leaving edges hanging over sides of dish. Pour in combined soup and potato mixture. Place top crust on; cut through both crusts around outside of dish with knife. Turn crust together on sides; cut slits in top for air to escape. Bake at 400° for 30 minutes or until browned.

Serves 4   Dora Ball

GOOEY CHICKEN

Flour
1 fryer, cut up
1 package onion soup mix

2 cups boiling water
¼ stick oleo

Flour chicken pieces and place in 9 x 13-inch dish. Mix soup, water and oleo; pour over chicken. Bake for 45 minutes at 350°, basting occasionally. This makes a delicious gravy with the chicken. Do not add salt. Serve with rice.

Serves 4   Mrs. Oma Shannon

GUARANTEED-CRISPY FRIED CHICKEN

1 quart Bulgarian buttermilk
1 tsp. baking soda
1 large frying chicken, cut-up
1 to 1½ cups all-purpose flour
  with salt and pepper to taste

Enough cooking oil to cover half
  of chicken

Mix buttermilk and soda in deep, large mixing bowl. Wash and partially dry chicken. Soak chicken in buttermilk mixture 30 minutes. Pour chicken and buttermilk into colander to drain. Roll chicken in flour. Fry in hot oil in covered electric skillet at about 375° for approximately 15 minutes on each side.

Serves 4-6

LEMON CHICKEN

4-6 chicken breast halves,
  skinned
3 Tb. butter or margarine
Dash of garlic powder

¼ to ⅓ cup lemon juice
1 ten and ¾-ounce can cream
  of mushroom soup
Salt and pepper to taste

Brown chicken breasts in butter until chicken is white. Remove and place in casserole. Sprinkle with garlic powder; pour lemon juice on the meat. Spread soup on top. Mix lightly with juice in pan. Cover and bake for 45 minutes in 350° oven. Baste once, midway through baking time. May be garnished with parsley and pimiento. Serve on a bed or rice.

Especially good on Mahatma yellow rice.

Serves 4-6   Cindy Staley

MASON SEARCY'S GRILLED CHICKEN

Chicken quarters (1-10)
1 stick oleo, melted
⅓ of 1 oz. jar garlic powder

⅓ cup salt
Pepper to taste
3 Tb. Worcestershire Sauce

Place chicken quarters on hot grill. Melt oleo and add all other ingredients. Baste chicken with sauce as often as desired while grilling. (May also be cooked under broiler.) Cook with sauce until tender, 20-30 minutes.

The basting sauce keeps well, if covered, in refrigerator for several weeks.

Serves 1-10   Marilyn Eudy

ORIENTAL CHICKEN

4 chicken breasts, skinned
  and boned
¼ cup oil
1 small onion, chopped
2 cups celery, sliced diagonally
1 seven-ounce can chicken broth or
  a chicken bouillon cube dissolved
  in water according to package
  directions

⅓ cup soy sauce
1 tsp. ginger
Garlic powder to taste
1 seven-ounce can water
  chestnuts, drained and sliced
1½ Tb. cornstarch dissolved
  in ¼ cup water

Cut chicken breasts into very thin strips and brown in hot oil. As chicken begins to turn white, add chopped onion. When onion is clear, add celery and stir-fry very quickly. Add bouillon, soy sauce, ginger and garlic. Cook 5 more minutes. Add sliced water chestnuts and cook only until they are heated through. Add cornstarch and water mixture and continue cooking until gravy thickens. Serve over cooked rice. May be topped with slivered, toasted almonds.

Serves 4-6   Suzie Thompson

OVEN FRIED CHICKEN Á LA CREOLE

¼ cup butter	½ cup flour
1 frying chicken, cut up	1 cup uncooked rice
1½ tsp. salt	½ cup chopped bell pepper
1 tsp. paprika	½ cup chopped onion
¼ tsp. poultry seasoning	3 cups hot chicken broth
⅛ tsp. black pepper	

Melt butter in 9 x 13-inch glass dish in oven. Shake chicken in a bag with salt, paprika, poultry seasoning, black pepper and flour. Place in butter skin side down. Bake for 30 minutes at 375°. Remove chicken from dish. Spread rice, bell pepper, onion, pich of salt and pepper in dish. Place chicken on top of rice mixture. Pour hot broth over all. Bake 45 minutes at 375° or until rice and chicken are done.

Serves 4-6

Sheila Hammond

PARMESAN CHICKEN

8 chicken breasts, boned	Pinch salt
1 cup flour	1 egg
1 cup Parmesan cheese	1 Tb. water
	Butter

Mix flour, Parmesan cheese and salt. Beat egg and 1 Tb. water. Dip chicken breasts in liquid and then in cheese and flour mixture. Dab with butter. Bake at 350° about 1 hour, basting with butter.

This dish can be made several hours ahead of time or the morning before serving.

Serves 8

Patty Pyron

PINEAPPLE CHICKEN

6 pieces chicken	¼ cup brown sugar, firmly
Salt and pepper to taste	packed
2 Tb. butter or margarine	¼ cup white vinegar
½ cup flour	¼ tsp. ginger
1 fifteen and ¼-ounce can	2 Tb. soy sauce
pineapple chunks	Thickener: 3 tsp. cornstarch
Liquid from pineapple	dissolved in ¾ cup water

Wash and skin chicken. Salt and pepper each piece. Lightly coat with flour and brown in melted butter. Place in large, shallow baking dish. Drain pineapple chunks, reserving liquid. Place liquid in saucepan; add sugar, vinegar, ginger, soy sauce and thickener. Bring to boil while stirring. Pour over chicken, add pineapple and bake covered 1 hour at 350°. Remove cover and bake additional 5 minutes. Serve over rice.

Serves 3-4

Susan Langley

ROBB'S SPECIAL CHICKEN

4 pieces chicken
1 ten and ¾-ounce can cream
  of mushroom soup
Ground pepper

4-8 ounces red or white wine
½ cup chopped green onions
Spices as desired

Into double thickness of foil put 4 pieces or 2 halves of chicken. Add cream of mushroom soup, a generous amount of freshly ground pepper, 4 ounces of wine and chopped green onions. Other spices may be added if desired. Seal foil tightly. Bake for 2 hours at 325°.

Serves 2   Sidney M. Nisbet

ROLLED CHICKEN BREASTS

4 chicken breasts
30 Ritz crackers, made into
  crumb meal

1 eight-ounce can cream of
  chicken soup
½ cup Wesson oil

Grind the Ritz crackers into crumbs or meal. A food processor may be used. Dip chicken breasts in oil; roll in crushed Ritz crackers. Place breasts close together in 9-inch pan and bake at 350° for one hour. Pour soup around chicken and bake for one more hour.

Serves 4   Mrs. James Heath

SHERRIED CHICKEN

½ cup flour
2 tsp. salt
1 three-pound chicken, cut-up
¾ cup butter
½ cup dry sherry

2 Tb. soy sauce
2 Tb. lemon juice
¼ cup finely chopped ginger
  (preserved)

Combine flour and salt; coat chicken with mixture. Melt ½ cup butter; brown chicken on all sides and place into a covered baking dish. In a saucepan, combine remaining butter, sherry, soy sauce, lemon juice and ginger. Bring to a boil, stirring, and pour over chicken. Bake in a preheated 350° oven for 1 hour or until tender. Turn chicken once during baking.

Serves 4   Frances Lance

STUFFED CHICKEN BREASTS

4 twelve-ounce chicken breasts,
   skinned and boned or 8 halves
½ cup green onions, sliced
¼ pound mushrooms, sliced
½ cup butter
3 Tb. all-purpose flour
¼ tsp. thyme
½ cup chicken broth

½ cup milk
½ cup dry white wine
Salt and pepper to taste
1 pound crab meat
⅓ cup parsley
⅓ cup bread crumbs
1 cup Swiss cheese, shredded

Pound chicken breasts between wax paper to ¼-inch thickness. Sauté onions and mushrooms in butter. Stir in flour, thyme, broth, milk and wine. Stir until thick. Season to taste with salt and pepper. Add crab meat, parsley and crumbs. Spoon equally onto chicken pieces; roll and secure with toothpicks. Place seam side down in buttered baking dish. Pour remaining sauce over chicken and sprinkle with cheese. Bake 40-45 minutes at 375°.

Serves 8   Janice Harris

TERIYAKI CHICKEN

⅔ cup soy sauce
⅓ cup sherry or white wine
2 Tb. oil
1½ tsp. ground ginger

½ cup lemon juice
Brown sugar
4-6 whole chicken breasts

Combine first four ingredients. (A bottle of prepared teriyaki sauce can be substituted for this.) Place chicken breasts skin side down in a dish deep enough to hold sauce. Pour lemon juice over breasts. Next pour sauce over the meat. Sprinkle 1 tsp. of brown sugar over each chicken breast. Cover and let marinate for 2-3 hours, turning every 15 to 20 minutes. Cook on charcoal grill, turning and basting often. For juicer chicken cook with skin on.

Serves 4-6   Cindy Staley

A pinch of salt in the skillet keeps grease from popping when frying chicken.

SPECIAL CHICKEN CRÊPES

2 cups milk
6 Tb. butter
6 Tb. flour
Salt and pepper to taste
1 cup chopped onion
1 cup chopped celery

1 eight and ½-ounce can water
   chestnuts, sliced
8 large chicken breasts, cooked and
   cut into bite-size pieces
1 cup chopped mushrooms

Combine and blend first 4 ingredients well. Add remaining ingredients. Simmer just until thick. Place a crêpe in 9 x 13-inch glass baking dish. Put a little chicken filling in it and roll it up. Turn seam side down. Put a little sauce on top and bake at 350° for 35 minutes. Serve with remaining sauce.

BASIC CRÊPES

1 cup flour
4 eggs
½ cup evaporated milk, chilled

½ cup chicken stock
½ tsp. salt
2 Tb. melted butter

Measure all ingredients except flour into large mixing bowl. Beat on medium speed, gradually adding flour until all ingredients are combined. If small lumps are present, pour batter through strainer before preparing crêpe.

SAUCE

6 Tb. butter
1 Tb. flour
8 ounces chicken stock

1 pint half and half
White dry wine for thinning

Melt butter and stir in flour. Gradually add chicken stock, cooking on medium heat until thick. Blend in cream and cook over low heat until mixture thickens again. Use wine for thinning if necessary.

For dessert crêpes use ½ cup water instead of chicken stock. Add 2 Tb. sugar and 1 tsp. vanilla.

Filled crêpes can be frozen and served later if sauce has not been added.

Serves 12-14

Pam Gustavus

Vegetables

ASPARAGUS CASSEROLE

1 ten and ½-ounce can asparagus
  tips with juice
3 eggs, well-beaten
1 cup milk

1 cup cracker crumbs
½ stick butter, melted
1 cup grated mild Cheddar cheese

Place asparagus in 2 quart casserole. Mash asparagus. Add remaining ingredients. Save some cheese to sprinkle on top. Bake uncovered in slow oven (350°) for 45 minutes.

Serves 6-8   Mrs. J. B. Lambert

ASPARAGUS ELEGANTÉ

2 pounds fresh asparagus
1 Tb. butter
1 Tb. flour
1 cup half and half
1 cup diced ham

1 tsp. lemon juice
¼ tsp. salt
Dash nutmeg
¼ cup grated Swiss cheese

Cut ends off asparagus and remove scales with a vegetable peeler. Cook asparagus, covered, in a small amount of boiling water until crisp and tender (about 5 minutes). Drain and arrange on serving platter. Melt butter in a saucepan over low heat. Blend in flour and cook 1 minute, stirring constantly. Gradually add half and half; cook over medium heat until thick, stirring constantly. Add ham, lemon juice, salt, nutmeg, and cheese. Stir until cheese melts. Serve sauce with asparagus.

Serves 6   Vicki Lackie

MEXICAN CHILI-BEAN WARM UP

½ cup chopped onion
1 Tb. butter
1 four-ounce can Ortega diced
  green chilies

1 one-pound can refried beans
2 cups grated Cheddar cheese
Taco sauce

Sauté onion in butter. Add chilies, refried beans and 1 cup cheese. Mix and spoon into a buttered 1½ quart caserole. Top with remaining cheese and a few sprinkles of taco sauce for color. Bake in preheated oven at 350° for 15 minutes or until heated through. Bake uncovered.

Debi Beasley

RED BEANS AND RICE

1 pound dried red beans
  (soaked overnight)
½ pound salt pork
2 quarts water
2 small chopped onions
2 Tb. dried parsley
2 garlic pods, crushed
1 Tb. salt

3 dashes Tabasco sauce
1 tsp. black pepper
1 Tb. Worcestershire sauce
½ tsp. oregano
¼ tsp. basil
1 pound smoked sausage
Cooked rice

Cook beans in salted water over low heat 45 minutes. Add salt pork, onions, and seasonings. Cook slowly 1 hour, stirring occasionally. Add sausage and cook 45 minutes more. Remove from heat and let stand 1-2 hours. Reheat and bring to a boil. Reduce heat and simmer slowly 45 minutes. Serve over boiled rice.

Serves 8-10   Madeline Johnson

ORANGE BEETS

1½ cups light brown sugar
2 Tb. cornstarch
1 six-ounce can frozen orange
  juice concentrate
¾ cup cider vinegar

2 twenty-ounce cans small whole
  beets, drained (save liquid)
1 Tb. butter
¾ cup beet juice

Blend brown sugar and cornstarch. Combine orange juice concentrate, vinegar, and beet juice. Add to brown sugar and cornstarch. Bring to a full boil stirring constantly. Add beets and butter.

Flavor improves if beets are allowed to stand in liquid before serving. Keeps well in refrigerator for a week. Simply reheat.

Serves 8   Janice Davies

BOBBIE'S BROCCOLI

2 ten-ounce packages frozen
  broccoli spears
1 stick oleo
1 Tb. Worcestershire

1 Tb. prepared mustard
Dash cayenne pepper
Dash pepper

Cook broccoli until done (no salt). Melt margarine and add next four ingredients. Pour over broccoli and serve.

Bobbie Phelps

BROCCOLI CASSEROLE

**2 ten-ounce packages frozen
broccoli cuts
1 stick oleo**

**1 eight-ounce package cream cheese
½ package Pepperidge Farm
Herb stuffing**

Cook broccoli as directed on package, drain and mash. Add ½ stick oleo and the cream cheese; mix well. Place into casserole. Melt the other ½ stick oleo and add it to the stuffing. Put on top of broccoli. Bake uncovered at 350° for 30 minutes.

Variations: Green beans may be used instead of broccoli.

Marianne Gosser

BROCCOLI SOUFFLÉ

**1 ten-ounce package frozen
broccoli, chopped
1 cup cream sauce (3 Tb. butter,
3 Tb. flour and 1 cup milk)
1 tsp. salt**

**Pinch of pepper
2 heaping Tb. salad dressing
or mayonnaise
4 eggs, separated**

Cook broccoli according to package directions and drain well. Make cream sauce and cook until thickened. Add salt and pepper. Combine sauce, broccoli, salad dressing or mayonnaise, and beaten egg yolks in a saucepan. Stop and let mixture cool. Fold in stiffly beaten (but not dry) egg whites. Pour into greased 1½ quart casserole or soufflé dish. Put dish, uncovered, in a shallow pan of hot water and bake at 350° for 1 hour. Serve immediately.

Betty Mabrey

A great casserole topping; herb flavored stuffing mix and a few pats of butter.

BETTER BRUSSELS SPROUTS

2 ten-ounce packages frozen
  brussels sprouts
1 cup water
2 tsp. instant chicken bouillon
½ tsp. salt
1 ten and ¾-can cream of
  chicken soup, undiluted

1 two-ounce jar diced
  pimiento, undrained
⅛ tsp. whole thyme leaves
⅛ tsp. pepper
2 Tb. butter or margarine
½ cup sliced almonds

Place brussels sprouts, water, bouillon, and salt into a medium saucepan. Cook over medium-high heat until mixture comes to a boil; reduce heat and cover. Simmer 8-10 minutes or until tender. Drain. Combine soup, pimiento, and seasonings; stir in brussels sprouts. Spoon into a greased 1½ quart casserole dish. Melt butter in a small skillet; add almonds and cook 3 minutes. Remove butter mixture from heat and spoon over top of casserole. Bake at 350° for 20 minutes or until hot. Bake uncovered.

Serves 6   Sandy Levin

STIR-FRY CABBAGE

1 medium cabbage, coarsley chopped
2 stalks celery, thinly sliced
1 medium onion, chopped
1 small bell pepper, chopped

2 Tb. margarine or butter
½ tsp. salt
⅛ tsp. pepper

Stir-fry cabbage, celery, onion, bell pepper in margarine or butter in heavy Dutch oven for 5 minutes over high heat. Cover and remove from heat; let steam until cabbage is tender (about 5-10 minutes). Stir in salt and pepper.

Serves 8   Vicki Lackie

AUNT THELMA'S COLD CARROTS

2 pounds raw carrots
2 tb. minced onion
1 Tb. salt
½ cup salad oil

1 Tb. liquid from cooked carrots
¾ cup sugar
  (or 3 tsp. sweet 'n low)
½ cup vinegar

Clean and slice carrots crosswise. Cook carrots in unsalted water 15-20 minutes or until done. Reserving 1 Tb. carrot liquid, drain carrots. Put minced onion over hot carrots. Mix salt, salad oil, liquid from cooked carrots, sugar, vinegar and stir until dissolved. Pour over carrots and let stand in refrigerator overnight.

Serves 10-12   Margaret Wilkins

CARROT CASSEROLE

2 cups cooked, mashed carrots
  or 4 jars baby-food carrots
1 cup sugar
½ stick oleo
¾ cup milk

2 rounded Tb. flour
5 tsp. cinnamon
3 beaten eggs
1 tsp. baking powder
½ cup chopped nuts (optional)

Mix all ingredients together. Bake uncovered at 350° until casserole sets, approximately 30 minutes.

Can be prepared a day ahead. Excellent with any meal; particularly good with chicken, turkey or wild game.

Barbara St. Onge

CARROT RING

3½ cups sliced raw carrots
1 cup cracker crumbs
1 cup milk
½ cup soft butter

¼ cup finely chopped onion
¾ cup grated Cheddar cheese
1 tsp. salt
¼ tsp. pepper

Cook carrots until tender. Drain and mash. Add all other ingredients and mix. Place in buttered 1½ quart ring mold or casserole dish. Bake uncovered 40-45 minutes at 350°. If ring mold is used, unmold and fill center with small cooked peas.

Serves 8

Saundra Hatch

SUNSHINE CARROTS

5 medium carrots, cooked
1 tb. sugar
1 tsp. corn starch
¼ tsp. ginger

¼ tsp. salt
¼ cup orange juice
2 Tb. butter

Chop carrots and cook until tender. Mix next five ingredients and cook over low heat, stirring constantly, until thick. Stir in butter and pour over carrots.

Serves 4-6

Ruth Wilson

CAULIFLOWER CASSEROLE

1 large head cauliflower
1 onion
½ pound bacon
1 cup sour cream

1 cup grated sharp cheese
½ pound mushrooms, sliced
Salt and pepper to taste
¼ cup Parmesan cheese

Separate cauliflower into small florets; wash in cold water. Cook cauliflower in lightly salted water until tender-crisp. Drain well. Slice the onion and bacon; fry together until soft but not crisp. Mix all ingredients except the Parmesan and place in a buttered baking dish. Sprinkle the top with Parmesan. Bake uncovered in a preheated 350° oven for 30 minutes.

Serves 4-6   Cathy Simpson

FRENCH FRIED CAULIFLOWER

1 head cauliflower
1 egg
1 Tb. water

Cracker crumbs (crushed very fine)
Salad oil

Wash cauliflower and break into florets. Cook, covered, in boiling, salted water about 10 minutes. Drain. Combine egg and water. Beat well. Dip florets in cracker crumbs, and then in egg mixture. Dip again in cracker crumbs. Deep fry at 375° till golden brown. Serve with cheese sauce.

CHEESE SAUCE:

2 Tb. butter
2 Tb. flour
1 cup milk

¼ tsp. salt
⅛ tsp. pepper
1 cup shredded Cheddar cheese

Melt butter in small saucepan over low heat. Add flour and stir until smooth. Gradually add milk and stir constantly until thick. Add salt, pepper, and cheese. Stir until cheese melts. Yield: 1 cup.

Serves 6   Madeline Johnson

CREOLE CORN

2 cups frozen or canned corn
¼ cup chopped onion
¼ cup chopped bell pepper

3 Tb. butter
Salt and pepper to taste
1 fresh tomato, diced

Cook corn for about 10 minutes or until corn is tender. Add the remaining ingredients to the corn and cook 15-20 minutes or until onion and pepper are tender.

Serves 4   Martha Haguewood

CORN FREMONT

1 one-pound 1-ounce can
cream-style corn
1 cup cracker crumbs
½ cup chopped celery
¼ cup chopped onion
⅔ cup grated Cheddar cheese
1 tsp. salt
Dash of pepper

2 beaten eggs
1½ cups milk
2 Tb. melted butter
Dash of sugar
Dash of paprika
1 four-ounce jar pimientos (optional)
¼ cup chopped olives (optional)

Mix all ingredients well. Pour into a buttered casserole. Cover and bake 1 hour at 350°.

Gerrie Fletcher

CORN PUDDING

¼ cup butter or margarine
¼ cup finely chopped celery
¼ cup finely chopped onion
2 Tb. flour
½ tsp. salt
¼ tsp. paprika

1 cup milk
1 twelve-ounce can whole
kernel corn
2 Tb. snipped parsley
2 eggs

Melt butter over medium heat. Add onions and celery and sauté until soft. Blend in flour, salt and paprika; heat until mixture bubbles. Add milk, stirring constantly. Bring to a boil and continue cooking 2 more minutes. Add corn and parsley. Fold in eggs. Turn into a buttered shallow 1½ quart casserole. Bake uncovered at 350° for 35 minutes or until a knife inserted halfway between center and edge of dish comes out clean.

Serves 4-6

Suzie Thompson

No tears! Put onions in freezer 30 minutes before chopping.

BAKED EGGPLANT

2 large eggplants
1¾ cup chopped onion
¼ cup olive oil (do not use
   vegetable oil)
1¾ cup Parmesan cheese
1¾ cup cracker crumbs

Pepper to taste
½ tsp. leaf oregano
1½-2 tsp. sugar
¾ tsp. garlic powder
1 twenty-eight ounce can tomatoes,
   coarsely chopped, including juice

Peel and cut eggplant into one inch squares. Soak in cold salted water for one hour. Drain. Cook in boiling salted water for 3 minutes. Drain. In a small pan, sauté onion in the olive oil until yellow. Set aside. In a large mixing bowl, slightly mash the cooked eggplant. Add all other ingredients including the onions and olive oil. Stir well. Pour into lightly-greased casserole dish. Bake uncovered in preheated 375° oven for about one hour.

Serves 10

Andrea Davenport

BAKED SPANISH EGGPLANT

3 medium-sized eggplants
3 eggs, beaten
3 cups canned tomatoes, drained
6 Tb. melted butter or margarine

6 Tb. chopped onions
3 cups dry bread crumbs
4 cups grated cheese

Pare eggplant and cut into 1-inch cubes. Cook in boiling, salted water 8 minutes. Drain. Add eggs, tomatoes, butter, onion, dry bread crumbs and grated cheese. Mix gently until cheese melts. Place in greased baking dish or foil pans in meal-size batches. Bake in moderate oven (350°) for 45 minutes. Makes about 3 medium-sized casseroles.

To freeze: Cool immediately. Wrap baking dishes in foil or seal in plastic bags. Label and freeze immediately. To serve: Remove from freezer and place immediately in 350° oven for 20-40 minutes, depending on size of baking dish. About 15 minutes before thawing is completed, sprinkle grated cheese over top. Return to oven and complete thawing. Will keep in freezer about 2 months.

Serves 18

Ruth Chronister
Kay Donham

BAKED STUFFED EGGPLANT

1 large, firm eggplant
1 green pepper
3 celery ribs
3 Tb. butter
1 hard-boiled egg
3 cooked chicken livers
1 raw egg, beaten

2 Tb. cracker crumbs
Pinch of cayenne pepper
Salt
Freshly ground black pepper
Cracker crumbs and butter
   for topping

Slice top off eggplant and scoop out inside, leaving enough so that eggplant will retain its shape when boiled in salt water for about 10 minutes. Boil scooped out portion in salt water until tender. Pour off water and mash well. Chop vegetables and sauté gently in butter until tender. Add mashed eggplant. Cook for 5 minutes. Grate the hard-boiled egg and chop the chicken livers. Add to above with rest of ingredients in order given. Fill eggplant shell with mixture. Sprinkle top with cracker crumbs and bits of butter. Bake in 375° oven until top is brown. Serve on platter and garnish with parsley.

Serves 4

Sam Peck

SHRIMP-STUFFED EGGPLANT

1 large eggplant, halved
2 Tb. peanut oil
2 cups fresh shrimp in shells
¾ cup butter
1 bunch green onions, chopped
1 large onion, finely chopped
4-6 cloves garlic, crushed

¾ cup fresh chopped parsley
½ ten and ½-ounce can of
   chicken broth
2 slices Swiss cheese
1 cup bread crumbs
Salt and pepper to taste

Score halves of eggplant. Do not cut through skin. Salt heavily and let drain one hour, or soak in heavily salted water for one hour. Rinse several times. Oil generously on all surfaces with peanut oil. Bake at 350° for one hour or until tender. Blanch and peel shrimp. Refrigerate while preparing stuffing. Sauté green onions, onion, garlic and parsley in butter; add chicken broth. Add chopped eggplant that has been scooped from shells, leaving shells intact. Add cheese, salt, pepper, bread crumbs, and shrimp (cut in thirds). Cook 3-4 minutes. Stuff the eggplant halves, top with more bread crumbs, and bake at 350° for 25-30 minutes until browned.

May be served as an entrée.

Serves 2

Sidney Nisbet

EGGPLANT CASSEROLE

1 large or 2 small eggplants,
  peeled and cubed
½ tsp. salt
Dash of pepper
½ cup chopped onion
¼ cup chopped celery

2 cups tomatoes
2 well-beaten eggs
2 cups cornbread crumbs
2 Tb. milk
1 cup grated Cheddar or
  Mozzarella cheese

Cook eggplant in water until tender. Drain thoroughly. Add salt and pepper and mash. In a skillet simmer onion, celery, and tomatoes until tender. In a greased casserole dish combine eggs, eggplant, cornbread crumbs, and cooked vegetables. Add milk to mixture. Top with grated cheese and bake uncovered at 350° for 30 minutes.

Serves 6

Susan Plunkett

BACON GARLIC CHEESE GRITS

6-ounce tube of bacon cheese
6-ounce tube of garlic cheese
4 cups water

½ tsp. salt
1 cut uncooked grits
¼ cup butter

Slice cheese into small pieces. Bring salted water to a boil; slowly add grits. Bring to a second boil; reduce heat and cook over medium heat for 4-5 minutes, stirring often. Add cheese and butter to grits, stirring until melted and blended. Pour into an ungreased 1½ quart casserole. Bake uncovered for 30 minutes at 350°.

A wonderful brunch dish!

Serves 6

Ginny Matthews

Lemon juice added to the cooking water will make rice white.

GREEN BEANS AND ARTICHOKES

2 sixteen-ounce cans whole
    green beans
1 fourteen-ounce can artichokes
    hearts

1 onion, sliced and
    separated into rings
1 Tb. vinegar
1 Tb. salad oil

Drain beans and artichokes and toss with onion rings, vinegar and oil. Sprinkle with salt and pepper. Marinate at least 2 hours. Before serving, add the dressing and serve cold.

DRESSING:

1 cup sour cream
½ cup mayonnaise
1 tsp. lemon juice
1 tsp. horseradish
1 tsp. onion juice

2 tsp. chopped chives
¼ tsp. dry mustard (rounded)
1 eight-ounce can water
    chestnuts, drained and
    sliced

Mix all ingredients well.

Serves 6

Edna Grace Finch

BUFFET GREEN BEANS

3 sixteen-ounce cans cut
    green beans
8 slices bacon

1 large white onion, sliced
½ cup sugar
½ cup vinegar

Drain beans and pour into a 9 x 13-inch baking dish. Place in 200° oven to warm. Fry bacon and sliced onions together until done, but not too dark. Remove onions and bacon from drippings and set aside. Mix sugar and vinegar together well, and pour into bacon drippings. Bring to a boil and pour over green beans. Place onions and bacon on top and return to oven which has been placed on warm. Prepare at least 3 hours before serving. Serve warm.

Serves 8-10

William E. George

GREEN BEAN BUNDLE

2 sixteen-ounce cans whole
   green beans
Bacon
¾ stick oleo

½ cup brown sugar
Garlic powder to taste
Salt and pepper to taste

Cut bacon slices in half. Wrap around bunch of green beans and secure with a toothpick to fasten. Make a glaze from the oleo, brown sugar, garlic powder, salt and pepper. Pour over beans. Bake covered at 375° for 45 minutes. Uncover the last few minutes.

Serves 6   Margaret Tester

DELICIOUS GREEN BEANS

1 pound frozen French style
   green beans
2 Tb. butter
2 Tb. flour
1 tsp. salt
½ tsp. sugar

¼ tsp. pepper
½ tsp. grated onion
1 cup sour cream
½ pound grated Cheddar cheese
1½ cups cornflakes
2 Tb. melted butter

Cook green beans according to the package directions and drain. In a saucepan, melt 2 tablespoons butter. Stir in dry ingredients and onion. Gradually stir in sour cream. In an 8 x 8 x 2-inch greased baking dish, place a layer of green beans followed by sauce and then cheese. Top with cornflakes. Sprinkle 2 tablespoons melted butter over top. Bake uncovered for 20-25 minutes, at 400°.

Debi Beasley

FRENCH BEAN CASSEROLE

2 sixteen-ounce cans French-cut
   green beans
5 thick slices bacon
   (7 slices if thin)
2 small onions, chopped
1 bell pepper, chopped

3 stalks celery, chopped
1 four-ounce can mushrooms,
   chopped
1 ten and ¾-ounce can
   tomato soup

Drain beans. Add salt and pepper to taste. Fry bacon slices; reserve drippings. Crumble bacon over beans. Cook onions, bell pepper and celery in bacon drippings at low heat. When softened, drain and add to beans. Add mushrooms to beans. Mix. Pour tomato soup into mixture and mix again. Put in casserole and bake uncovered at 350° for 1 hour.

Serves 12   Judy Wilson

STUFFED GREEN PEPPERS (NORTHERN ITALY)

6 bell peppers, washed, cut in
half lengthwise, with stems and
membranes removed
2 sixteen-ounce cans spinach
2 loaves French bread,
soaked in water
6-7 average-sized garlic buttons,
finely chopped

1½ cups olive oil (do not use
vegetable oil)
2 cups Parmesan cheese, grated
⅓ cup parsley flakes (fresh may
be used)
9 eggs, well beaten
salt
pepper

Boil peppers in water for 5 minutes. Remove from water and drain. With hands, squeeze as much liquid from spinach and bread as possible. In a small pan, lightly toast chopped garlic in the olive oil. Remove pan from heat. Combine the cheese and parsley with the beaten eggs. Mix well. To this mixture, add the bread, spinach, olive oil and garlic. Mix well. Add salt and pepper to taste and mix well again. Fill the pepper halves with desired amount of mixture. Place filled peppers into a 2½-quart baking dish, and add about one inch of water. Cover dish with aluminum foil. Bake at 350° for 45 minutes. Uncover and bake 15 minutes longer. Serve hot.

Serves 6   Andrea Davenport

HOMINY CASSEROLE

2 Tb. bacon fat
2 Tb. flour
1 - 2 Tb. chili powder
1 one-pound can tomatoes
2 cups water
1 tsp. salt

¼ tsp. oregano
2 two and a half-pound cans
white hominy
¼ cup margarine
1 six-ounce package Cheddar cheese
1 large onion, chopped

Combine fat, flour, chili powder, tomatoes, water, oregano and salt. Toast hominy in margarine till lightly brown in a large skillet. Layer ½ hominy, cheese, onion, and tomato-chili mixture in large baking dish. Repeat layers. Bake 25 minutes at 350° uncovered.

Serves 4-6   Ruth Wilson

211

DINNER CASSEROLE

1 pound lean ground beef
½ onion, diced
1 ten and ¾-ounce can cream of
  mushroom soup
½ cup milk

Salt and pepper
1 box Kraft Macaroni and Cheese
  Dinner
1 cup grated Cheddar cheese

Sauté meat and onion. Add milk and soup. Season with salt and pepper. Prepare Kraft dinner as directed on package. Put a layer of macaroni and cheese in 9 x 13-inch dish, a layer of meat mixture, and repeat layers. Sprinkle cheese on top and bake at 350° for 30 - 45 minutes or until bubbly.

Serves 6

Mrs. C. C. Criner

RAGLAND MACARONI

1 eight-ounce package macaroni,
  cooked
¼ cup chopped bell pepper
¼ cup chopped onion
¼ cup chopped pimiento

1 ten and ¾-ounce can cream of
  mushroom soup
1 cup mayonnaise
Grated Cheddar cheese

Heat soup and vegetables. Add mayonnaise and pour over the macaroni. Grate cheese over the top and heat at 350° for 20 minutes.

Serves 4

Betty Rodgers

MARINATED MUSHROOMS

1 pound fresh mushrooms
1 16-ounce bottle Italian dressing

1 four-ounce jar pimientos,
  chopped

Place mushrooms in large pan and cover with cold water. Boil and then simmer for 5 minutes. Drain well. Fill jars with mushrooms and cover with Italian dressing, adding chopped pimientos for color. Seal jar tightly and marinate at least 2 days in refrigerator.

Suggestions: Nice for Christmas gifts; a change from cookies!

Christy Simon

MUSHROOMS STUFFED WITH SPINACH

12 large mushrooms
3 Tb. butter
1 garlic clove
1 ten-ounce package frozen
   chopped spinach
Juice of 1 small lemon

1 tsp. salt
3 Tb. mayonnaise
3 Tb. grated Parmesan cheese
Dash of Tabasco sauce
½ tsp. Worcestershire sauce

Remove stems from mushrooms. Wash and dry. Sauté garlic clove in melted butter. Dip mushroom caps in this mixture and line a flat casserole with them. Cook spinach as directed on package. Drain thoroughly. Add remaining ingredients to spinach, mixing well. Fill mushroom caps with spinach mixture. Bake in 350° oven for 20 to 25 minutes.

Serves 6   Claudia Howe

FRIED OKRA

2 small onions
3 slices of bacon, chopped
Salt and pepper

1 quart of raw okra, chopped
Corn meal

Slice 2 small onions and sauté with bits of bacon. Lightly roll okra in corn meal and season with salt and pepper. Add okra to onion and bacon; fry until browned.

Serves 4   Vicki Lackie

FRENCH ONION SCALLOP

6 large onions, sliced
4 Tb. butter or margarine
4 Tb. flour
½ tsp. salt
¼ tsp. pepper
2 cups milk

1 tsp. Worcestershire sauce
6 slices Swiss cheese cut into pieces
   (from eight-ounce package)
6 slices buttered, slightly dry
   French bread, cubed

Cook slices of onion in boiling water. Cover 10-12 minutes, until just tender. Drain well and rinse with cold water. Arrange in buttered, shallow, six-cup baking dish. Melt butter in medium-size saucepan. Remove from heat. Blend in flour, salt and pepper. Slowly stir in milk and Worcestershire. Cook, stirring constantly, until sauce thickens. Boil one minute. Add cheese, stirring over low heat, until melted. Pour over onions; stir to mix. Arrange bread cubes around edges. Bake at 350° for 30 minutes or until bread is golden. Bake uncovered.

Serves 4   Barbara Hoffman

DELICIOUS FRIED ONION RINGS

2 large sweet Spanish onions
1¼ cups flour
1 tsp. baking powder
¼ tsp. salt
1 egg, beaten

1 cup beer
1 Tb. oil
Oil for frying
Salt

Peel onions and cut into ⅜-inch-thick slices. Separate into rings. Combine flour, baking powder, salt, egg, beer, and 1 Tb. oil. Blend until smooth. Heat oil to 375° in a heavy pan. Using a fork, dip onion rings into batter and coat well. Transfer one at a time to hot oil. Do not crowd the pan. Fry until light brown; turn and let other side brown. Drain on paper towel; repeat until all rings are fried.

To freeze, spread rings on a baking sheet and place in freezer. When rings are frozen, package them in small quantities in foil packets or vinyl freezer bags, and store. To reheat, spread rings on baking sheet and bake at 400° for 5 to 7 minutes. While hot, sprinkle with salt.

Yield: 5 dozen rings

Betty Croom

GLAZED CLOVE ONIONS

16 small white onions or
  2 seven and ½-ounce jars
  small onions

Whole cloves
¼ cup maple blended syrup
1 Tb. butter

If using fresh onions, boil 15 minutes or until tender. Place a clove in each onion and place in shallow baking dish. Pour syrup over onion; dot with butter. Bake uncovered at 350° for 30 minutes. Baste 3 times while baking.

Serves 4

Rose Thrash

BLACK-EYED PEAS

2 pounds fresh black-eyed
  peas, shelled
1 small onion, minced
1 clove garlic, minced

½ pound salt pork
½ tsp. chili powder
One yellow onion, chopped

Place salt pork and other ingredients in saucepan and bring to a boil. Reduce heat and simmer until peas are tender. Serve with finely chopped sweet onion.

Pam Gustavus

SCALLOPED GREEN PEAS AND ONIONS

¼ cup margarine
¼ cup flour
2 cups milk
½ tsp. salt
Dash pepper

3 cups quartered small onions
1 ten-ounce package frozen peas, partially thawed
1 cup shredded natural Swiss cheese

Melt margarine in a small saucepan. Add flour and stir until it makes a paste. Slowly add the milk, stirring constantly until the mixture boils. Add salt and pepper. Combine onions and peas. Place in greased 10 x 6-inch baking dish. Pour sauce over vegetables; top with cheese. Bake at 375° for 45 minutes.

Serves 6   Terri Caple

POTATO CASSEROLE

2 pounds frozen hash browns
½ cup melted butter
1 tsp. salt
¼ tsp. pepper
1 tsp. oregano
½ cup chopped onion

½ cup chopped celery
½ cup chopped green pepper
1 ten and ¾-ounce can cream of celery soup
1 pint sour cream with chives
2 cups grated Cheddar cheese

Defrost potatoes. Combine salt, pepper, oregano, soup and sour cream. Mix potatoes with onions, celery, green pepper and cheese. Place in a 3-quart casserole.

TOPPING:

2 cups Rice Chex or corn flakes   ¼ cup melted butter

Top with cereal and drizzle with melted butter. Bake 45 minutes at 350°. Can be made ahead and frozen.

Serves 16   Sherry Wright

POTATO STRIPS

6 medium baking potatoes   1 envelope onion soup mix
½ cup butter

Scrub potatoes and slice lengthwise in three or four slices. Spread with mixture of butter and soup mix and reassemble. Wrap with foil and bake 45 - 60 minutes at 400°.

Serves 6   Becky Witcher

215

OVEN POTATOES

6 medium potatoes
¼ cup butter, melted
½ tsp. salt

1 cup grated Swiss cheese
3 Tb. grated Parmesan cheese
⅛ tsp. pepper

Butter a square or rectangular glass baking dish. Peel potatoes and cut crosswise in thin slices. Arrange overlapping slices in rows in baking dish. Pour butter over potatoes and sprinkle with salt and pepper. Bake uncovered in 500° oven until potatoes are tender (about 20-30 minutes). Remove from oven and sprinkle with cheeses. Return to 500° oven until cheese is melted (about 5 minutes).

These can also be cooked on High in microwave for 10 - 15 minutes.

Serves 6

RICE CASSEROLE

1 Box Uncle Ben's Long Grain
   and Wild Rice
1 eight-ounce can water chestnuts

1 four-ounce can sliced mushrooms
5 slices bacon, cooked and drained
½ cup chicken stock (optional)

Cook box of rice according to directions. Before serving, add drained water chestnuts, sliced mushrooms and crumbled bacon. If you have any chicken stock on hand, about ½ cup added to rice makes it still better.

Serves 8-10   Frances Cox

GRANDMOTHER'S RICE DRESSING

1 cup uncooked rice
   (not instant rice)
2 tsp. butter or margarine
½ cup chopped onion
½ cup chopped celery
1 tsp. parsley
Clove garlic or ¼ teaspoon
   minced garlic or garlic powder

1 pound raw sausage or ½ pound
   hamburger and ½ pound sausage
2 eggs, well-beaten
½ tsp. sage
½ tsp. thyme
Salt and pepper to taste
2 tsp. cornstarch

Cook rice following cooking directions on package and add 1 teaspoon butter to it before water boils. Sauté the onion, celery, parsley and garlic in 1 teaspoon butter until onion is tender. Combine with cooked rice. Add meat/meats and mix well. Add eggs, sage, thyme, salt, pepper, and cornstarch. Mix well. Stuff 10- or 12-pound fowl and cook as directed for fowl or bake in loaf at 350° for 45-60 minutes.

Serves 10-12   Margaret Wilkins

MONTEREY JACK CHEESE AND RICE

3 cups cooked white rice
¾ - 1 pound grated Monterey
   Jack cheese
1 pint sour cream

1 four-ounce can regular green
   chili peppers, chopped
Parmesan cheese

Grease a 7 x 11-inch baking dish. Layer the rice, Monterey Jack cheese, and sour cream with chili peppers. Repeat, being sure to end with sour cream. Layers will be very thin. Sprinkle top with Parmesan cheese. Bake uncovered 20 - 25 minutes in a 350° oven. **Do not overbake** as the dish will become too dry.

Serves 8-10

Janice Davies

ORIENTAL FRIED RICE

5 - 6 slices bacon, chopped
1 onion, chopped
2 - 4 cups cooked rice
1 - 2 eggs
1 ten-ounce package frozen peas
   and carrots

1 two and ½ ounce jar
   mushrooms
Soy sauce to taste
1 jalapeno pepper, chopped

In electric skillet, fry chopped bacon and onions. Pour cooked rice into skillet; let fry 3 minutes. Stir. Add eggs to rice mixture. Stir. Add remaining ingredients, stirring occasionally until peas and carrots are done (about 5 minutes).

Serve as a vegetable or as a luncheon dish with salad.

Serves 8 - 10

Marcella Nofziger

WINNING RICE

¼ cup diced green pepper
⅓ cup chopped onion
2 Tb. bacon grease
1 cup uncooked rice
1 ten and ¾-ounce can consommé

1 ten and ¾-ounce can water
1 Tb. Worcestershire sauce
¾ tsp. salt
¾ tsp. cumin seed

Sauté onions, pepper, and rice in bacon grease until golden brown. Add consommé, water, Worcestershire sauce, salt, and cumin seed. Cover with a tight-fitting lid and bring to a boil. Turn burner low and cook 20 minutes. Can be made ahead and reheated.

Serves 6

Betty Croom

217

SPINACH AND ARTICHOKE CASSEROLE

3 ten-ounce packages frozen leaf
  spinach, thawed and drained well
1 ten-ounce package frozen
  artichokes, thawed and drained
1 ten and ¾-ounce can cream of
  celery soup

3 Tb. sour cream
½ onion, minced
1 heaping Tb. of "Rotel Dip" or
  1 inch of Jalapeño cheese tube
Dash garlic powder
Parmesan cheese

Cook and drain spinach. Add all other ingredients and place in well-buttered 13 x 9-inch baking dish. Sprinkle top with Parmesan cheese. Bake uncovered in 350° oven 30 - 35 minutes or until heated thoroughly.

Serves 8-10

Suzanne Godwin

SPINACH SQUARES

1 ten-ounce box frozen spinach
2 eggs
1 cup sour cream
½ cup Parmesan cheese or
  grated Mozarella cheese

1 Tb. flour
1 Tb. butter
1 tsp. salt
⅛ tsp. pepper

Cook spinach according to directions on package. Drain well. Add eggs, sour cream, cheese, flour, butter, salt, and pepper. Blend well. Bake in covered casserole dish at 350° for 30 minutes. Cut in squares to serve.

Serves 8

Suzanne Godwin

SPINACH SUPREME

2 packages frozen chopped
  spinach
4 green onions, chopped
1 small yellow onion, chopped
4 slices bacon, fried crisp
  (reserve drippings)

⅓ cup seasoned bread crumbs
1 three-ounce can mushrooms,
  pieces and stems
Salt and pepper to taste

Cook spinach according to the directions on the package. Drain well. In a sauce pan, sauté the onions in the bacon drippings until soft. Combine all the ingredients and mix well. Place in a casserole and bake at 350° for 20 minutes.

Serves 6-8

Judi Dietz

ACORN SQUASH A' LA FRUIT

2 medium acorn squash
Salt
2 cups chopped, unpeeled
  cooking apples
¾ cup fresh cranberries

½ cup broken pecans
¼ cup brown sugar
½ tsp. ground cinnamon
2 Tb. melted butter or margarine

Cut squash in half; remove seeds. Place cut side down in shallow baking dish. Add water, 1 inch deep. Bake 30 minutes at 350°. Turn cut side up and sprinkle with salt. Combine remaining ingredients. Spoon into squash halves. Bake at 350° for 30 - 40 minutes.

Serves 4   Vicki Lackie

BATTER FRIED SQUASH

4 - 6 small summer squash
⅓ cup buttermilk
½ - ¾ cup flour
  (Self-rising is best.)

¼ cup cornmeal
1 tsp. salt

Slice squash in ¼-inch slices. Cover with ice water for 30 minutes. Drain. Pour buttermilk over squash; toss to coat. Combine cornmeal, flour and salt in large paper sack. Toss squash, a few at a time, in cornmeal mixture. Deep fry in hot oil. Drain and serve immediately.

Serves 4   Marge Whitmore

SQUASH CASSEROLE

1½ pounds squash, sliced
1 ten and ¾-ounce can cream of
  chicken soup
1 eight-ounce sour cream
1 four-ounce jar pimientos

1 8 oz. can sliced water chestnuts
1 medium onion, finely chopped
1 stick butter
½ package herb stuffing mix
  (Pepperidge Farm four-ounce package)

Cook sliced squash 12 - 15 minutes until tender. Drain well. Add next 5 ingredients. Melt ¾ stick butter; add stuffing and mix well. Press stuffing mixture into bottom of 2 quart casserole dish. Reserve some stuffing for top of casserole. Pour squash mixture over stuffing. Sprinkle remaining stuffing on top. Dot with remaining butter. Bake at 350° for 30 minutes.

Serves 8 - 10   Charlotte Lloyd

SQUASH AND CORN CASSEROLE

⅔ stick margarine
1½ cups bread crumbs
   from toast
1 medium onion, chopped
½ green bell pepper, chopped
Chopped pimiento
2 cups cooked and mashed squash
   (about 8 medium)

1 cup cooked corn
3 eggs, beaten
2 Tb. sugar
1 tsp. salt
1 tsp. pepper
1 cup canned milk
1 cup grated cheese

Put margarine in a 9 x 13-inch baking dish and place in a 350° oven to melt. Add ½ cup bread crumbs; stir well. Save 1 cup crumbs to sprinkle over top of casserole. Sauté onion, bell pepper and pimiento in a large skillet. Mix the sauteed vegetables, ½ cup bread crumbs, squash, corn, eggs, sugar, salt, pepper and milk. Place in baking dish. Sprinkle top with 1 cup reserved bread crumbs. Bake at 350° for 1 hour. Remove. Sprinkle 1 cup grated cheese over top. Return to oven for about 5 minutes or until cheese melts.

Serves 12   Paulette Mercer

ZUCCHINI CASSEROLE

4 medium zucchini
1 medium onion
2 fresh tomatoes, peeled or
   1 twelve-ounce can of tomatoes,
2 - 3 Tb. olive oil
1 tsp. salt

½ tsp. pepper
½ tsp. basil
½ tsp. oregano
1 bay leaf
1 pound Mozzarella cheese
½ cup grated Parmesan cheese

Slice onion, zucchini, and tomato. Simmer in olive oil with seasonings for thirty minutes. Alternate layers of zucchini and mozzarella cheese in casserole. Sprinkle with Parmesan. Heat in 350° oven long enough to melt cheese.

Serves 8   Janice Davies

SWEET POTATO CASSEROLE I

6 medium sweet potatoes
6 Tb. butter
3 slightly beaten eggs
½ cup sugar
½ cup chopped pecans
½ cup flaked coconut

½ cup orange juice
½ tsp. salt
½ tsp. vanilla
10 orange slices
10 marshmallows

Cook potatoes until tender. Beat with mixer. Melt butter and add to potatoes. Add next 7 ingredients. Pour into buttered 8 x 10-inch casserole. Arrange orange slices on top. Bake uncovered 30 minutes at 350°. Remove from oven and place marshmallows on top. Return to oven until marshmallows melt.

Serves 8 - 10   Mrs. Bernard Moore

SWEET POTATO CASSEROLE II

2 cups mashed sweet potatoes
1¼ cups sugar
2 eggs
1 cup milk

½ tsp. cinnamon
¾ stick butter
½ tsp. nutmeg

TOPPING:

½ cup cup brown sugar
½ cup nuts

¾ cup crushed corn flakes
¾ stick butter

Bake sweet potatoes or steam on top of stove in a little water 10 minutes and drain. Mash potatoes and add remaining ingredients. Mix well. Pour into casserole and bake in 400° oven for 20 minutes.

Topping: Melt butter and combine with corn flakes, nuts, and brown sugar. Spread evenly over sweet potatoes and return to oven for 10 minutes.

Serves 8 - 10   Margaret Tester

SHERRIED SWEET POTATO CASSEROLE

8 medium sweet potatoes	2 cups orange juice
1 cup brown sugar	½ cup raisins
2 Tb. cornstarch	6 Tb. butter
½ tsp. salt	⅓ cup dry sherry
½ tsp. shredded orange peel	¼ cup chopped nuts

Cook potatoes in boiling salted water until just tender. Drain. Peel and cut lengthwise into ½-inch thick slices. Arrange in baking dish and sprinkle with salt. In saucepan combine brown sugar, cornstarch, and ½ tsp. salt. Blend in orange juice and orange peel; add raisins. Cook and stir over medium heat until thickened and bubbly. Cook one minute more. Add butter, sherry, and nuts. Stir until butter melts. Pour over potatoes. Bake uncovered at 325° for approximately 30 minutes, basting occasionally.

Garnish with parsley or mint sprigs.

Serves 8

Brenda Cerrato

TEMPURA VEGETABLES

1 cup flour	2 green peppers
2 eggs	½ pound mushrooms
¼ cup soy sauce	1 onion
½ cup water	½ pound broccoli
Vegetable oil for frying	1 sweet potato

Beat the eggs with the soy sauce and water and mix in the flour. Set aside for 20 minutes. Prepare the vegetables by cutting the green peppers into ½-inch-wide strips, onion into ½-inch slices , and sweet potato into ½-inch slices. Break the broccoli into small florets, and leave the mushrooms whole. Pour 4 inches of oil into a pan and heat. Dip the vegetables in the batter, drop in the hot oil, and fry until golden brown. Drain and serve with soy sauce passed separately.

Variations: Be imaginative. Try zucchini, cauliflower, carrots, or other vegetables.

Serves 4- 6

Vicki Lackie

SLICED GREEN TOMATO PIE

1¼ cup sugar
½ tsp. cinnamon
½ tsp. nutmeg
¼ tsp. salt
4 - 5 Tb. flour

2 Tb. lemon juice
4 cups peeled, thinly-sliced
    green tomatoes
Pastry for 2-crust pie

Blend together sugar, cinnamon, nutmeg, salt, flour, and lemon juice. Toss with green tomatoes. Place in pastry-lined 9-inch pie pan. Adjust top crust and flute edges. Cut vents. Bake at 425° 50-60 minutes or until tomatoes are soft and crust is brown.

Serves 6 - 8

Arlene Laman

TOMATOES ROCKEFELLER

12 thick slices tomato
2 ten-ounce packages frozen
    chopped spinach
½ cup soft bread crumbs
½ cup seasoned bread crumbs
1½ cups finely chopped
    green onions

6 eggs, slightly beaten
¾ cup melted butter or margarine
½ cup grated Parmesan cheese
½ tsp. minced garlic
1 tsp. salt
1 tsp. thyme
Hot sauce to taste

Arrange tomato slices in a lightly greased 13 x 9 x 2-inch baking dish. Cook spinach according to package directions; drain well and squeeze to remove excess water. Add remaining ingredients to spinach, stirring well. Mound mixture on tomato slices. Bake uncovered at 350° about 30 minutes or until spinach mixture sets. May be prepared ahead of time and refrigerated.

Serves 12

Frances Lance

VEGETABLE PLENTY

1 ten-ounce package frozen
chopped broccoli, thawed and
drained
2 cups shredded
Deluxe Choice American or
Old English process cheese

1 eight and ½-ounce can cream style
corn
½ cup cracker crumbs
⅓ cup chopped onion
2 medium tomatoes, cut
into wedges

Combine all ingredients except ½ cup process cheese and tomatoes; mix lightly. Layer half of vegetable mixture and tomatoes in a 1½ quart casserole. Cover with remaining vegetable mixture. Bake at 350° for 30 minutes. Top with remaining tomatoes and continue baking 15 minutes. Top with reserved process cheese.

Serves 6   Terri Caple

BAKED APPLES

6 large apples, cored
6 heaping Tb. brown sugar
1½ tsp. ground cinnamon

1½ tsp. ground nutmeg
6 pats butter

Place apples in 2 quart casserole; pour a heaping Tb. of brown sugar inside each apple. Sprinkle ¼ tsp. cinnamon and nutmeg on each apple. Place a pat of butter on top of each apple. Bake uncovered at 400° for 1 hour, basting occasionally with juice.

Serves 6

Cathy Simpson

APPLE CRISP

4 or 5 tart apples,
    peeled and sliced
½ cup butter

1 cup brown sugar
1 cup flour
Nutmeg or cinnamon

Fill a buttered glass pie plate (9-inch) with apples. Cream together butter, sugar and flour. Chill a few minutes. Take portions of the mixture and pat between hands until flat. Place over apples and continue until completely covered. Sprinkle top with cinnamon or nutmeg. Cook in 425° oven for 10 minutes. Reduce oven to 350° and bake for 20 minutes longer. Serve warm with vanilla ice cream.

Serves 6

Dottie Hankins

CHARLIE'S CHERRIES

2 Tb. butter
4 Tb. brown sugar
1 jigger vodka

1 sixteen and ½-ounce can dark
    pitted cherries, drained
1 jigger brandy

Melt butter in 9-inch skillet. Add 4 Tb. brown sugar, 1 jigger vodka and drained cherries. Continue to heat. Add 1 jigger brandy. Simmer for 3 minutes. Serve over vanilla ice cream.

Variations: You may use frozen strawberries or fruit cocktail instead of cherries. For a flaming dessert add more brandy and ignite.

Serves 6 - 8

Charlie Burks

BUTTER BAKED PEACHES

¼ cup butter
2 Tb. orange juice
1 one-pound, fourteen-ounce can
  cling peach halves

½ cup crushed sugar-coated
  corn flakes
½ cup whipping cream
1 Tb. sugar

In a shallow 1½-qt. baking dish melt butter in heated oven. Stir in orange juice. Roll peach halves in crumbs; place in baking dish. Bake in preheated 400° oven for 15 minutes. In a small mixing bowl, whip cream until almost stiff; add sugar. Whip until stiff. Serve peaches with dollops of whipped cream on top, spooning remaining butter mixture from bottom of baking dish over top of peaches.

Variations: Pour unwhipped cream over peaches or top with scoops of ice cream.

Serves 6 - 8   Margaret Kennedy

PEACH COBBLER SUPREME

¼ cup butter
1 cup all purpose flour
1 cup sugar
⅛ tsp. salt
1 Tb. baking powder

⅔ cup milk
1 twenty nine-ounce can
  sliced peaches
¼ tsp. nutmeg
¼ tsp. cinnamon

Melt butter in a 11 x 7-inch shallow baking dish. Mix dry ingredients and add milk. Stir well. Pour mixture into baking dish. Do not stir. Top with peaches, including juice. Sprinkle nutmeg and cinnamon over peaches, but do not stir. Bake 350° oven for 40 minutes or until golden brown.

Serves 6 - 8   Ann Cornwell

Sprinkle wax paper with powdered sugar before wrapping a frosted cake. Frosting will stick to the cake, not the paper.

FRUIT PIZZA

1 eighteen-ounce package Pillsbury
   refrigerator sugar cookie mix
1 eight-ounce package cream cheese,
   softened
⅓ cup sugar

½ tsp. vanilla
Any of your favorite fruits:
   Fresh strawberries, bananas,
   peaches, canned apricots and
   pineapple chunks, drained well

Cut cookie dough into ⅛ inch slices. Line ungreased 14 inch pizza pan with overlapping slices. Bake at 375° for 12 minutes. Cool. Combine softened cream cheese, sugar and vanilla. Spread this mixture over cookie crust. Arrange fruit on top of cream cheese mixture.

GLAZE:

½ cup apricot, peach, or
   orange marmalade

2 Tb. water

Glaze with marmalade and water mixture.

Atheta Ball

FLORENDINES

Pastry for 1 single-crust pie
¼ cup softened butter
½ cup sugar
2 eggs, beaten

¼ tsp. salt
½ cup stewed apricots, sweetened
½ cup stewed, pitted prunes,
   unsweetened

Roll out pastry as for pie crust. Cut into circles and fit into muffin tins. Cream butter and sugar. Blend in beaten eggs and salt. Fold in fruit, mixing well. There should be about 2 Tb. of juice in the total amount of fruit. Fill each pie crust cup about ⅔ full. Bake in 400° oven for about 25 minutes. If desired, top each with a spoonfull of whipped cream before serving.

Mrs. W. H. Snead
Maude, Texas

BAKLAVA

SYRUP:

¾ cup sugar
¾ cup water
1½ cups honey

2 inch cinnamon stick
4 lemon slices

In medium saucepan, combine sugar and ¾ cup water. Bring to boiling, stirring to dissolve sugar. Add honey, cinnamon stick and lemon slices. Reduce heat. Simmer, uncovered, for 10 minutes. Strain. Cool. Set aside. Should measure 2½ cups.

1 one-pound package prepared phyllo
3 cups finely chopped or ground
  pecans
¾ cup sugar

½ tsp. ground cinnamon
¼ tsp. ground nutmeg
1½ cups sweet butter, melted

Preheat oven to 325°. Remove pastry leaves from package. In small bowl, mix pecans, sugar, cinnamon and nutmeg. Place two pastry leaves in a 15½ x 10½ x 1 inch pan. Brush top leaf with some of the melted butter. Continue stacking leaves, 14 in all, buttering every other leaf. (Keep remainder covered with damp towels to prevent drying.) Sprinkle with ⅓ of nut mixture. Add six more leaves, brushing every other one with butter. Sprinkle with ⅓ of nut mixture. Layer six more leaves, brushing every other one with butter. Sprinkle with the last ⅓ of nut mixture. Stack any remaining pastry leaves on top, brushing every other one with remaining melted butter and buttering top pastry leaf. Trim edges, if necessary. With sharp knife, cut through top layer on long side. Make eight diagonal cuts at 1½ inch intervals. Then starting at one corner, make nine cuts, on diagonal at 1½ inch intervals to form diamonds. Cut through top layer only. Do not cut through layers. Bake 60 minutes. Remove and pour cooled syrup over baklava. Following diamond pattern, cut all the way through baklava. Cool in pan to absorb syrup.

Yield: 35 pieces

Micki Thurow

To keep cake fresh, put a cut apple in the container.

GRAHAM CRACKER SANDWICHES

1 one-pound box graham crackers	½ cup milk
1 cup sugar	1 cup coconut
1 egg	1 cup chopped pecans
2 sticks margarine	1 cup graham cracker crumbs

Lay out graham crackers to completely cover a 17 x 11 x 1-inch cookie sheet. Cream sugar and egg. Blend in margarine and milk. Bring to a boil and remove from heat. Add coconut, pecans and graham cracker crumbs. Mix well and spread over graham crackers. After spreading, place graham crackers over top to form sandwich.

ICING:

¾ stick margarine, melted	4 Tb. milk
2 cups confectioner's sugar	1 tsp. vanilla

Cream all ingredients. Spread over cookies and refrigerate. When cool, cut into squares or strips.

Yield: 5 dozen   Judy Wilson

PECAN TASSIES

CRUST:

¼ pound butter	1 cup flour
1 three-ounce package cream cheese, softened	½ cup pecans, chopped

Combine first three ingredients and mix well. Divide into walnut size balls (about 36). Press each ball into bottom and sides of very small muffin tins. Sprinkle nuts on crust.

FILLING:

2 eggs	½ tsp. vanilla
2 Tb. melted butter	Pinch of salt
1½ cup brown sugar	½ cup pecans, chopped

Beat eggs lightly and add butter, sugar, vanilla and a pinch of salt. Mix well. Fill each cup and sprinkle with nuts. Bake at 325° for 15 minutes. Reduce heat to 225° and bake 10 minutes longer.

Yield: 36   Colleen Wallace

TOFFEE DESSERT

CRUST:

1½ cups crushed vanilla wafers (reserve some for topping)

Sprinkle crushed vanilla wafers on bottom of 9 x 13-inch pan.

FILLING:

1 cup butter (not margarine)	**2 eggs**
2 cups powdered sugar	**1 cup pecans**
2 Tb. cocoa	**1 Tb. butter**
½ tsp. salt	**2 tsp. vanilla**

Cream butter, sugar, cocoa and salt. Beat eggs until light. Add to mixture. Toast pecans in butter in preheated 350° oven for 10 minutes. Cool and add to mixture, along with vanilla. Stir well. Pour over crust. Chill for several hours.

TOPPING:

½ pint whipping cream	**1 tsp. vanilla**
2 tsp. powdered sugar	

Whip cream with powdered sugar. Add vanilla. Put on top of filling and sprinkle remaining crushed wafers lightly over cream. Refrigerate until ready to serve. Cut into squares.

Serves 10   Florine Tyler

BRANDY ALEXANDER SOUFFLÉ

2 envelopes gelatin	**8 ounces cream cheese, softened**
2 cups cold water	**3 Tb. Creme de Cocoa**
1 cup sugar	**3 Tb. brandy**
Dash of salt	**1 cup cream, whipped**
4 eggs, separated	**½ cup slivered almonds, toasted**

Soften gelatin in 1 cup water. Stir over low heat until dissolved. Add remaining water and remove from heat. Blend in ¾ cup sugar, salt and the beaten egg yolks. Return to heat and cook 2 to 3 minutes or until slightly thickened. Gradually add mixture to softened cream cheese and blend well. Stir in Creme de Cocoa and brandy. Chill until slightly thickened. Beat egg whites to peaks; add remaining sugar (¼ cup), and beat until stiff. Fold egg whites and whipped cream into cream cheese mixture. Wrap a two inch wide collar of oiled foil around a 1½ quart souffle dish. Pour mixture into dish, and chill until firm. Top with almonds. Remove foil and serve with after dinner coffee. This can be made a day ahead.

Gerrie Fletcher

232

DOUBLE LEMON FRUIT CUP

1 six-ounce package lemon gelatin	1½ cups miniature marshmallows
2 cups boiling water	1 cup banana slices
1 six-ounce can frozen lemonade, thawed	1 cup strawberry slices
	¼ cup chopped pecans
1⅓ cups mandarin oranges, drained	1 cup Cool Whip

Dissolve gelatin in boiling water. Add lemonade and mix. Pour into six parfait or sherbet glasses and fill half-full. Chill until firm. Combine next 5 ingredients. Fold in the Cool Whip. Pat fruit mixture on top of firmed gelatin mixture. Chill until serving time.

A nice light dessert.

Serves 6   Vicki Lackie

PRETZEL JELL-O

CRUST:

3 Tb. sugar	2⅔ cup coarsely crushed
¾ cup margarine	large pretzels

Cream sugar and margarine. Add crushed pretzels. Press into a 9 x 13-inch pan. Bake 10 minutes at 350°. Cool.

FILLING:

1 eight-ounce package cream cheese, softened	1 scant cup sugar
	1 eight-ounce carton Cool Whip

Cream cheese and sugar. Add Cool Whip. Mix thoroughly. Spread over cooled pretzel crust.

TOPPING:

1 six-ounce package strawberry Jell-o	1 sixteen-ounce package frozen
2 cups boiling water	strawberries, thawed

Dissolve Jell-o in boiling water. Add frozen berries to Jell-o. Allow to partially set. Pour over cream cheese mixture. Refrigerate until firm.

Serves: 10 - 12   Linda King

ANGEL COCONUT PUDDING

1 Angel food cake mix
2 6-ounce packages instant
  vanilla pudding
5 cups milk
3 or 4 Tb. Sherry
1 seven-ounce can Angel
  Flake coconut

1 nine-ounce container Cool Whip
1 seven-ounce bottle maraschino
  cherries, sliced
1 cup chopped pecans
  (optional)

Bake cake by mix instructions and cool. Crumble cake into bite size pieces and place in a glass bowl. Prepare pudding using milk and sherry. Pour over cake and tumble a bit. Sprinkle with coconut. Spread with Cool Whip and top with sliced cherries. Refrigerate several hours.

Pretty in cut-glass for serving.

Serves 12-15   Margaret McIlwain

LAYERED CHOCOLATE DESSERT

FIRST LAYER:

1 stick butter, melted
1 cup flour

Dash salt
1 cup chopped nuts

Mix all ingredients. Press thinly into a 9 x 13-inch pan. Bake for 20 minutes at 350° until lightly browned. Cool completely.

SECOND LAYER:

1 eight-ounce package cream cheese
1 cup powdered sugar

1 cup Cool Whip from a
  9-ounce carton

Cream ingredients in second layer together and spread on top of first layer.

THIRD LAYER:

2 three and ¾-ounce boxes of
  instant chocolate pudding

3½ cups milk

Mix chocolate pudding with milk. Beat for 3 minutes and pour over second layer.

FOURTH LAYER:

Remaining Cool Whip

Spread Cool Whip over top. Refrigerate at least 5 hours.

LEMON CAKE TOP PUDDING

2 eggs, separated
1 Tb. oleo, melted
3 Tb. lemon juice
2 tsp. grated lemon rind

¼ tsp. salt
3 Tb. flour
1 cup sugar
1 cup milk

Pre-heat oven to 375°. Grease 6 custard cups. Beat egg whites until stiff, but not dry. In mixing bowl, blend oleo, egg yolks and lemon juice. Stir in lemon rind, salt, flour and sugar. Beat until smooth. Stir in milk. Fold egg whites into mixture and pour into greased custard cups. Set in shallow pan in 1-inch of hot water. Bake 30-35 minutes at 375°.

Betty Croom

CHOCOLATE TORTILLA TORTE

1 six-ounce package semi-sweet
  chocolate bits
2 cups sour cream
3 Tb. powdered sugar

4 flour tortillas
1 two-ounce milk chocolate
  candy bar

Melt together in double boiler the chocolate bits, 1 cup of sour cream, and 1 Tb. powdered sugar. Stir until well blended. Place 1 tortilla on a plate. Spread ⅓ of chocolate mixture out to edges of tortilla. Place another tortilla on top. Repeat. Top with fourth tortilla. Blend 1 cup sour cream with 2 Tb. powdered sugar. Spread over stack of tortillas until completely covered. Chill. Scrape chocolate bar with vegetable peeler into curls, or thin bits, and sprinkle over top of torte. To serve, cut torte into narrow wedges.

Very rich!

Serves 8 - 10

Shirley Hale

When baking a cake, use the butter wrapper to grease the pan.

MOCHA BROWNIE TORTE

1 package fudge brownie mix
¼ cup water
2 eggs
½ cup chopped pecans

1½ cups chilled whipping cream
⅓ cup brown sugar, packed
1 Tb. instant coffee powder
Shaved chocolate

Heat oven to 350°. Grease and flour 3 eight-inch cake pans. Blend brownie mix, water, and eggs. Stir in nuts. Spread in pans. Bake 20 minutes. Remove from pans and cool completely. In chilled bowl, beat cream until it begins to thicken. Gradually add sugar and coffee powder. Continue beating until stiff. Fill layers with cream mixture, saving enough to frost sides and top. Sprinkle with shaved chocolate. Chill at least one hour.

Variation: Brittle Torte — omit brown sugar, instant coffee and shaved chocolate. Fold ¾ cup finely crushed peanut brittle into whipping cream. Sprinkle torte with chopped peanuts.

Deborah Blodgett Deacon

PUMPKIN DATE TORTE

½ cup chopped dates
½ cup chopped black walnuts
2 Tb. flour
¼ cup butter
1 cup brown sugar
⅔ cup cooked pumpkin
1 tsp. vanilla

2 eggs
½ cup sifted or pre-sifted flour
½ tsp. baking powder
½ tsp. cinnamon
½ tsp. nutmeg
¼ tsp. ginger
¼ tsp. baking soda

Mix dates, nuts and flour. Set aside. Melt butter over low heat. Blend in brown sugar. Remove from heat. Stir in pumpkin and vanilla. Beat in eggs, one at a time. Sift together dry ingredients. Add to pumpkin mixture, mixing thoroughly. Stir in floured dates and nuts. Turn into greased 9 x 11 x 2″ round baking pan. Bake in 350° oven 20 to 25 minutes. Serve warm with topping.

TOPPING:

Whipped cream
½ tsp. nutmeg

1 tsp. whiskey

Mix whipped cream with ½ tsp. nutmeg and 1 tsp. bourbon whiskey.

Evelyn Graham

STRAWBERRY FRENCH TORTE

CRUST:

2 cups flour
1 cup nuts, chopped

½ cup light brown sugar
2 sticks oleo

Mix pie crust and pat into 9 x 13-inch or larger pan. Bake 15 minutes at 400°. **Do not overbake.** Cool.

FILLING:

1 eight-ounce package cream cheese
1 tsp. vanilla
1 cup Confectioner's sugar

1 eight-ounce carton Cool Whip
Strawberry glaze (below) or
  1 can fruit pie filling

Mix cheese, vanilla, and sugar with mixer. Add Cool Whip and spread onto cooled crust. Chill 12 hours. Before serving, spread top with 1 can blueberry or other fruit pie filling or the strawberry glaze listed below.

STRAWBERRY GLAZE:

1 ten-ounce package frozen
  strawberries

2 Tb. sugar
2 Tb. cornstarch

Thaw and drain frozen strawberries. Add sugar and cornstarch. Bring to boil. When mixture turns red, add strawberries. Cool. Spread on torte before serving.

Serves 12

Agnes Dean

To prevent breaking and crumbling when removing a cake from a tube pan, cut an X in the center of a paper plate. Slide it over the tube down to the cake. Turn the cake over and onto the cake plate.

STRAWBERRY TORTE

1 cup sifted flour	1 tsp. vanilla
1 tsp. baking powder	3 Tb. milk
¼ tsp. salt	¼ tsp. almond extract
½ cup butter	¾ cup sugar
½ cup sugar	½ cup toasted, slivered almonds
5 eggs, separated	

Butter and lightly flour bottoms of 2 nine-inch layer cake pans. Sift flour, baking powder and salt onto waxed paper. Cream butter with ½ cup sugar in medium sized bowl until fluffy. Beat in egg yolks, one at a time, until blended. Next beat in vanilla and milk. Fold in flour mixture until blended. Spread evenly in pans. Beat egg whites with ¼ tsp. of almond extract in a large bowl until foamy and doubled in volume. Sprinkle in ¾ cup of sugar, beating constantly until sugar dissolves completely and meringue stands in firm peaks. Spread evenly over batter in pans. Sprinkle with almonds. Bake in oven at 350° for 30 minutes or until meringue is delicately browned. Cool layers in pans for 5 minutes. Loosen around edges with a knife. Turn each out onto palm of hand and place, meringue side up on wire rack. Cool completely.

TOPPING:

2 pints strawberries	¼ cup sugar
2 cups cream for whipping	½ tsp. almond extract

Quarter strawberries. Beat cream with sugar and almond extract until stiff. Place one cake layer on a large serving plate. Top with half of the whipped cream and then strawberries. Repeat with second cake layer and remaining whipped cream and strawberries.

Serves 8 — Patti Brady

FROZEN PEPPERMINT PIE

½ cup butter or margarine	3 cups rice crispies
1 6-ounce package chocolate chips	½ gallon peppermint ice cream

Melt butter and chocolate chips. Stir in rice crispies and press mixture into two 9-inch buttered pie plates or one oblong cake pan. Chill. Fill crusts with softened ice cream. Freeze.

Note: If peppermint ice cream is unavailable, a half gallon softened vanilla ice cream mixed with ½ cup crushed peppermint candy may be substituted.

Serves 12 — Donna Bosley

CARAMEL ICE CREAM DESSERT

2 cups flour
½ cup oatmeal
½ cup brown sugar
2 sticks melted butter
1 cup chopped nuts

2 twelve-ounce jars caramel
ice cream topping
½ gallon vanilla ice cream,
softened

Mix flour, oatmeal and brown sugar together. Add butter and nuts. Mix well. Spread on a cookie sheet like a big cookie and bake at 400° for 15 minutes. Crumble while hot. Cool. Sprinkle half of crumbs on bottom of large 9 x 13 x 3-inch pan. Drizzle one jar caramel topping over crumbs. Then spread ice-cream on top. Sprinkle the other half of crumbs over ice cream and drizzle the other jar of caramel topping over that. Cut in squares and serve.

This keeps in freezer indefinitely if the family doesn't know it's there!

Eva Hunt
Eloise Evans

OREO FROZEN DESSERT

24 oreo cookies, crushed
½ cup margarine, melted

½ gallon vanilla ice cream

Mix oreo cookies and margarine. Pat into the bottom of a 9 x 13-inch pan. Soften ice cream. Pat on top of cookie crust. Freeze.

SAUCE:

1 bar German chocolate
½ cup oleo
⅛ tsp. salt
⅔ cup sugar
⅔ cup evaporated milk
(5.33 ounce can)

1 tsp. vannilla
1 eight-ounce carton Cool Whip
Chopped nuts, optional

Melt chocolate with oleo, salt, sugar and evaporated milk. Cook until thick, approximately 4 minutes. Add vanilla. Let cool. Spread this on the ice cream. Top with Cool Whip and chopped nuts.

Serves 15 - 20

Carolyn Cobb

239

BUTTER NUT ICE CREAM

4 eggs
2½ cups sugar
2 Tb. vanilla
½ tsp. salt

1 cup crunchy peanut butter
3 to 4 large Butterfinger
candy bars, crushed
6 cups milk

Cream eggs, sugar, vanilla, salt and peanut butter. Add crushed candy bars. Add milk and pour into freezer and freeze.

Pam Holt

MILKY WAY ICE CREAM

12 one and ¾-ounce Milky
Way Bars, cut up
1 14-ounce can Eagle Brand Milk

3 quarts milk
1 cup Hershey's Chocolate Syrup

Combine candy bars and Eagle Brand in sauce pan. Stir constantly until candy melts. Let cool completely (put in refrigerator until cold, approximately 1 hour). Add 1 quart of milk to cool mixture and beat with mixer until smooth. Pour mixture into ice cream freezer. Add chocolate syrup and remaining milk. Stir well. Freeze. Let stand about 1 hour in freezer to harden.

MICROWAVE DIRECTIONS:

Combine candy bars and Eagle Brand. Put in microvave on high for 2 minutes.

Yield: 1 gallon

Madeline Johnson

PIÑA COLADA ICE CREAM

6 eggs
2 cups sugar
1 fourteen-ounce can condensed milk
2 thirteen-ounce cans evaporated milk
2 Tb. vanilla

1 fifteen and ¼-ounce can
crushed pineapple
1 fifteen and ½-ounce can
Cream of Coconut

Beat eggs until thick. Add sugar. Beat until lemon colored, at least 4 to 5 minutes. Add the can of condensed milk, 2 cans of evaporated milk, vanilla, pineapple and Cream of Coconut. Beat slowly until well blended. Pour into a 6-quart ice cream freezer. Fill to line with milk. Freeze until firm. Let set for at least 30 minutes before serving.

Serves 15 - 20

Donna Bosley
Carol Ann Allison

VANILLA ICE CREAM

9 eggs
2 cups sugar
1 quart heavy cream

2 Tb. vanilla
Whole milk

Beat eggs and sugar together. Add cream to egg mixture, and mix thoroughly. Add vanilla, and pour into ½ gallon freezer. Add enough milk to make freezer ¾ full. Freeze.

Serves 8 - 10

Suzie Thompson

HEAVENLY HOT FUDGE SAUCE

4 squares unsweetened chocolate
1 stick butter
3 cups sugar

Pinch of salt
1 thirteen-ounce can evaporated milk

Melt chocolate and butter together over low heat. Stir in sugar gradually, about ⅓ of the quantity at a time. Make sure sugar is completely moistened after each addition. Mixture will become very thick and dry. Add salt and slowly stir in evaporated milk, a little at a time. It will be completely smooth and satiny. Serve hot over ice cream. Refrigerate left-over sauce.

Yields: 1 quart

Harryette Shue

MOCHA FUDGE SAUCE

1 fourteen-ounce can sweetened
  condensed milk
¼ cup butter or margarine
¼ tsp. salt
1 six-ounce package semi-sweet
  chocolate pieces

1 tsp. vanilla
⅓ cup Kahlua
½ cup chopped nuts

Mix everything but Kahlua and nuts in top of double boiler until chocolate melts. Add Kahlua and nuts. Keep warm. Rich and delicious over ice cream or pound cake. Makes 2½ cups.

Brenda Cerrato

241

VINEGAR PIE CRUST

1 cup plus 3 Tb. shortening	1 egg, beaten
3 cups flour	5 Tb. cold water
1 tsp. salt	1 tsp. vinegar

Blend together shortening, flour, and salt with pastry blender. In a bowl mix well the eggs, water, and vinegar. Add egg mixture to flour mixture and blend well. Roll out and place in pie pans. Bake at 425° until golden. Makes enough pastry for 3 nine-inch single-crust pies. Pastry will keep in refrigerator 4 weeks.

Always flaky!

Yield: 3 single pie crusts   Suzie Thompson

MILE-HIGH MERINGUE

3 egg whites	1 Tb. cornstarch
⅛ tsp. salt	2 Tb. sugar
1 tsp. vanilla	½ cup water
6 Tb. sugar	

Beat egg whites until foamy. Add salt, vanilla, and 6 Tb. sugar, one Tb. at a time, beating well after each addition until mixture is thick and holds a peak. Set aside. Combine cornstarch and 2 Tb. sugar, mixing well. To mixture add water and cook over low heat, stirring constantly until clear in color. Combine with egg white mixture, beating again until thick (about two minutes). Pile on any cream pie, sealing the edges. Bake at 400° for 15 minutes or until golden brown.

Well worth the extra time and effort!

Carol Ann Allison

For "eggscellant" meringue, start with egg whites at room temperature.

APPLE CREME PIE

CRUST:

1 stick butter
1½ cups graham cracker crumbs
½ cup sugar

½ cup crushed almonds
1 tsp. cinnamon

Melt butter in large saucepan. Add graham cracker crumbs, sugar, almonds, and cinnamon. Press hard into buttered pie plate. Bake at 350° for 8 minutes. Cool and fill.

FILLING:

1 envelope unflavored gelatin
⅔ cup sugar
⅔ cup apple juice
2 three-ounce packages cream cheese

1 Tb. fresh lemon juice
2 medium apples, peeled and
   quartered
½ cup whipping cream

Combine gelatin and sugar in saucepan. Stir in apple juice and cook over medium heat until mixture is clear and sugar is dissolved. Refrigerate until slightly thick. In mixing bowl, combine cream cheese and lemon juice, beating until very smooth. Mix gelatin mixture with cream cheese mixture and refrigerate until thick. Grate apples over chilled cream cheese mixture. Stir mixture. Beat whipping cream until stiff, and fold into cheese mixture. Pour into pie crust and chill until set, a minimum of 6 hours. If desired, whip the remaining cream and use to top pie.

This crust is good for many other pies; a favorite!

Serves 8   Susie Walker

BLUEBERRY PIE SUPREME

2 nine-inch baked pie crusts
1 envelope Dream Whip
1 eight-ounce package cream cheese,
   softened at room temperature

1 cup sugar
4 bananas, sliced
1 can blueberry pie filling

Prepare Dream Whip according to directions on package. Cream together cream cheese and sugar. Combine Dream Whip and cream cheese mixture and beat. Line baked pie crusts with sliced bananas. Spoon cheese mixture over bananas and top with pie filling. Refrigerate at least two hours before serving.

Yield: 2 pies
Serves: 12 - 14   Bobbie McKenzie

243

CHIFFON CHEESE PIE

1 thirteen-ounce can evaporated milk	1 cup sugar
1 three-ounce package lemon gelatin	3 Tb. lemon juice
1 cup boiling water	2 nine-inch graham cracker crusts
1 eight-ounce package cream cheese, softened	1 ten-ounce package frozen strawberries

Chill evaporated milk and **large** glass bowl in refrigerator the day before serving.

Dissolve gelatin in boiling water. Chill until mixture is thick as honey. Cream together cream cheese, sugar and lemon juice. Add gelatin to cheese mixture. Whip chilled evaporated milk in large bowl until stiff like whipped cream. Fold gelatin and cheese mixture into whipped milk. (This takes a large bowl and will be a pale yellow when folded well.) Pour into pie crusts. Chill several hours. Garnish wih strawberries when serving.

This is a very light version of cheese cake and keeps for a week.

Yields: 2 pies or 16 servings   Deborah Dorsa Carman

CHOCOLATE ANGEL PIE WITH MERINGUE CRUST

MERINGUE CRUST:

2 egg whites	½ cup sifted granulated sugar
⅛ tsp. cream of tartar	½ cup finely chopped pecans
⅛ tsp. salt	½ tsp. vanilla

Beat egg whites with cream of tartar and salt until foamy. Add sugar gradually, beating until very stiff peaks hold. Fold in nuts and vanilla. Spread in greased 8-inch pie pan. Build up sides to ½ inch above pan. Bake at 300° for 50-55 minutes. Cool.

CHOCOLATE FILLING:

1 package German sweet chocolate	1 tsp. vanilla
3 Tb. water	1 cup whipping cream, whipped

Melt chocolate in water over low heat, stirring constantly. Remove from heat and let cool until thickened. Add vanilla and fold the mixture into whipped cream. Pile into cooled shell and chill two hours before serving.

Judy Meador
Conway, Arkansas

COCONUT CREAM PIE

2 Tb. butter
1 tsp. vanilla
Grated coconut (fresh) to taste
1 nine-inch baked pie shell

1½ cups milk
½ cup sugar
¼ tsp. salt
4 Tb. flour
2 egg yolks

Scald 1 cup milk over boiling water. Mix sugar, salt, flour, and remaining milk together. Stir into hot milk and cook until thickened, stirring constantly. Cover and cook over boiling water 5 minutes. Add mixture slowly to beaten egg yolks. Cook 1 minute longer and remove from heat. Add butter and vanilla. For more flavor add coconut to filling while hot. Pour into baked pie shell. Add meringue. Sprinkle coconut on top of meringue and bake in 350° oven until desired shade of brown.

MERINGUE:

4 Tb. sugar   2 egg whites

Whip egg whites until very stiff, adding sugar 1 Tb. at a time.

Variation: This cream mixture may be used without the coconut for banana pie. Place sliced, sweetened bananas in the shell and cover with cooled filling. Top with whipped cream.

Bess Vestal

EGG CUSTARD PIE

1 cup sugar
¼ tsp. salt
1 tsp. vanilla
¼ tsp. cinnamon

1 Tb. butter or oleo
5 eggs
2 cups milk
1 large unbaked pie crust

Mix sugar, salt, vanilla, cinnamon, and butter. Add eggs and beat well. Add milk; mix until well-blended. Pour into uncooked pie crust. Bake at 450° 7 minutes. Reduce heat to 325° and bake 25 - 30 minutes or until done. Test with knife inserted into center of pie. If knife comes out clean, pie is done.

Serves 6

FUDGE PIE

½ cup margarine
1 cup sugar
2 eggs
½ cup flour

1 tsp. vanilla
1 square chocolate, melted, or
 ¼ cup cocoa

Cream margarine, sugar, and eggs. Cocoa should also be added at this time if it is used instead of melted chocolate. Add flour, vanilla, and chocolate, mixing all ingredients well. Bake in 8-inch greased pie plate at 325° for 25 minutes. Let cool. Serve with peppermint ice cream or whipped cream.

This pie creates its own crust.

Serves: 8

PEANUT BUTTER CREAM PIE

CRUST:

½ cup creamy peanut butter
1 nine-inch pastry shell, baked and
 cooled

¾ cup powdered sugar

Combine powdered sugar and peanut butter until mixture resembles coarse crumbs. Reserve 3 Tb. crumb mixture; sprinkle remaining crumb mixture over bottom of baked pastry shell.

FILLING:

½ cup granulated sugar
3 Tb. cornstarch
½ tsp. salt

3 egg yolks, slightly beaten
2½ cups milk
½ tsp. vanilla

In medium sauce pan, combine ½ cup granulated sugar, cornstarch, and salt. Combine egg yolks and milk. Stir into granulated sugar mixture until well-blended. Cook over medium heat, stirring constantly, until mixture comes to a boil. Cook and stir one minute longer. Remove from heat. Stir in vanilla and cool to room temperature. Pour into prepared pastry shell. Preheat oven to 425°.

TOPPING:

3 egg whites

6 Tb. granulated sugar

Beat egg whites with electric mixer at medium speed about 1 minute or until soft peaks form. Gradually add 6 Tb. granulated sugar, 1 Tb. at a time, beating at high speed until stiff peaks form. Spread beaten egg whites over filling, sealing the edges; top with reserved crumb mixture. Brown in oven 5 - 8 minutes. Cool and store covered in refrigerator.

Judy Fletcher
Jeanie Weir

MILE-HIGH PIE

½ pound butter
2 eggs
2 cups powdered sugar
4 bananas
1 eight-ounce carton Cool Whip
1 fifteen and ½-ounce can crushed
  pineapple

½ cup chopped pecans or
  slivered almonds
7 cherries
Shredded milk chocolate (optional)
1 ten-inch graham cracker crust,
  baked and cooled

Beat butter, eggs and powdered sugar until smooth and pour over crust. Drain pineapple well and layer over filling. Slice bananas and layer over pineapple. Spread Cool Whip over layers. Garnish with nuts, cherries, and chocolate. Chill 2 - 3 hours before serving.

Very rich — serve in small slices. They'll love it! (Low-calories, too!)

Serves 8 - 10

Deborah Carman

SOUTHERN PECAN PIE

Unbaked pastry for a single-crust,
  9-inch pie
3 Tb. butter or margarine
1 tsp. vanilla
¾ cup sugar

3 eggs
½ cup chopped pecans
1 cup dark corn syrup
Pinch salt
½ - ¾ cup pecan halves

Line pie pan with pastry; set aside. Cream butter with vanilla; add sugar gradually. Mix well. Add eggs one at a time. Blend in chopped pecans, syrup, and salt. Pour into pie shell and bake in preheated 450° oven for 10 minutes. Reduce heat to 350°. Remove pie from oven and arrange pecan halves on top of filling. Return to oven and bake for 30 - 35 minutes more.

Plan to make more than one of these. It is the BEST pecan pie recipe I have ever tried — well worth the extra trouble!

Serves 8

Suzie Thompson

PRALINE PUMPKIN PIE

PRALINE CRUNCH:

¼ cup butter or margarine   1 cup pecans, chopped
½ cup sugar

Cook margarine, sugar, and pecans over low heat, stirring until sugar turns golden brown. Turn out onto foil to cool. Crumble into pieces when cool.

FILLING:

1 envelope unflavored gelatin   ½ tsp. salt
½ cup cold water   1 tsp. cinnamon
¾ cup brown sugar   ¾ tsp. nutmeg
1 eighteen-ounce can pumpkin   ½ pint cream, whipped
¼ cup milk   9-inch baked pie crust

Sprinkle gelatin into water and dissolve over low heat. Add brown sugar and stir. In a large bowl, combine all remaining ingredients except whipped cream and crust. Blend in gelatin mixture and fold in whipped cream. To assemble pie, sprinkle 1 cup praline crunch over bottom of pie crust. Pour filling over crunch and top with remaining praline mixture. Refrigerate.

Serves: 6 - 8   Robin Dean

RASPBERRY PIE

1 three-ounce package raspberry-   1 three-ounce package cream cheese
  flavored gelatin   ⅓ cup powdered sugar
¼ cup sugar   1 tsp. vanilla
1¼ cups boiling water   Dash of salt
1 ten-ounce package frozen   1 cup whipping cream
  raspberries   1 nine-inch baked pie shell
1 Tb. lemon juice

Dissolve gelatin and sugar in boiling water. Add frozen berries and lemon juice. Chill until partially set. Meanwhile blend cream cheese, powdered sugar, vanilla and salt. Whip the cream and fold into cheese mixture. Spread half of cheese mixture over baked pie shell. Cover with half the gelatin mixture. Repeat layers. Chill until set.

Serves 6 - 8   Bobbie Phelps

STRAWBERRY ICEBOX PIE

VANILLA WAFER CRUST:

1⅔ cups crushed vanilla wafers

¼ cup margarine, melted
¼ cup sugar

Combine and press into 8 or 9-inch pie pan.

FILLING:

½ pound marshmallows
½ pint whipping cream

½ cup sliced strawberries and liquid
½ cup nuts

Melt marshmallows with 7 Tb. liquid from strawberries. Let cool while whipping the cream. Combine marshmallow mixture, strawberries, and nuts; fold into whipped cream. Pour into vanilla wafer crust. Chill for at least 1 hour before serving.

Variations: Any well-drained fruit (fresh, frozen, or canned) may be used instead of strawberries. Also delicious in a regular baked pie shell.

Serves 6   Bernice Witt

SWEET POTATO PIE

2 cups sweet potatoes, cooked and mashed
½ cup melted margarine
1 cup sugar
2 eggs
1 cup evaporated milk

¼ tsp. cinnamon
¼ tsp. nutmeg
¼ tsp. ground cloves
½ cup coconut
1 unbaked pie crust

Mix potatoes, margarine and sugar. Whip in eggs; add milk, spices, and part of coconut, saving a little to sprinkle on top. Mix well and pour into pie crust. Sprinkle with coconut. Bake 35 - 60 minutes at 375°. Test with a clean knife.

Serves 6 - 8   Rose Wilshire

GERMAN APPLE CAKE

CAKE:

2 cups sugar
1 cup salad oil
2 eggs (3 if small)
2 tsp. cinnamon
1 tsp. soda

½ tsp. salt
1 tsp. vanilla
2 cups flour, sifted
4 cups apples, peeled and thinly sliced
½ - 1 cup walnut pieces, optional

Mix all ingredients with spoon. **Do not use mixer.** Mix sugar, oil, eggs, cinnamon, soda, salt and vanilla. Gradually add flour. Stir in apples. Spread into greased and floured 13 x 9 x 2-inch pan. Bake at 350° for 50 - 55 minutes.

ICING:

2 three-ounce packages cream
   cheese, softened
3 Tb. melted butter

1 tsp. vanilla
1½ cups powdered sugar

Melt butter and mix cream cheese, vanilla and powdered sugar (adding gradually). Spread over cooled cake.

Serves: 16

Gayle Anderson
Sondra Lyons

BERNICE McNEILL'S FRESH APPLE CAKE

CAKE:

1½ cups oil
2 cups granulated sugar
3 cups flour
1 tsp. salt
1 tsp. soda
1 tsp. nutmeg

1 tsp. cinnamon
¼ tsp. cloves
3 eggs, beaten
1 tsp. vanilla
3 apples, chopped
1 cup chopped pecans

Mix oil and sugar. Add dry ingredients. Add beaten eggs and vanilla. Fold in apples and pecans. Bake in a greased and floured tube pan for 90 minutes at 325°. Test cake with a toothpick. Remove from pan to cool.

ICING:

1 cup brown sugar
¼ cup evaporated milk

1 stick oleo

Cook brown sugar, evaporated milk and oleo in double boiler for 5 minutes. Allow to cool for approximately 5 minutes and then spread.

Serves 15 - 20

Betsy Davies

FRESH APPLE CAKE

CAKE:

4 cups chopped apples
2 cups sugar
1 cup Wesson oil
2 eggs
3 cups flour
2 tsp. soda

1½ tsp. cinnamon
1 tsp. salt
½ tsp. allspice
1 tsp. vanilla
1 cup raisins
1 cup nuts

Pour sugar and oil over chopped apples; let stand for 1 hour. Beat eggs. Pour over apples and stir. Sift together all dry ingredients. Add to apples and mix well. Add vanilla, raisins and nuts. Pour in a 9 x 13-inch greased pan. Bake in preheated oven at 325° for 45 - 60 minutes. Cut into squares and serve rum sauce over cake. Top with whipped cream.

RUM SAUCE:

2 Tb. corn starch
1 cup water
1 cup sugar

2 Tb. butter
2 - 3 Tb. rum
Whipped Cream

Cook sugar, corn starch, water and butter until clear and sauce begins to thicken. Cool a few minutes and add rum.

Serves 15

Mildred Swain

APRICOT NECTAR CAKE

1 box yellow cake mix
¾ cup Wesson oil
1 three-ounce package lemon gelatin
¾ cup apricot nectar
4 eggs

2 Tb. lemon juice
1½ cups powdered sugar
½ cup lemon juice or
    ¼ cup apricot nectar and
    ¼ cup lemon juice

Beat the cake mix, oil, gelatin, apricot nectar, eggs and 2 Tb. lemon juice with mixer for 4 minutes. Bake at 325° for 45 minutes. Punch holes in hot cake with toothpick. Mix the powdered sugar and lemon juice and pour over cake.

This is like a pound cake and works well in a bundt pan. It becomes more moist as it sits.

Serves: 8 - 10

Bobbie Phelps

SOUR CREAM BANANA CAKE

CAKE:

¼ cup shortening
1⅓ cups sugar
2 eggs
1 tsp. vanilla
2 cups flour
1 tsp. baking powder

1 tsp. soda
¾ tsp. salt
1 cup sour cream
1 cup mashed bananas
½ cup chopped pecans

Grease and flour 13 x 9 x 2-inch cake pan. Preheat oven to 350°. Cream shortening and sugar until light and fluffy. Add eggs and vanilla to this mixture. In a separate bowl, combine flour, baking powder, soda and salt. Add dry mixture to the creamed shortening and sugar alternately with the sour cream, beginning and ending with the dry ingredients. Next add bananas and pecans. Mix these until just blended. Cook approximately 30 minutes or until the center of the cake springs back when lightly touched.

CREAM CHEESE FROSTING:

1 eight-ounce package cream
   cheese, softened
¼ cup melted margarine

1 tsp. vannila
1 one-pound box powdered
   sugar

Combine all ingredients and mix well. Spread over cool cake.

Serves 16 - 20

Bobbie Brinkley
Anne Glover

When baking a chocolate cake, grease and "cocoa" the pans rather than flour them.

CARROT-PINEAPPLE CAKE

CAKE:

1½ cups sifted all-purpose flour
1 cup sugar
½ tsp. salt
1 tsp. soda
1 tsp. baking powder
1 tsp. cinnamon

⅔ cup salad oil
2 eggs
1 cup shredded carrot
½ cup crushed pineapple and syrup
1 tsp. vanilla

Sift dry ingredients. Add oil, eggs, carrots, pineapple and vanilla. Stir until well mixed. Bake in a greased and floured 9 x 9 x 2-inch pan at 350° for 35 minutes.

CREAM CHEESE FROSTING:

1 three-ounce package cream cheese
1 Tb. butter
1 tsp. vannila

2 cups sifted powder sugar
Milk (if necessary)
½ cup chopped pecans

In small bowl combine cream cheese, butter and vanilla. Beat at low speed until light. Gradually add powdered sugar. If necessary, add milk. Stir in chopped pecans. This frosts one 9" cake.

Serves 9   Christy Simon

CHOCOLATE CAKE PUDDING

CAKE:

¾ cup sugar
1 cup sifted flour
¼ tsp. salt
2 tsp. baking powder

2 Tb. cocoa
½ cup milk
3 Tb. melted butter or oleo, cooled
1 tsp. vanilla

TOPPING:

½ cup sugar
½ cup brown sugar

¼ cup cocoa
1½ cups water

Sift sugar, flour, salt, baking powder and cocoa together into a 9-inch square baking pan. Stir in milk, butter or oleo and vanilla. Spread batter evenly in pan. Mix topping sugars and cocoa and sprinkle over batter. Pour water over all and bake in a 350° oven for 45 minutes or until top springs back when slightly touched. Serve warm or cool with ice cream, whipped cream or sour cream.

Serves 6 - 8   Sheila Hammonds

OLD-FASHIONED CHOCOLATE CAKE

CAKE:

4 ounces semi-sweet chocolate
1 cup milk
1 cup light brown sugar
3 egg yolks
½ cup sweet butter
1 cup granulated sugar

2 cups sifted cake flour
1 tsp. baking soda
½ tsp. salt
¼ cup water
1 tsp. vanilla
2 egg whites

Preheat oven to 375°. Grease and flour two 9-inch cake pans. Melt the chocolate with milk and brown sugar in top of double boiler. Beat in 1 egg yolk. Add to mixture and stir until smooth. Cool. Cream the butter with the granulated sugar and beat in the other egg yolks, one at a time. Stir in the cooled chocolate mixture. Sift the flour with the baking soda and salt. Mix water with vanilla. Add the chocolate mixture in 3 parts, alternating with thirds of water/vanilla mixture. Beat egg whites until stiff and fold in the batter. Pour into cake pans and bake approximately 25 minutes. Watch carefully. Remove when done and cool.

ICING:

3 ounces bitter chocolate
1 fourteen-ounce can sweetened
  condensed milk

½ stick butter,
  cut into small pieces
1 beaten egg yolk

Melt chocolate with condensed milk in top of double boiler. When smooth, cut in the butter and beat in the yolk. Stir until thick. Cool for a few minutes before icing cake.

Marion Grant
Conway, Arkansas

PIÑA COLADA CAKE

1 yellow Duncan Hines cake mix
1 eight and ½-ounce can cream of
  coconut
1 fourteen-ounce can sweetened
  condensed milk

1 six-ounce package frozen coconut
1 eight-ounce carton Cool Whip

Prepare cake according to package directions and bake in a 9 x 13-inch cake pan. While cake is baking, blend condensed milk and cream of coconut in a bowl. As soon as cake is removed from the oven, puncture it with as many holes as possible using a fork. Pour the milk/cream of coconut mixture into the holes. Mix coconut with Cool Whip and ice cake. Refrigerate until cool.

ONE-HOUR CHOCOLATE CAKE AND FROSTING

CAKE:

1 stick oleo
½ cup shortening
4 Tb. cocoa
1 cup hot water
2 cups flour
2 cups sugar

½ cup buttermilk
2 eggs
2 tsp. soda
1 tsp. vanilla
½ tsp. salt
1 tsp. cinnamon

Place oleo, shortening, cocoa and water in saucepan and bring to a boil. Remove from heat and add all other ingredients and beat until smooth. Pour into a greased and floured jelly-roll pan. Bake in preheated 400° oven for 20 - 30 minutes. After 15 minutes, begin preparing frosting.

FROSTING:

1 stick oleo
4 Tb. cocoa
6 Tb. milk

1 one-pound box powdered sugar
1 tsp. vanilla
1 cup chopped pecans

Combine oleo, cocoa and milk in saucepan. Bring to a boil. Remove from heat and add sugar and vanilla. Beat until smooth. Add pecans. Ice cake in pan while still hot. When cool, slice into small pieces.

Serves 25

KALUHA CAKE

CAKE:

1 box Duncan Hines deep chocolate
  cake mix
½ cup Wesson oil
1 four and ¼-ounce package instant
  chocolate pudding

4 eggs
¾ cup strong coffee
¾ cup combined Kaluha and
  créme de cocoa

Combine ingredients and mix well. Pour into greased bundt pan. Bake at 350° for 45 - 50 minutes. Remove from pan and cool. Punch holes in cake with fork and spoon topping over cake.

TOPPING:

1 cup sifted powder sugar
2 Tb. strong brewed coffee

2 Tb. Kaluha
2 Tb. créme de cocoa

Mix topping ingredients and spoon over cake. When serving, put small amount of Cool Whip on each piece.

Serves 18 - 20

Jan Casali
Jonesboro, Arkansas

CHOCOLATE CHEESECAKE

CRUST:

⅓ cup sugar
1 eight and ½-ounce box chocolate
  sugar cookies, crushed

½ - ¾ cup butter, melted
1½ tsp. cinnamon
1 tsp. almond extract

Combine ingredients thoroughly. Press on bottom of 10-inch springform pan. Chill.

FILLING:

1 twelve-ounce package semi-sweet
  chocolate bits
2 eight-ounce packages cream
  cheese softened
2 cups sugar

4 eggs
3 tsp. cocoa
3 tsp. vanilla extract
2 cups sour cream

Preheat oven to 350°. Melt chocolate in top of double boiler over warm water. In large mixing bowl, beat cream cheese until fluffy. Add sugar. Add eggs one at a time, beating after each addition. Add cocoa and vanilla. Blend thoroughly. Stir in sour cream. Stir in melted chocolate bits and pour into chilled crust. Bake 1 hour 10 minutes. The cake will be slightly runny, but will become firm as it chills. Cool 20 minutes.

TOPPING:

2 cups sour cream
1½ tsp. vanilla

½ cup sugar

Combine ingredients and pour over cake. Bake 5 minutes at 450°. Cool to room temperature and chill at least 5 hours before serving. Freezes well.

Serves: 12 - 16

Mrs. Sidney Nisbet

VANILLA CRUMB CAKE

1 twelve-ounce box vanilla wafers,
  crushed
2 sticks butter
2 cups sugar

6 eggs
½ cup milk
1 seven-ounce can coconut
1 cup pecans, chopped

Crush the vanilla wafers. Cream butter and sugar well. Beat eggs in one at a time. Add vanilla wafer crumbs and milk alternately. Mix well and fold in coconut and pecans. Pour in a greased and floured tube pan. Bake at 275° for 2 hours.

Dottie Hankins
Thelma Chronister

GRASSHOPPER CAKE

CAKE:

4 one-ounce squares chocolate, melted
½ cup boiling water
¼ cup sugar
2½ cups cake flour, sifted
1½ cups sugar
3 tsp. baking powder

1 tsp. salt
½ cup oil
7 eggs, separated
¾ cup cold water
1 tsp. vanilla
1 tsp. cream of tartar

Blend together melted chocolate, boiling water and ¼ cup sugar. Let cool while sifting flour, sugar, baking powder and salt. Add oil, egg yolks, cold water and vanilla to flour mixture. Beat until smooth. Stir in chocolate mixture. Beat egg whites and cream of tartar until stiff peaks are formed. Fold chocolate mixture into egg whites. Pour into 10-inch ungreased tube pan. Bake at 350° for 1 hour. Invert on a bottle to cool, preferably overnight. Split into three layers.

FROSTING:

1 envelope unflavored gelatin
¼ cup cold water
⅓ cup créme de cocoa

½ cup green créme de menthe
2 two-ounce packages Dream Whip
topping

Soften gelatin in ¼ cup cold water. Heat créme de cocoa and créme de menthe until warm. Add softened gelatin, stirring until dissolved. Cool. Prepare Dream Whip topping according to package directions; fold into gelatin mixture. Chill until mixture mounds, stirring often, about 30 minutes. Frost between layers and on top only. Chill frosted cake uncovered for at least 1 hour before serving.

Carol Ann Allison

ITALIAN CREAM CAKE

½ cup shortening
2 cups sugar
5 egg yolks
1 stick oleo
2 cups sifted plain flour

1 tsp. soda dissolved in
 1 cup buttermilk
1 cup chopped pecans
1 seven-ounce can coconut
5 egg whites, beaten

ICING:

1 eight-ounce package cream cheese
1 stick oleo

1 one-pound box powdered sugar
1 tsp. vanilla

Mix all ingredients in order given and fold in beaten egg whites. Bake in 3 nine-inch pans for 20 - 25 minutes at 350°. Cool. Mix icing ingredients in order given. Beat until of spreading consistency.

Judy Wilson
Saundra Hatch

257

FESTIVE CAKE

3 cups all purpose flour
2 cups sugar
1 tsp. baking soda
1 tsp. salt
1 tsp. cinnamon
1 cup chopped almonds

3 eggs
1½ cup vegetable oil
1 tsp. almond extract
2 cups chopped firm ripe bananas
1 eight-ounce can crushed pineapple

Mix and sift flour, sugar, baking soda, salt and cinnamon. Stir in almonds. Beat eggs slightly. Stir in oil, almond extract, bananas and undrained pineapple. Add to dry ingredients. Mix thoroughly but do not beat. Spoon into well-oiled 10-inch tube pan. Bake at 325° for 1 hour 25 minutes. Remove from oven and let stand 10 to 15 minutes. Invert on cake rack. Remove pan. Cool thoroughly before frosting.

FROSTING:

1 eight-ounce package cream cheese
½ cup margarine

1 pound confectioner's sugar

Soften cream cheese and margarine to room temperature. Cream together with confectioner's sugar. Frost top and sides. Store in refrigerator.

Bonnie Low

COCONUT RUM CAKE

CAKE:
2 sticks butter
½ cup shortening
3 cups sugar
5 whole eggs
1 tsp. coconut extract

1 tsp. rum extract
3 cups flour
½ tsp. baking powder
½ tsp. salt
1 cup milk

Cream butter and shortening with sugar. Add eggs one at a time. Mix well after each. Add extracts and blend. Add flour which has been sifted with baking powder and salt. Alternate with milk, beginning and ending with flour. Pour into well greased and lightly floured bundt pan. Put any remainder in loaf pan. Bake at 300° for 45 minutes. Increase temperature to 325° and bake 10 - 15 minutes longer.

GLAZE:
1 cup sugar
½ cup water

1 tsp. almond extract

Boil sugar and water together and set aside to cool. When cake and glaze are cool, add almond extract to glaze. Mix well. Brush on all sides of cake with pastry brush.

Serves 10 - 12

Virginia Bankston

COCONUT CAKE SUPREME

CAKE:

1 box white cake mix
⅓ cup oil
3 eggs

1 eight-ounce carton sour cream
1 eight and ½-ounce can cream of
   coconut

Blend cake mix, oil, eggs, sour cream and cream of coconut together with electric mixer. Bake in greased 9 x 12-inch pan at 350° for 30 minutes.

ICING:

1 eight-ounce package cream cheese
1 box or 3½ cups powdered sugar
2 Tb. milk

1 tsp. vanilla
1 three and ½-ounce can
   Angel Flake coconut

Blend powdered sugar into softened cream cheese and work in milk and vanilla. Spread icing over cooled cake. Sprinkle coconut over iced cake.

Serves 15   Patty Lowe

MILKY WAY CAKE

CAKE:

6 Milky Way Bars, regular size
1 stick margarine
½ cup chopped pecans
¾ cup Crisco
2 cups sugar
4 eggs

1¼ cups buttermilk
2½ cups flour
½ tsp. soda
1 tsp. salt
2 tsp. vanilla

Melt candy bars with margarine. Add chopped nuts and set aside to cool. Cream Crisco and sugar. Add eggs, one at a time, beating after each addition. Blend in candy-nut mixture. Add dry ingredients and buttermilk, alternately. Add vanilla. Bake in three layers in 9-inch pans at 350° for 25 - 30 minutes.

FROSTING:

2 cups sugar
1 stick margarine
1 cup Carnation milk
¼ tsp. salt

1 five-ounce jar marshmallow cream
1 six-ounce package semi-sweet
   chocolate bits

Combine sugar, margarine, milk and salt. Bring to soft ball stage (240°). Remove from heat. Add marshmallow cream and chocolate bits. Beat until cool and of right consistency to spread.

Serves 12 - 16   Florine Tyler

259

COCA-COLA CAKE

CAKE:

2 cups unsifted flour
2 cups sugar
2 sticks oleo
3 Tb. cocoa
1 cup Coca-Cola

1 tsp. soda
½ cup buttermilk
2 eggs, beaten
1 tsp. vanilla
1½ cups miniature marshmallows

Combine flour and sugar in bowl. Heat oleo, cocoa and Coca-Cola to boiling and pour over flour and sugar mixture. Dissolve soda in buttermilk and add to first mixture. Also add eggs, vanilla and marshmallows. (This makes a thin batter and the marshmallows will be floating to the top.) Bake in a 13 x 9" greased pan at 350° for 30 - 35 minutes. Check with a toothpick for doneness. Ice while hot.

ICING:

1 stick oleo
6 Tb. Coca-Cola
3 Tb. cocoa

1 one-pound box confectioner's sugar
1 tsp. vanilla
1 cup chopped pecans, toasted

Combine oleo, Coca-Cola and cocoa and heat to boiling. Pour over sugar. Beat well and add vanilla and pecans. Spread over hot cake.

Serves 12   Hazel Cook

GRANDMA WARD'S FRUIT CAKE

1 cup flour
1 cup sugar
1 tsp. baking powder
4 ounces candied pineapple, green
   or red
4 ounces candied pineapple, natural

4 ounces candied cherries, red
4 ounces candied cherries, green
1 pound dates
1 pound pecan halves
4 eggs, beaten slightly
1 tsp. vanilla

In large bowl mix sugar, flour and baking powder thoroughly. Add fruit that has been cut into small pieces, reserving a few for decorating top of cake. Stir to coat fruit. Add dates (cut into small pieces), stir to coat. Add nuts and stir. Beat eggs slightly and add vanilla. Add to fruit and flour mixture. Stir thoroughly and let stand while preparing cake pan. Grease an 8 x 8 x 2-inch cake pan and line with wax paper. Stir mixture again. Put cake mixture into pan one or two large spoonfuls at a time; press down firmly. Repeat until all the mixture is in the pan. Place reserve fruit and nuts on top for decorations. Bake at 325° for 1 hour and 15 minutes. Cover with foil last 30 minutes to prevent excessive browning. Remove cake from pan immediately and remove wax paper. Let cool on rack.

This cake can be made months in advance and kept in a freezer up to four months. The cake can also be made in small 1-pound loaf pans for individual cakes. Makes a wonderful gift.

Yields: 4-pound cake   Sandra Levin

FEUD CAKE

CAKE:

8 whole eggs	1 cup flour
2 cups sugar	4 tsp. baking powder
1 Tb. vanilla	5 cups pecans, chopped

Beat eggs at high speed of mixer for 5 minutes. Add sugar, vanilla, flour and baking powder. Beat another 5 minutes. Add 5 cups of pecans at low speed to moisten well (about 1 minute). Pour into three greased and paper lined 9-inch cake pans. Bake at 350° for 20 minutes. Remove immediately from pans to wire cake racks and cool.

TOPPING:

1½ quarts whipping cream	¼ cup pecans, chopped
1 cup powdered sugar	

Whip 1½ quarts whipping cream. Add 1 cup powdered sugar. Frost layers, top and sides of cake and sprinkle generously with ¼ cup chopped pecans.

Marvelous! We have it Christmas Eve and the presents wait! Legend tells that two neighbors both claimed the honor of being the originators of this cake. The argument turned into a family feud. The two families are forgotten — but not the cake.

Serves 15   Betsy Davies

FROZEN FRUIT CAKE

2 eggs, separated	1 cup whipped cream
½ cup sugar	2 cups macaroons, crumbled
¼ cup flour	1 cup chopped pecans
¼ tsp. salt	½ cup candied cherries, chopped
2 cups milk or coffee cream	1 cup raisins or ½ cup raisins plus
1 tsp. vanilla	½ cup citron

Make a custard with egg yolks, sugar, flour, salt and milk. Cook 10 minutes. Stiffly beat egg whites. After custard is cooked, fold in vanilla and the beaten egg whites. Set aside to cool. Fold together the whipped cream, macaroons, pecans, cherries, and raisins. Fold this mixture into the custard. Freeze in a loaf pan or freezing trays. Serve with whipped cream laced with 2 tsp. orange cointreau, if desired.

Serves: 12 - 14   Roberta R. Herlocker

EXTRA-MOIST LEMONADE CAKE

CAKE:

1 package lemon cake mix
1 three and ¾-ounce package lemon
   instant pudding

4 eggs
1 cup water
¼ cup oil

LEMON GLAZE:

1 six-ounce can frozen Country
   Time Lemonade, thawed

2 cups unsifted powdered sugar

Combine cake mix, pudding mix, eggs, water and oil in large mixer bowl. Beat at medium speed of electric mixer for 4 minutes. Pour into greased and floured 10-inch fluted tube pan (bundt). Bake at 350° for 50 - 55 minutes. Do not underbake. Cool in pan for 5 minutes. Thoroughly prick warm cake completely through to bottom of cake. Combine frozen drink and 2 cups powdered sugar; blend well. Gradually spoon this glaze mixture over cake until completely absorbed. Cool 15 minutes; remove from pan. Sprinkle with powdered sugar.

Sheila Hammonds

OATMEAL CAKE

1¼ cup boiling water
1 cup quick cooking oats
1 cup brown sugar
1 cup granulated sugar
1 stick oleo
1 tsp. vanilla

2 eggs
1⅓ cups flour
1 tsp. soda
1 tsp. cinnamon
1 tsp. nutmeg

TOPPING:

¾ cup sugar
3 Tb. oleo
1 cup chopped nuts

1 cup Angel Flake Coconut
3 Tb. milk
1 egg, well beaten

Pour boiling water over oats; stir well, cover and let stand until cool. Beat brown sugar, granulated sugar and oleo until creamy. Add cooled oatmeal, vanilla and eggs and beat well. Sift together flour, soda, cinnamon and nutmeg. Add to creamed mixture and beat 1 minute. Pour into a greased and floured 13 x 9 x 2-inch pan. Mix topping ingredients and pour over batter. Bake at 350° for 35 to 40 minutes. The topping will be thick and difficult to spread.

Judy Fletcher

ORANGE-RAISIN CAKE

CAKE:

1 cup raisins
1 cup buttermilk
1 cup sugar
½ cup shortening

2 eggs
2 cups flour
1 tsp. soda
½ tsp. salt

GLAZE:

2 large oranges

1 cup sugar

Soak raisins in the buttermilk. Cream sugar and shortening. Add eggs and beat. Add dry ingredients and stir. Add soaked raisins. Put in 7 x 12-inch greased and floured baking dish. Bake at 325° for 1 hour. While cake is baking, grate the rinds of the oranges. Add juice of oranges and sugar and dissolve. Pour over cake after baking is completed.

This cake can be kept for a week and may be warmed over without affecting it.

Margaret Tester

PINEAPPLE DELIGHT

CAKE:

2 cups sugar
2 eggs
2 cups flour
2 tsp. baking soda

¼ cup oil
1 fifteen and ¼-ounce can crushed
   pineapple, undrained

Mix all cake ingredients and bake in a 9 x 13 x 2-inch pan at 325° for 35 - 40 minutes.

TOPPING:

1 five and ⅓-ounce can evaporated
  milk or ¾ cup regular milk
1 cup sugar

1 stick margarine
1 cup nuts, chopped (optional)
1 cup coconut (optional)

Combine all topping ingredients in saucepan and boil slowly 10 minutes. Pour over cake while hot.

Serves: 12 - 15

Pat Landers

GOOEY CAKE

1 box yellow cake mix
3 eggs
1 stick oleo, melted

1 one-pound box powdered sugar
1 eight-ounce package cream cheese

Blend cake mix, 1 egg and oleo. Press into 9 x 13-inch pan. Mix together powdered sugar, cream cheese and 2 eggs and pour on crust. Bake at 350° for 40 minutes.

Serves 20

Nedra Wood
Jonnie Schulte

PINEAPPLE JAM CAKE

CAKE:
1 cup Crisco shortening
1½ cups sugar
4 eggs
3 cups sifted flour
1 tsp. soda
1 tsp. salt

1 tsp. allspice
1 tsp. ground cloves
1 tsp. cinnamon
1 cup buttermilk
1 cup strawberry jam

FILLING:
1 fifteen and ½-ounce can
   crushed pineapple
1½ cups cups sugar

1 Tb. flour
2 Tb. butter

Cream shortening and sugar. Add eggs one at a time, beating after each. Add soda, salt and spices to flour and sift again. Add dry ingredients to egg mixture alternately with buttermilk. Beat after each addition. Stir in strawberry jam. Bake in three 9-inch layer pans which have been greased and floured. (Wax paper liners on bottom of pans will keep jam from sticking.) Bake 25 - 30 minutes at 350°. While cake is baking, mix filling ingredients. Boil 1 minute. Spread between layers while cake is still warm.

FROSTING:
1 stick butter or margarine
1 cup light brown sugar, firmly packed
¼ cup canned milk

1 tsp. vanilla
2 cups powdered sugar, sifted

Bring butter and brown sugar to boil, stirring constantly. Boil 1 minute. Remove from heat and add milk. Return to boil. Cool slightly. Add vanilla. Let cool to lukewarm before adding sifted powdered sugar. Cover top and sides of cake. If frosting is too thick, add small amount of milk; if too thin, more sugar.

This makes a very large cake. It will stay moist a very long time if well covered.

Serves: 16 - 20

Mrs. Alfred Stone
Nashville, Arkansas

264

VERY SPECIAL LEMON CAKE

1 package lemon cake mix
  (Duncan Hines preferred)
1 three and ¾-ounce package lemon
  instant pudding mix
½ tsp. nutmeg

4 eggs
¾ cup Wesson oil
¾ cup dry sherry
Powdered sugar

Place all ingredients except powdered sugar in large mixing bowl. Beat 10 minutes, with electric mixer at medium speed. Pour mixture into greased, floured bundt pan. Bake at 350° until golden brown, about 55 minutes. Sprinkle with powdered sugar while still hot.

A delicious lemon cake with a very delicate taste.

Serves: 8 - 10

Shirley Hale

STRAWBERRY DELIGHT

1 box yellow cake mix
1 three-ounce box strawberry gelatin
1 four-ounce box vanilla instant
  pudding

2 ten-ounce packages frozen
  strawberries, partially drained
1 eight-ounce carton Cool Whip

Bake cake in a 9 x 13-inch pan according to directions on box. While cake is baking, mix gelatin and chill. Cool cake 10 minutes and then punch holes with ice pick over cake. Slowly pour gelatin over cake and let soat in. Put cake in refrigerator about 1 hour. Mix pudding and let chill about 20 minutes. Spread pudding on top of cake, sprinkle strawberries on top of pudding and add a layer of Cool Whip. Refrigerate cake until serving.

Kathy Jolly

EXCELLENT POUND CAKE

3 cups sugar
1 pound butter, softened
6 eggs (at room temperature)
4 cups all-purpose flour

¾ cup milk
1 tsp. almond extract
1 tsp. vanilla extract

Combine sugar and butter; cream until light and fluffy. Add eggs, one at a time, beating well after each. Add flour to creamed mixture alternately with milk, beating well after each addition. Add flavorings. Pour batter into a well-greased and floured 10-inch tube pan. Bake at 300° for 1 hour 40 minutes or until cake tests done.

Dottie Hankins

STRAWBERRY CAKE

CAKE:

1 box white cake mix
1 three-ounce box strawberry gelatin
4 eggs
¾ cup milk

¾ cup Wesson oil
½ ten-ounce box frozen strawberries
½ cup coconut
½ cup chopped pecans

Mix dry ingredients together. Add eggs, milk and oil. Beat well. Fold in strawberries, coconut and pecans. Bake in 3, 9-inch layer pans that have been greased and floured. Bake at 350° for 25 - 30 minutes.

ICING:

1 one-pound box powdered sugar
¼ cup butter
½ ten-ounce box frozen strawberries

½ cup coconut
½ cup chopped pecans

Soften butter and mix remaining ingredients together. Spread on cooled cake.

Serves: 16 - 20

Judy Casali
Pine Bluff, Arkansas

PRUNE CAKE

3 eggs
2 cups sugar
1 cup Wesson oil
1 cup buttermilk
2 cups flour
1 tsp. soda

1 tsp. cinnamon
1 tsp. nutmeg
1 tsp. allspice
½ tsp. cloves
1 cup chopped nuts
1 cup cooked prunes

Mix all ingredients and beat well, adding the prunes and nuts last. Pour into buttered bundt pan. Bake for 1½ hours at 300°.

ICING:

½ cup sugar
½ stick oleo

¼ cup buttermilk

Cook 5 - 7 minutes, stirring constantly. Spoon on cake.

This cake keeps beautifully.

Ruth Morley

CHOCOLATE POUND CAKE

1½ sticks butter	¼ tsp. salt
1½ sticks oleo	¾ tsp. baking powder
3 cups sugar	½ cup cocoa
5 eggs	1¼ cups milk
3 cups flour, plain	1 tsp. vanilla

Let butter and oleo soften. Add sugar and cream well. Add eggs one at a time and continue beating. Mix dry ingredients and alternate adding to creamed mixture with milk. Add vanilla. Bake at 300° for 1½ hours. Test often with straw. Cool.

This makes one large tube pan or two smaller tube pans. Smaller pans take about 1 hour 15 minutes.

Serves: 18 - 20

Joyce Holsted

FIVE-FLAVOR POUND CAKE

CAKE:

2 sticks oleo	½ tsp. baking powder
½ cup shortening	1 cup milk
3 cups sugar	1 tsp. of following extracts: coconut,
5 eggs, well beaten	rum, butter, lemon and vanilla
3 cups all-purpose flour	

Cream oleo, shortening and sugar until light and fluffy. Add eggs which have been beaten until lemon colored. Combine flour and baking powder and add to creamed mixture alternately with milk. Stir in flavorings. Spoon mixture into greased and floured 10-inch tube pan. Bake at 325° for 1½ hours or until cake tests done. Add glaze while cake is still hot.

GLAZE:

1 cup sugar	1 tsp. of following extracts: coconut,
½ cup water	rum, butter, lemon, vanilla and
	almond

Combine all glaze ingredients in sauce pan and bring to a boil. Stir until sugar is melted. Pour over hot cake.

Bonnie Stowers
Vicksburg, Mississippi

APRICOT DATE BAR

½ cup margarine or butter
1½ cups graham cracker crumbs
1 eight-ounce package chopped
  dates
1 four and ¾-ounce can or jar
  strained apricot baby food

1 fourteen-ounce can sweetened
  condensed milk
1 three and ½-ounce can flaked
  coconut
¾ cup nuts, chopped

Preheat oven to 350°. (325° if using glass baking dish). In 13 x 9-inch pan melt butter and sprinkle crumbs evenly over butter. In small bowl combine dates and apricots. Spoon evenly over crumbs. Pour condensed milk evenly over dates. Top evenly with coconut and nuts, pressing down gently. Bake 30 - 35 minutes, or until lightly browned. Cool thoroughly before cutting.

Margaret Kennedy

BLACK BOTTOM CUPCAKES

WHITE MIXTURE:

1 eight-ounce package cream cheese
1 egg, beaten
⅓ cup sugar

⅛ tsp. salt
1 cup mini-chocolate chips

CHOCOLATE MIXTURE:

1½ cups flour
1 cup sugar
¼ cup cocoa
½ tsp. salt
1 tsp. baking soda

⅓ cup cooking oil
1 Tb. vinegar
1 tsp. vanilla
1 cup water

Beat well cream cheese, egg, sugar and salt of white mixture ingredients and stir in chocolate chips. Set aside. Sift together flour, sugar, cocoa, salt and baking soda of chocolate mixture. Add oil, vinegar, vanilla and water and beat well. Fill mini-muffin tins half full of chocolate mixture and add 1 teaspoon white mixture. Bake at 350° for 20 minutes.

Yield: 3 to 4 dozen

Jean Anne Twombly
Wiesboden, Germany

BROWNIES

½ cup butter
1 cup sgar
4 eggs
1 sizteen-ounce can Hershey's
  chocolate syrup

1 cup flour
½ cup nuts

Beat butter, sugar, eggs and syrup. Add flour and beat until smooth. Add nuts, and bake in a jelly roll pan for 15 to 20 minutes at 350°.

ICING:

1½ cups sugar
6 Tb. butter

6 Tb. milk
1 cup chocolate chips

Melt butter and sugar. Add milk. Boil for 30 seconds. Add chips. Beat until smooth. Frost brownies.

Barbara Hoffman

CHOCOLATE PEPPERMINT BROWNIES

COOKIE:

½ cup butter
2 ounces semi-sweet chocolate
2 eggs
1 cup sugar

¼ tsp. peppermint extract
½ cup flour
⅛ tsp. salt
½ cup chopped pecans

Preheat oven to 350°. Melt butter and chocolate. Beat eggs and sugar. Add egg mixture to chocolate mixture. Stir in remaining ingredients. Bake in buttered 8 or 9-inch square cake pan for 15 minutes. Cool.

FROSTING:

1 cup powdered sugar
2 Tb. butter
1 Tb. evaporated milk

½ tsp. peppermint extract
Green food coloring

Mix powdered sugar, butter, evaporated milk, peppermint extract and food coloring. Spread on cooled cookie and chill.

GLAZE:

2 ounces chocolate

2 Tb. butter

Melt chocolate and butter for glaze. Spread over frosting. Store in refrigerator in warm weather. Recipe doubles easily.

Jayne White

269

HAVE-ON-HAND BROWNIE MIX

MIX:

4 cups flour

6 cups sugar

2½ cups cocoa (8 ounces)

4 tsp. baking powder

3 tsp. salt

2 cups Crisco shortening

Stir together all dry ingredients. Mix well. Cut in Crisco until evenly mixed throughout. Store in air tight container on shelf. Can be stored for up to 6 months. Will make about 10 batches.

ONE BATCH:

2 cups mix

2 eggs

1 tsp. vanilla

Mix together mix, eggs and vanilla. Batter will be stiff. Spread in an 8 x 8-inch pan. Bake in preheated oven at 350° for 20 minutes.

Carol Long

CARAMEL LAYER CHOCOLATE SQUARES

14 ounces light caramels, (50 pieces)

⅔ cup evaporated milk, divided

1 package German Chocolate Cake Mix

¾ cup butter or oleo

1 cup chopped nuts

1 cup semi-sweet chocolate

chips, (6 ounces)

In heavy saucepan, combine caramels and ⅓ cup evaporated milk. Cook over low heat, stirring constantly until caramels are melted. Set aside. Grease and flour 9 x 13-inch baking pan. In large mixing bowl, combine by hand the cake mix, butter or oleo, ⅓ cup evaporated milk and nuts, stirring until dough holds together. Press half the dough into prepared pan. Reserve remaining dough for topping. Bake at 350° for 10-12 minutes. Sprinkle chocolate chips over baked crust. Spread caramel mixture over chocolate chips. Crumble reserved dough over all. Return to oven and bake 18 to 20 minutes. Cool slightly. Refrigerate about 30 minutes to set caramel layer. Cut into bars.

Yields: 36 bars

CHOCOLATE CHIP BARS

½ cup margarine

1¼ cup brown sugar

1 egg

1 Tb. water

1 cup flour

¼ tsp. salt

1 tsp. baking powder

½ tsp. vanilla

½ cup semi-sweet chocolate bits

½ cup nuts

Mix all ingredients together and bake at 350° for 25 minutes in a square pan.

Sandra Cook

CREAM CHEESE CUPCAKES

**3 eight-ounce packages cream
cheese, softened**
1 cup sugar

1 tsp. vanilla
5 eggs

ICING:

1 cup sour cream

8 Tb. sugar

Cream together cream cheese, sugar and vanilla. Add eggs one at a time beating after each one. Spoon into baking cups. Bake 40 minutes at 300°. Remove from oven and let stand 5 minutes so that centers indent. Mix sour cream together with 8 Tb. sugar. Spoon on cupcakes and bake at 350° for 5 minutes.

Serves: 24

Nedra Wood

MAPLE BARS

1 cup graham cracker crumbs
¼ cup butter or margarine, melted
¼ cup brown sugar, well-crumbled

2 cups flaked coconut
1 cup Eagle Brand milk
9 x 9-inch pan

Combine graham cracker crumbs, butter and brown sugar with a fork in the 9 x 9-inch pan. When mixture is evenly mixed, press into the pan for a crust. In a large mixing bowl, combine coconut with Eagle Brand milk. Let mixture set for about 15 minutes. Spread coconut mixture over crumb mixture and bake 30 minutes at 300°. Coconut mixture should be golden brown on top. When cool, frost with maple frosting.

FROSTING:

½ cup butter
1 cup brown sugar

¼ cup evaporated milk
1½ cups powdered sugar

Combine butter, brown sugar and evaporated milk in saucepan. Cook until it comes to a full boil. Remove from heat and sift in powdered sugar, stirring constantly.

Reba Workman
Fort Smith

QUICK CHEWY BARS

1 can of Pilsbury Crescent rolls
1 fourteen-ounce can of Eagle
  Brand milk

1 box of Coconut Pecan
  Frosting mix
½ cup melted butter or margarine

Onto a large greased cookie sheet with deep sides, spread 1 can of crescent rolls, flattened into a sheet. Spread a can of Eagle Brand milk on the rolls. Sprinkle on top of Eagle Brand milk a box of Coconut Pecan Frosting Mix. Melt one cup of butter or margarine and pour on top. Bake at 400° for 12 to 15 minutes. Cut into bars. Makes two dozen.

Debbie Birch

ADVENTURE COOKIES

½ cup butter
1 cup chopped dates
¾ cup white sugar
1 egg, well beaten
1 Tb. milk

1 tsp. vanilla
½ tsp. salt
½ cup chopped nuts
½ cup Rice Krispies
Coconut

In a double boiler on low heat combine the butter, dates and sugar. Add egg, milk, vanilla and salt to above; heat again, stirring constantly, until well-blended. Remove from heat; add the nuts and Rice Krispies. Form into small balls and roll in finely cut coconut. Cookies are not baked. Store in the refrigerator.

Yield: 3 dozen cookies

Theresa Keene

ALMOND COOKIES

1 pound butter
2 cups sugar
4 cups flour

1 cup beaten egg yolks
  (approximately 10 egg yolks)
2 ounces sliced almonds

Cream together butter, sugar and flour. Roll out on lightly floured surface to ⅛-inch thickness; cut with glass or cutter. Cookies should be 2 inches in diameter. Brush with egg yolks and place 3 sliced almonds on each cookie. Place 2 inches apart on ungreased cookie sheet. Bake at 350° for 10-12 minutes.

Yield: 4 dozen cookies

Barbara Althoff

BUTTER COOKIES

2 sticks butter or 1 each
  butter and margarine
1 cup sugar
1 egg

1½ cups cake flour
½ tsp. salt, scant
½ tsp. vanilla

Cream butter and sugar. Add unbeaten egg to butter and sugar. Beat well and add flour sifted with salt. Blend well. Add vanilla and mix. Drop on lightly greased cookie sheet by teaspoonfuls. Press with prongs of fork. Bake 6 - 10 minutes at 350°. Watch closely; cookies are done when edges begin to brown. Let harden.

Variations: substitute lemon juice for vanilla. Sprinkle cookies with cinnamon sugar, powdered sugar, orange sprinkles, coconut, etc.

Impossible to eat fewer than five at a time!

Yield: 3 dozen cookies

Claudia Howe

CARAMEL NUT SLICES

1 cup soft shortening
2 cups brown sugar
2 eggs
3½ cups sifted flour

½ tsp. salt
1 tsp. soda
1 cup finely chopped nuts

Mix shortening, sugar, and eggs well. Sift together flour, salt and soda. Stir all ingredients together; add nuts. Shape into 2 rolls, 2 inches in diameter and chill. Preheat oven to 400°. Slice ⅛ inch thick and bake on ungreased cookie sheet 8 - 10 minutes.

Yield: 12 dozen cookies

Sara Nichols

CHOCOLATE DROP COOKIES

1½ cups sifted flour
⅓ tsp. salt
1 tsp. baking bowder
2 ounces chocolate (squares)
½ cup shortening, melted

1 cup brown sugar
1 egg
½ cup milk
1 tsp. vanilla

Sift flour, salt and baking powder together. Melt shortening and chocolate together. Add sugar, egg, milk and vanilla and then add sifted ingredients. Mix. Let stand 10 minutes. Drop from teaspoons onto greased baking sheet and bake at 375° for 12 - 15 minutes. Frost if desired.

Yield: 3 dozen cookies

Lucille Rebholz

CHRISTMAS COOKIES

1 cup sugar	1 tsp. soda, dissolved in ¼
⅔ cups butter	cup boiling water
2 eggs	½ cup whiskey (bourbon)
2½ cups flour	2 cups chopped pecans
1 tsp. cinnamon	1 pound dates, chopped
1 tsp. cloves	1 pound candied cherries, chopped
1 cup white raisins	1 pound candied pineapple, chopped

Cream sugar and butter in large mixing bowl. Beat in eggs. Sift flour, cinammon, and cloves together. Add flour mixture, soda and whiskey, to sugar, butter and egg mixture. Stir in pecans, dates, cherries and pineapple. Drop by small teaspoonfuls on greased cookie sheet. Bake at 300° for 10 - 15 minutes. Should be rather soft. Store in tin.

Yield: 200 bite-sized cookies   Atheta Ball

HOLIDAY COOKIES

2 eggs	3½ cups flour
⅔ cup Crisco	2 tsp. baking powder
⅔ cup margarine, softened	1 tsp. salt
1½ cups sugar	2 tsp. vanilla

Beat eggs slightly in large bowl. Add remaining ingredients; blend with mixer on low speed about 1 minute. Mix on medium speed about 3 minutes until all ingredients are well-blended. Form dough into a ball with hands and refrigerate until ready for use (at least 1 hour). Roll dough to ⅛ inch thick on floured board. Cut with cutters and place on ungreased cookie sheets. Bake at 375° for 8 - 10 minutes or until light brown. Sprinkle with sugar or ice as desired.

Yield: 5 dozen cookies   Colleen Wallace

LEMON SQUARES

1½ sticks butter or oleo	1½ cups granulated sugar
(room temperature)	3 Tb. flour
⅓ cup powdered sugar	⅓ cup lemon juice
1½ cups flour	Powdered sugar
3 eggs	

Mix butter, powdered sugar and 1½ cups flour with pastry blender and pat into 9 x 13-inch pan. Bake 20 minutes at 350°. Mix eggs, sugar, and 3 Tb. flour until well blended. Add lemon juice and mix well. Pour over baked crust and bake again for 20 minutes at 350°. Remove from oven. Sprinkle powdered sugar on top. Cool and cut into squares.

Serves: 12 - 15

LEMON COOKIES

1 cup butter, softened
½ cup sifted powdered sugar
2 cups flour

⅛ tsp. salt
1 tsp. lemon extract

Cream butter and gradually add ½ cup powdered sugar, beating until fluffy. Combine flour and salt; add to cream mixture, beating well. Stir in lemon flavoring. Flour hands and shape dough into ¾-inch balls. Place 2 inches apart on ungreased cookie sheets and flatten each slightly with a fork. Bake at 400° for 8 - 10 minutes or until browned. Cool. Spoon ¼ - ½ teaspoon lemon filling on half of the cookies and top with the other half of cookies to make a sandwich. Sprinkle with powdered sugar.

LEMON FILLING:

1 egg, beaten
⅔ cups sugar
3 Tb. lemon juice

2 Tb. softened butter
1½ tsp. grated lemon rind

Combine all ingredients in top of double boiler and bring water to a boil. Reduce heat to low and cook, stirring constantly until thick. Chill one hour.

Yield: 3 dozen cookies

Edwina Whalen

MOLASSES COOKIES

¾ cups Crisco
1 cup sugar
¼ cup molasses
1 egg
2 tsp. soda
2 cups flour

½ tsp. cloves
½ tsp. ginger
1 tsp. cinnamon
½ tsp. salt
Sugar

Melt shortening over low heat. Remove; set aside for 5 minutes. Add sugar, molasses, and egg; mix. Add soda, flour, spices, and salt. Beat well with mixer. Chill several hours or overnight. Form dough into 1-inch balls; roll in sugar. Bake on greased cookie sheet 8 - 10 minutes at 375°.

Yield: 3 dozen cookies

Becky Witcher

OATMEAL CRISPIES

1 cup margarine
1 cup brown sugar
1 cup sugar
2 eggs
1 tsp. vanilla

1 tsp. salt
1½ cups flour
1 tsp. soda
3 cups quick-cooking oats
½ cup chopped nuts or coconut

Cream margarine and sugars. Add eggs and vanilla, and beat well. Add salt, flour and soda; mix. Fold in oats and nuts or coconut. Shape into roll. Wrap in wax paper and chill. Slice. Bake on ungreased cookie sheet at 350° for 8 - 10 minutes. Do not over-bake cookies.

Yield: 5 dozen cookies

Marianne Gosser
Marcella Nofziger

PEANUT BLOSSOMS

1¾ cups flour
1 tsp. soda
½ tsp. salt
½ cup sugar
½ cup brown sugar
½ cup shortening

½ cup peanut butter
1 egg
2 Tb. milk
1 tsp. vanilla
Bag of Hershey Kisses

Mix all ingredients except Kisses. Roll batter into balls the size of a jacks ball. Roll balls in sugar and place on a non-greased baking sheet. Bake until slightly cracked in 350° oven. Place opened Hershey Kisses on top of cookies while hot.

Yield: 5 dozen cookies

Cathy Olsen

GRANDMOTHER'S PEANUT BUTTER COOKIES

1 cup sugar
1 cup brown sugar
1 cup shortening
1 cup peanut butter

2 eggs
2½ cups flour
1 tsp. soda
¼ tsp. salt

Cream sugars with shortening. Add peanut butter and eggs and mix well. Add flour, soda and salt. Make into balls and flatten tops with a fork. Bake at 350° for 8 - 10 minutes.

Yield: 4 - 5 dozen cookies

Madeline Johnson

PECAN PIE COOKIES

1 cup margarine
½ cup sugar
½ cup dark corn syrup

2 eggs, separated
2½ cups flour

Stir margarine and sugar in a large bowl. Add corn syrup and egg yolks; beat until thoroughly blended. Stir in flour gradually. Chill several hours. Beat egg whites slightly. Using one tablespoonful of dough for each cookie, roll into balls. Brush very lightly with egg white. Place 2 inches apart on greased cookie sheet. Bake at 375° for five minutes. Remove from oven. Roll ½ teaspoon of chilled pecan filling into a ball and firmly press into the center of each cookie. Return to oven; bake 5 minutes longer or until lightly browned.

PECAN FILLING:

½ cup powdered sugar
¼ cup margarine

3 Tb. dark corn syrup
½ cup chopped pecans

Combine sugar, margarine and corn syrup in saucepan; stir to blend. Cook over medium heat, stirring occasionally, until mixture reaches a full boil. Remove from heat and stir in pecans. Chill.

Yield: 4 dozen cookies

Laura Harper

PRALINE CANDY COOKIE

1 stick margarine
2 cups sugar
1 five and 3/10-ounce can
  evaporated milk
20 large marshmallows

Dash salt
1¾ cup graham cracker crumbs
1 cup chopped pecans
1 tsp. vanilla

Combine margarine, sugar and evaporated milk in 2½-quart saucepan. Stir to mix well; bring to a boil over medium heat. Boil for 3 minutes, stirring constantly. Remove from heat and add marshmallows and salt. Very quickly add graham cracker crumbs, pecans, and vanilla; beat vigorously until well-blended. Quickly drop by tablespoonfuls onto wax paper. Let cool. Store in airtight container.

Yield: 3 - 4 dozen cookies

Becky Witcher

FROSTED PUMPKIN SPICE COOKIES

½ cup shortening	1 tsp. salt
1 cup sugar	2½ tsp. cinnamon
2 eggs, beaten	½ tsp. nutmeg
1 cup solid-pack pumpkin	¼ tsp. ginger
2 cups sifted flour	1 cup raisins
1 tsp. baking powder	1 cup chopped nuts

Cream shortening with sugar. Add eggs and pumpkin; mix well. Sift flour, baking powder, salt and spices together. Add to pumpkin mixture; mix well. Add raisins and nuts. Drop by heaping teaspoonfuls onto greased cookie sheet. Bake in 350° oven about 15 minutes or until firm to touch. Cool and frost.

FROSTING:

2 cups confectioners' sugar	1 Tb. grated lemon rind
1 Tb. lemon juice	Milk

Combine sugar, lemon juice and lemon rind. Add enough milk to frosting to spread easily.

Yield: 4 dozen cookies

Kay Redman

SESAME WAFERS

⅔ cup sesame seeds	1 egg
½ cup butter, room temperature	1 cup sifted flour
½ cup sugar	1 tsp. vanilla
½ cup packed dark brown sugar	⅛ tsp. salt

Preheat oven to 275°. Place sesame seeds in pie plate and bake until toasted; about 10 minutes. Let cool. Preheat oven to 350°. Grease baking sheets. Cream butter with sugars in large bowl. Stir in egg. Add flour, vanilla, salt and sesame seeds; mix well. Drop onto cookie sheets by rounded half-teaspoonfuls about 3 inches apart. Bake wafers until caramel-colored, about 10 - 12 minutes.

Yield: 6 dozen cookies

Edwina Whalen

When transporting a pie with meringue, place a wet pie plate over the pie and the meringue won't pull off.

OLD FASHIONED SUGAR COOKIES

4¼ cups flour
1 tsp. soda
1 tsp. cream of tartar
1 cup margarine
1 cup sugar

1 cup powdered sugar
2 eggs, beaten
1 tsp. salt
1 cup oil
2 tsp. lemon extract

Sift together flour, soda and cream of tartar. Cream margarine, sugar and powdered sugar. Mix dry and creamed ingredients together. Chill for 1 hour. Remove from refrigerator, roll in walnut-sized balls, and place on cookie sheet. Dip bottom of a glass in oil and then in sugar; flatten cookie with end of glass. Bake at 350° for 10 - 15 minutes.

Yield: 6 dozen cookies

Sue Lackie

WEDDING COOKIES

1 cup margarine, softened
1 cup powdered sugar
½ tsp. vanilla

1¾ cups all-purpose flour
½ cup finely chopped pecans

Cream margarine and ½ cup sugar until light and fluffy. Add vanilla and flour; continue beating until well-mixed. Stir in nuts. Cover and chill dough overnight. Preheat oven to 350°. Shape into 1-inch balls and place on ungreased cookie sheet. Bake for 15 minutes. Remove from cookie sheet to cool. Roll in remaining powdered sugar. Wait several minutes and roll again in powdered sugar.

Yield: 3 dozen cookies

Laura Harper

Keep cookies soft by placing a piece of bread or cut apple into the container.

APRICOT BALLS

1½ cups ground dried apricots   ½ cup sweetened-condensed milk
2 cups coconut

Mix thoroughly and roll into small balls. Roll in powdered sugar.

Servings 80   Margaret Kennedy

BRANDY BALLS

2½ cups crushed vanilla   ½ cup chopped walnuts
    wafers   ¼ cup brandy
1 cup sifted powdered sugar   ¼ cup light corn syrup
2 Tb. cocoa powder   Granulated sugar

Combine vanilla wafers, powdered sugar, cocoa, and nuts. Stir in brandy and corn syrup. Add about ¼ tsp. water if necessary to form mixture into ¾-inch balls. Roll in granulated sugar. Store in tightly covered container.

Yield: 4 dozen   Edwina Whalen

CARAMEL CORN

5 quarts popped corn, seasoned   ½ cup light corn syrup
    (about 1 cup unpopped)   ¼ tsp. cream of tartar
2 cups brown sugar   ½ tsp. baking soda
½ cup oleo

Combine brown sugar, oleo, corn syrup, and cream of tartar. Bring to boil over medium heat, stirring constantly until sugar is dissolved. Cook rapidly for 5 minutes, stirring occasionally. Remove from heat. Add soda and stir. As foam begins to go down, pour over popped corn. Stir well to coat all the corn. Place corn in two 9 x 13-inch pans and bake in 200° oven for two hours. Stir occasionally.

Patty Lowe

CHOCOLATE COVERED BON-BONS

1 fourteen-ounce can sweetened-
  condensed milk
1 stick butter, softened
2 packages confectioner's sugar
8 ounces Angel Flake coconut

1 cup finely chopped pecans
¼ pound paraffin (1 sheet)
1 twelve-ounce package semi-sweet
  chocolate chips

Mix milk, sugar and butter well. Stir in coconut and pecans. Chill in mixing bowl for 20 minutes. After chilling, shape into quarter-sized balls on cookie sheet. Cover top with wax paper and chill 30 minutes. Melt chocolate and paraffin in double-boiler. Dip balls in chocolate with toothpicks and return to cookie sheets. After about an hour, these can be stored in containers in a cool place (not refrigerator) indefinitely.

Servings: 5 dozen

Rosemary Russell

DATE LOAF CANDY

3 cups sugar
1 cup evaporated milk
2 Tb. white Karo syrup
3 Tb. butter

1 eight-ounce package dates,
  finely chopped
1 cup chopped nuts

Place sugar, milk, syrup, butter and dates in pan and cook until soft ball stage. Remove from heat, add nuts, and beat with mixer. Wrap in damp cloth in a long roll. Chill for at least 2 hours. Slice and serve.

Serves: 4 dozen

Susan Plunkett

DIVINITY

2½ cups sugar
½ cup light corn syrup
2 egg whites

¼ tsp. salt
½ cup water
½ cup chopped pecans (optional)

In 2-quart saucepan, combine sugar, corn syrup, salt, and water. Cook to hard-ball stage (260°). Stir only until sugar dissolves. Beat egg whites until they form stiff peaks. Gradually pour syrup over egg whites. Beat at high speed. Add vanilla (and nuts, if desired) and beat until candy holds shape (4 - 5 minutes). Quickly drop by teaspoonfuls onto wax paper. For best results prepare candy on a sunny day.

Elizabeth Edwards

281

MILLION DOLLAR FUDGE

12 one-fourth-ounce plain Hershey
  bars
1 twelve-ounce package Hershey
  chips
1 small jar marshmallow cream

1 Tb. butter
1 tsp. vanilla
4½ cups sugar
1 thirteen-ounce can evaporated milk
1½-2 cups pecans

Mix the following ingredients in a 6 - 8 quart container: Hershey bars, (break into pieces), Hershey chips, marshmallow cream, butter, and vanilla. Mix the following ingredients in a 4 - 6 quart sauce pan: 4½ cups sugar and 1 thirteen-ounce can evaporated milk. Let sugar and milk come to a boil. After it starts to boil, cook 6 minutes. Pour mixture of sugar and evaporated milk over remaining ingredients. Blend until smooth and creamy. After mixture is completely blended, add the pecans. Fold in pecans and pour into greased pans. Let stand 4 - 6 hours. Chill.

Makes 6 pounds   Susan Plunkett

MILLIONAIRES

1 fourteen-ounce package
  Kraft caramels
3 Tb. milk
2 cups broken pecan pieces

Margarine or butter
1 Tb. shortening
1 twelve-ounce package milk
  chocolate morsels

Melt carmels with milk over low heat. Add pecans and stir. Drop by teaspoonfuls onto buttered Saran Wrap. Chill in refrigerator on cookie sheet about one hour, until hard. Melt shortening and morsels in saucepan over low heat. Remove from heat. Dip candy pieces into chocolate and return to plastic wrap on cookie sheet. Chill again.

Variation: Use semi-sweet morsels instead of milk chocolate or mix the two. Fudge caramels may be used for double chocolate taste.

Servings: 3 - 3½ dozen   Susan Langley

ORANGE SUGAR-COATED NUTS

1½ cups sugar
½ cup orange juice

2 cups nuts

Cook sugar and orange juice until mixture reaches soft-ball stage (240°). Remove from heat and add 2 cups nuts. Stir until syrup begins to look cloudy. Drop onto wax paper. Store in container.

Cathy Simpson

OLYMPIA CREAM

3 cups sugar
2 cups milk
½ cup white Karo

2 Tb. butter
1 tsp. vanilla
1 cup chopped nuts

Mix sugar, milk, Karo, and butter in extra-large sauce pan (mixture will boil up high). Cook over medium low heat until a firm ball forms in a cup of cold water. Remove from heat. Let stand until pan is warm to touch of hand. Beat with electric beater or by hand until mixture loses gloss. Add nuts. May be turned into buttered dish or onto two squares of buttered wax paper. Pour half of mixture on each square and roll up. Chill and slice.

Serves: 4 dozen

Liz Laughter

PEANUT BRITTLE

2 cups sugar
1 cup light corn syrup
½ cup water
1 cup butter

3 cups raw peanuts
2 tsp. soda
Salt

Mix sugar, corn syrup and water in sauce pan and cook till clear. Add butter. Heat to soft crack stage. Add peanuts. Heat to hard crack (305°). Add soda, stir, and pour onto buttered cookie sheets. Sprinkle with salt.

Mary Lou Hindsman

PEANUT BUTTER BARS

2 sticks oleo
1 cup grapham cracker crumbs
4 cups powdered sugar

1 cup peanut butter
1 large package milk chocolate
   chips

Melt oleo. Mix oleo, crumbs, powdered sugar and peanut butter in 13 x 9-inch pan. Pat down to cover pan. Melt chips in double boiler. Pour over crumb mixture. Cool and slice.

Servings: 15 - 20

Sally Boyd

283

PEANUT BUTTERSCOTCH TURTLES

2 packages butterscotch chips
½ cup crunchy peanut butter

1 five and ¾-ounce can LaChoy
Noodles

Melt butterscotch chips and peanut butter in double boiler. Remove from heat. Stir in noodles. Spoon onto wax paper. Will stiffen in 15 minutes.

Servings: 60

Nedra Wood

SUE'S PECAN PRALINES

1⅔ cups white sugar
⅔ cup water
¼ pound butter (do not substitute)

⅔ cup white sugar
3 cups pecans
1 tsp. vanilla

Combine sugar, water and 2 tablespoons butter in large pan and bring to a boil. Melt ⅔ cup sugar in a skillet until golden, being careful not to let the sugar become too brown. When melted, add to sugar and water. Stir until dissolved. Add pecans and cook until soft ball is formed when dropped into cold water. Remove from heat. Add balance of butter and vanilla. Beat until color changes and candy thickens. Drop by tablespoonfuls onto wax paper. Put in cool place. (If candy thickens too soon, add 1 teaspoon milk and heat until thin).

Servings: 42

Mary Snead

ENGLISH TOFFEE

1 cup butter (not margarine)
1 cup sugar
3 Tb. water
1 tsp. vanilla

½ cup shaved or grated Hershey bar
(Shave chocolate when very hard
or frozen.)
¼ cup finely chopped pecans

Stir together butter, sugar, and water until sugar melts and is amber in color. Candy thermometer should read 320°. Remove from heat and add vanilla. Pour into buttered pan immediately, as mixture will harden fast. Sprinkle with shaved chocolate and chopped pecans. Twist pan to crack candy.

Barbara Althoff

Microwave

RULES FOR CONVERTING CONVENTIONAL RECIPES TO MICROWAVE

Many of your favorite recipes can be easily converted to microwave recipes. By following some simple steps and guidelines, you will be able to turn your own often-used recipes into microwave delights.

—Start with a familiar recipe while learning the techniques of conversion. Knowing how the food should look and taste will assist you in adapting it.

—Find a written-for-microwave recipe similar to your conventional one, and follow it as a guide using the ingredients called for in your recipe.

—To establish microwave cooking times, start with one-fourth the conventional time. For example, if a recipe cooks conventionally in sixty minutes, fifteen minutes will be a rule of thumb for microwaving. If more time is needed, a minute or two can always be added.

—Always undercook and check for doneness. Add additional cooking time if necessary. Overcooking is the major problem for beginning microwavers: it is the most common cause of failure with microwave cooking.

—Reduce liquid to about ¾. Microwave's faster cooking does not permit the evaporation of liquid that we have come to expect from conventional cooking. More liquid may be added during cooking if it is needed to make the microwave version match conventional results.

—In microwave cooking foods continue to cook up to 5 minutes after the programmed cooking time. Always allow this standing time; if food is not done, then additional microwave time is necessary.

NUTS AND BOLTS

6 Tb. butter
1 one-ounce envelope Italian salad
   dressing mix with cheese
1 tsp. Worcestershire sauce
⅛ tsp. garlic powder

⅛ tsp. Tabasco
4 cups Corn Chex or Wheat Chex
3 cups pretzel sticks
1 cup salted mixed nuts

Melt butter in glass mixing bowl on MEDIUM for 1 minute. Add dressing mix, Worcestershire sauce, garlic powder and Tabasco. Stir. Add remaining ingredients and toss. Microwave on MEDIUM for 3 - 5 minutes, stirring once. Let cool and store in airtight container.

Yield: 8 cups

CHEESE AND ONION QUICHE

CRUST

1 cup flour	⅓ cup plus 1 Tb. butter
½ tsp. salt	3 to 4 Tb. ice water

Toss flour and salt together. Cut in butter with a pastry knife. Sprinkle with water, 1 Tb. at a time, using only enough to form a firm ball of dough. Chill. Roll out to fit an 8 or 9-inch pie plate. Ease dough into plate without stretching. Trim dough overhang and fold under. Flute folded edge. Prick well with a fork. Microwave on HIGH 2 minutes. Prick again and push up crust if it has slipped. Microwave on HIGH 2 minutes or until crisp.

FILLING

1 onion, finely chopped	1 cup shredded Cheddar or
2 Tb. butter	Gruyere cheese
5 to 6 slices bacon, fried crisp	¼ tsp. salt
in microwave	Pinch of white pepper
2 or more eggs	½ tsp. mustard
¾ cup evaporated milk or	¼ tsp. thyme
light cream	

Place onions and butter in 2-cup measure. Microwave 2 minutes on HIGH or until onions are transparent. Spread in bottom of baked quiche shell, and sprinkle with crumbled bacon. Beat eggs lightly. Stir in milk or cream, cheese, salt, pepper, mustard and thyme. Pour over onions and bacon. Microwave on HIGH 6 - 7 minutes, until knife inserted near center comes out clean. (Other ingredients, such as cooked broccoli, cooked spinach, mushrooms, etc. may be added before final baking.)

Serves: 6 - 8   Marcella Nofziger

RICE AND CHEESE BAKE

2 eggs, beaten	¼ tsp. black pepper
¾ cup half-and-half	Dash of ground red pepper
3 cups cooked rice	1 cup grated Swiss or Cheddar
½ tsp. salt	cheese
½ tsp. onion powder	2 Tb. chopped parsley
½ tsp. dry mustard	

Combine ingredients in shallow 2-quart dish. Cook on HIGH 3 minutes. Stir well. Cook 3 - 4 minutes more on HIGH.

Serves: 6   Becky Hight

SWISS BROCCOLI CASSEROLE

1 bunch fresh broccoli
1 ten and ¾-ounce can cream of
  celery soup
½ soup can milk

1 three-ounce can French-fried
  onion rings
½ cup grated Swiss cheese

Wash broccoli, removing large outer leaves and tough stalks. Slit stems to speed cooking. Arrange broccoli in a 9 x 13-inch dish with stems to outside. Cover. Microwave on HIGH for 10 - 12 minutes. Combine soup and milk. Pour over broccoli. Sprinkle with grated cheese and onion rings. Microwave on MEDIUM for 1½ minutes.

Jeanne Dimond

TANGY MUSTARD CAULIFLOWER

1 medium head cauliflower
2 Tb. water
½ cup mayonnaise

1 tsp. prepared mustard
¼ tsp. minced onion
½ cup shredded Cheddar cheese

Place cauliflower in 1½-quart casserole. Add 2 Tb. water. Cook covered 7 or 8 minutes on HIGH or until just about tender. Combine mayonnaise, onion and mustard. Spread mayonnaise mixture over top and about halfway down sides. Sprinkle with cheese. Cook uncovered 1 minute to heat topping and melt cheese.

Variation: The topping can be spooned over cooked cauliflower florets. For 10-ounce package use half of topping amounts.

Serves: 6

Janice Davies

POTATO CASSEROLE

4 cups potatoes, peeled, sliced
  and quartered
¼ cup water
¼ cup margarine
½ Ten and ¾-ounce can cream of
  chicken soup

1 cup shredded Cheddar cheese
½ cup sour cream
2 Tb. minced onion
3 Tb. margarine, melted
½ cup cornflakes, crushed

Combine potatoes and water in 1½-quart glass dish. Microwave, covered, on HIGH for 10 minutes, stirring once. Combine margarine and soup in a 2-cup glass measure. Microwave on HIGH for 1 minute. Stir until smooth. Stir in cheese, sour cream, and minced onion. Stir in potatoes. Microwave, covered, on HIGH for 3 - 4 minutes. Allow to stand, covered, 10 minutes. Mix melted margarine and cornflakes. Sprinkle on potatoes.

Serves: 4 - 6

Becky Hight

SQUASH CASSEROLE

2 pounds (7-8 cups) yellow
  squash, sliced
⅓ cup chopped onion
⅓ cup chopped celery
¼ cup water
1 egg

⅔ cup bread or cracker crumbs
1 pound Velveeta process cheese,
  grated
⅔ cup Pepperidge Farm cornbread
  stuffing
4 Tb. margarine, melted

Combine squash, onion, celery and water in a 2-quart glass casserole. Microwave, uncovered, on HIGH for 13 - 15 minutes or until tender. Drain well. Mash. Stir in egg, cracker crumbs, and cheese. Blend well.* Mix stuffing mix with melted margarine. Sprinkle evenly over top of squash. Microwave, uncovered, on HIGH 6 - 7 minutes.

*Can be frozen at this point. When ready to serve, defrost on 30% power for 7-10 minutes. Stir well and add crumb topping. Microwave on HIGH 6 - 7 minutes.

Serves: 8

Linda Adams
Whirlpool Microwave Specialist
North Little Rock

MICROWAVE ZUCCHINI

1 medium-size zucchini
½ - ¼ cup oil
¼ cup Parmesan cheese

¼ cup bread crumbs
Dash of salad seasoning

Cut zucchini into lengthwise quarters. Roll in oil; roll in mixture of Parmesan, bread crumbs, and seasonings. Place on a plate and microwave on HIGH for 4 or 5 minutes until just soft.

BAKED CHICKEN

½ stick butter
1 whole fryer

1 Brown-in-Bag
1 package onion soup mix

Melt butter in cup. Brush over entire chicken. Place chicken in Brown-in-Bag. Pour onion soup over chicken and shake. Twist ends of bag together, and tuck under chicken. (Do not use twister seal with metal.) Puncture bag on top so that it will not explode. Place in glass dish. Microwave on HIGH 18 - 20 minutes. (In older ovens bake 10 minutes; then rotate ½ turn and bake 10 more minutes.) When chicken is done, remove from bag and dish. Thicken juice with two Tb. flour or corn starch to make delicious gravy.

Serves: 6 - 8

Marcella Nofziger

CHICKEN PARMESAN

2½ - 3 pounds chicken, cut up
1 egg, beaten
1 ten and ¾-ounce can condensed
  golden mushroom soup

⅓ cup milk

CRUMB MIXTURE:

½ cup cornflake crumbs
½ cup Parmesan cheese

¼ tsp. oregano
Dash each: salt, pepper, thyme

Dip chicken in beaten egg and roll in crumb mixture. In a 2-quart baking dish, arrange chicken with meaty pieces to outer edges. Microwave on HIGH for 10 minutes. Combine soup and milk and pour over chicken. Microwave on HIGH 8 minutes. Sprinkle with parsley and remaining crumbs.

Lou Kelly

SWEET AND SOUR MEATBALLS

1 pound ground beef
1 egg, lightly beaten
¼ cup onion, finely chopped
1¼ cup bread crumbs
1 tsp. salt

⅛ tsp. pepper
1 Tb. parsley flakes
1 fourteen-ounce bottle catsup
1 cup red currant jelly

Lightly but thoroughly combine first seven ingredients. Shape into 40-48 small bite-sized meatballs. Arrange about 24 meatballs on a glass pie plate. Cover with paper towel. Microwave on HIGH 4 - 5 minutes, turning meatballs over. Rearrange on dish halfway through cooking. Drain well. Repeat procedure with remaining meatballs. Put meatballs in a microwave-safe fondue pot or chafing dish. Place catsup and jelly in a 2-cup measuring cup. Microwave 1 minute on HIGH. Stir well. Pour over meatballs. Microwave on HIGH 3 - 4 minutes or until meatballs are of serving temperature.

Linda Adams
Whirlpool Microwave Specialist
North Little Rock

A wet newspaper can be dried in the microwave on low setting.

Hot compress: It's easier to wring out a cold, wet towel than a hot one. Heat a wet towel in microwave for about 1 minutes. Place carefully on those aches and pains.

MEAT LOAF

2 pounds ground beef
1 package dry onion soup mix
1 egg, beaten
½ cup cracker crumbs, crushed

½ tsp. salt
⅛ tsp. garlic salt
1 eight-ounce can tomato sauce
1 two-ounce can chopped mushrooms

Combine meat, soup mix, eggs, crackers, and seasonings. Press into casserole in ring shape. Cover with wax paper. Microwave on HIGH for 14 minutes. Remove drippings. Pour combined tomato sauce and mushrooms into ring. Microwave on HIGH for 2 - 3 minutes. Let stand, covered, 4 minutes.

Serves: 4 - 6

Becky Hight

MEXICAN CASSEROLE

1 pound ground beef
1 small onion, chopped
1 ten and ¾-ounce can cream a
  chicken soup
1 ten-ounce can Ro-Tel tomatoes
  and Green Chilies

1½ cups grated cheese
1 nine-ounce package of tortilla
  chips, crushed

Crumble beef and onion in glass bowl. Microwave on HIGH for 5 minutes. Stir and drain once. Mix soup, Ro-Tel, and cheese. In large casserole layer chips, beef mixture and Ro-Tel mixture. Repeat. Microwave on MEDIUM 10 - 12 minutes.

Serves: 6

Mary Lee Henderson

VEGETABLE SOUP

2 cups beef broth
1 cup hot water
1 sixteen-ounce can whole tomatoes,
  chopped
¾ cup shredded carrot
¼ cup chopped onion

¾ cup chopped celery
1 bay leaf
1 tsp. salt
⅛ tsp. pepper
Dash marjoram
Dash thyme

In large casserole, combine all ingredients. Heat, covered, on HIGH 9 - 10 minutes. Heat, covered, on MEDIUM 20 minutes. Let stand, covered, 5 minutes before serving.

Mary Lee Henderson

CRUSTLESS SAUSAGE QUICHE

1 sixteen-ounce package seasoned
   bulk pork sausage
8 eggs
½ cup milk
¼ tsp. salt
⅛ tsp. pepper
1 cup shredded Cheddar cheese
1 cup shredded Swiss cheese

Crumble sausage into glass quiche dish or 8-inch round casserole. Microwave, covered with a paper towel, on HIGH power for 5 - 6 minutes or until meat is no longer pink, stirring to break apart after half the time. Break sausage into small pieces; drain well. Spread evenly. Set aside. Beat eggs, milk, salt, and pepper in 2-quart dish. Reduce power to MEDIUM (50%). Microwave 5 - 7 minutes or until eggs are set but still very moist, stirring every 2 minutes. Stir in cheeses; pour over sausage. Cover with wax paper. Microwave on MEDIUM (50%) 6 - 8 minutes, or until center is set, but slightly moist on top, rotating ¼ turn at 3 minutes. Allow to stand, covered, 5 minutes before serving.

Leftovers are easily reheated in the microwave. For each serving microwave on HIGH, uncovered, 45 - 60 seconds.

Serves: 6 - 8

Linda Adams
Whirlpool Microwave Specialist
North Little Rock

VEAL ARTICHOKE HASH

3 Tb. flour
½ tsp. salt
¼ tsp. pepper
1½ pounds ground veal
2 Tb. butter
½ tsp. leaf basil
1 tsp. paprika
1 Tb. parsley flakes
1 clove garlic, minced
1 four-ounce can mushroom
   stems and pieces
1 two-ounce jar chopped pimientos,
   drained
1 nine-ounce can artichoke
   quarters, drained
2 Tb. corn starch
1 thirteen and ½-ounce can
   chicken broth

Blend flour, salt, pepper, and veal in a bowl. Melt butter in a casserole. Add meat mixture and microwave on MEDIUM, covered, for 10 minutes. Add basil, paprika, garlic, parsley, mushrooms, pimientos and artichokes. Stir into meat mixture. Blend cornstarch and broth in small bowl. Pour over meat and vegetable mixture. Cover and microwave on LOW 26 - 28 minutes. Let stand, covered, 5 minutes. Stir well before serving.

Delicious served over rice.

Serves: 4 - 6

Carolyn Crews

SLOPPY JOES

1 pound ground beef
½ cup finely chopped onion
½ cup catsup

¼ cup sweet pickle relish
4 hamburger rolls

Crumble ground beef into round baking dish. Add onion. Heat on HIGH 5 - 7 minutes, stirring once or twice. Drain. Add catsup and relish and heat on HIGH 3 - 4 minutes. Stir. Heat on MEDIUM 4 minutes, stirring once. Serve over hamburger rolls.

Serves: 4

Mary Lee Henderson

CHERRIES JUBILEE

1 sixteen-ounce bag
   unsweetened, frozen, pitted,
   dark sweet cherries
1 Tb. plus 1 tsp. corn starch

⅓ cup currant jelly
2 Tb. sugar
¼ cup cherry brandy
Vanilla ice cream

Thaw frozen cherries and drain juice into 2-quart dish. Mix in corn starch. Add jelly and sugar. Cook on HIGH, uncovered, 2½ minutes or until thickened, stirring 2 - 3 times. Add cherries and any remaining juice. Cook on HIGH, uncovered, for 3 minutes or until cherries are hot. Put brandy in a glass measuring cup. Heat on HIGH for 25 seconds. Pour brandy over cherry sauce and ignite. Spoon over ice cream.

Serves:6

Carol Long

BANANAS FOSTER

⅓ cup butter or oleo
3 Tb. granulated brown sugar or
   1½ Tb. liquid brown sugar
¼ tsp. cinnamon

¼ cup light corn syrup
3 Tb. lemon juice
4 bananas, cut into 1-inch pieces

Mix first 5 ingredients and microwave, uncovered, on HIGH for 1½ minutes or until mixture is melted and bubbly. Add bananas and microwave on HIGH for 2 minutes or until fruit is warmed. Stir until bananas are glazed well. Serve warm over vanilla ice cream.

If desired, flame ⅓ cup rum on top before serving over ice cream.

Bobbie McKenzie

RAVE REVIEWS

EASY FUDGE

1 one-pound box confectioners'
    sugar
½ cup cocoa
¼ tsp. salt
¼ cup evaporated milk

½ cup (¼ pound) butter or
    margarine
1 Tb. vanilla
1 cup chopped nuts

Mix sugar, cocoa, salt, and milk together in a 1½-quart microwave-safe casserole. Mixture will be stiff and not thoroughly blended. Place butter or margarine over top of mixture in center of dish. Microwave 2 minutes on HIGH. Butter or margarine will not be completely melted. Stir vigorously. Add vanilla and chopped nuts. Stir until blended and pour into a wax paper-lined 8 x 4 x 3-inch dish. Chill for 1 hour in the refrigerator or 25 minutes in the freezer. Cut into squares.

Yield: 24 squares

Wincie Hughes
Home Economist, G.E.

EASY PEANUT BRITTLE

1 cup raw peanuts
1 cup sugar
½ cup white corn syrup
⅛ tsp. salt

1 tsp. vanilla
1 tsp. butter or oleo
1 tsp. baking soda

In two-quart microwave-safe casserole, stir together first 4 ingredients and microwave on HIGH for 8 minutes. Stir well at 4 minutes. Add vanilla and oleo and stir. Microwave 1½ - 2 minutes on HIGH. Add baking soda and stir quickly until light and foamy. Pour immediately onto lightly buttered baking sheet. Spread thin. When cool, break into pieces.

Easy and foolproof idea for Christmas gifts.

Bobbie McKenzie

Put an open box of hard brown sugar in the microwave with 1 cup of hot water. Cook on HIGH 2 minutes for ½ pound, 3 minutes for 1 pound.

Heat liqueur for flaming desserts on HIGH 10 - 15 seconds. Pour over dessert and ignite.

IMPOSSIBLE PUMPKIN PIE

1 cup sugar
½ cup Bisquick baking mix
2 Tb. margarine, melted
1 thirteen-ounce can evaporated
   milk, less ¼ cup

2 eggs
1 sixteen-ounce can pumpkin
2½ tsp. cinnamon
2 tsp. vanilla

Mix all ingredients together and beat until smooth. Pour into a buttered 10-inch pie plate. Microwave 20 - 22 minutes on MEDIUM power (70%). If center of pie looks undercooked at the end of the cooking time, let stand up to five minutes. If a knife inserted into the center does not come out clean, microwave the pie for another minute or two. Let pie cool. Serve with whipped cream.

Serves: 8 - 10

Wincie Hughes
Home Economist, G.E.

To dry herbs, place 4 - 6 washed branches between 2 paper towels. Cook on HIGH 2 - 3 minutes or until brittle and dry. Separate leaves from stalks, place between 2 sheets of wax paper and crush with rolling pin. Store in glass jars with tight lids.

High-protein foods should not be cooked on full power in the microwave.

Warm baby food in original containers. Remove lid and microwave on HIGH
25 - 35 seconds. (Not recommended for egg yolks or meat dinners.)

Fast Caramel Apples: Place unwrapped caramels in a 1-quart bowl and microwave on HIGH 2½ minutes, stirring 3 times. Dip apples.

Vegetables are usually cooked on HIGH 7 minutes per pound.

Soften a stick of butter in microwave 1 minute on LOW.

To soften cream cheese, remove foil wrapper and microwave at MEDIUM for 1 - 1½ minutes.

Index

A

Acorn Squash à la Fruit 219
Adventure Cookies 272
Almond Cookies 272
Almond Pita Sandwiches, Chicken 123
Andrean-Style Sweet Roast Pork 16
Angel Coconut Pudding 234
APPETIZERS
  Artichoke Dip 47
  Baked Stuffed Mushrooms 53
  Black-Eyed Pea Dip 47
  Cajun Mistakes 56
  Cheese Ball 44
  Cheese Dip 47
  Cheese Krispies 61
  Cheese Puffs 62
  Chicken Liver and Water Chestnuts
    Hors D'Oeuvre 62
  Chinese Egg Roll Crêpes 62
  Cocktail Weiners 60
  Crab Meat Dip 48
  Cream Cheese 43
    Seafood Spread 43
    Pickapeppa Sauce 43
    Pepper Jelly 141
    Jezebel Sauce 140
  Cucumber Dip 49
  Cucumber Sandwiches 56
  Curried Mushrooms 53
  Curry Dip 49
  Delicious Cocktail Dip 49
  Dip for Raw Vegetables 50
  Dried Beef Cheese Ball 44
  Drunken Meat Balls 59
  Fiesta Appetizer Pie 50
  Frosted Nuts 54
  Glazed Pecans 55
  Good Seasons Italian Dip 50
  Granola 55
  Guacamole Dip 51
  Ham Ball 44
  Ham Cheese Ball 45
  Home Made Party Salami 57
  Hot Cheese Dip with Crab Meat 48
  Hot Dogs 61
  Hot Sauce 53
  Hot Spiced Meat Balls 59
  Jalapeño Cheese Ball 45
  Jalapeño Cheese Dip 48
  Jalapeño Cheese Squares 45
  Little Links in Oriental Sauce 61
  Mexican Pizza Dip 51
  Mexico Chiquito Cheese Dip 51
  Nix-Nax Party Mix 55
  Nuts and Bolts 287
  Olive-Tuna Canape Spread 57
  Party Nuts 56
  Party Rye Bread 57
  Paté 58
  Pineapple Cheese Ball 46
  Pizza Spread 58
  Sausage Balls 60
  Shrimp Ball 46
  Shrimp Cocktail Sauce 143
  Shrimp Dip 52
  Shrimp Log 46
  Smoky Salmon Cheese Spread 58
  Stuffed Mushrooms 54
  Stuffed Mushrooms with Bacon 54
  Sweet and Sour Meatballs 60
  Tamale Dip 52
  Torta Risa (Northern Italy) 43
  Water Chestnut Dip 52
Apple Bread 78
Apple Cake, Bernice McNeill's Fresh .. 250
Apple Cake, Fresh 251
Apple Cake, German 250
Apple Creme Pie 243
Apple Crisp 227
Apple Muffins, Favorite 87
Apple Pancake, Big-Mama's 88
Apple Pie Filling 36
Apples, Baked 227
Apricot Balls 280
Apricot Casserole, Baked 93
Apricot Date Bars 268
Apricot Nectar Cake 251
Apricot Salad I 93
Apricot Salad II 94
Arkansas Omelette 129
Artichoke Casserole, Spinach and 218
Artichoke Dip 47
Artichoke Hearts, Veal and 163
Artichoke Soup, Cream of 115
Artichoke Veal Hash 293
Artichokes, Green Beans and 209
Asparagus Casserole 199
Asparagus Casserole,
  Party Shrimp and 156
Asparagus Elegante' 199
Aunt Mary's Chicken-Rice Casserole .. 181
Aunt Thelma's Cold Carrots 202
Avocado, Crab Stuffed 108
Avocado Sandwich 19
Avocado Shell, Creamed Chicken in ... 188
Avocado Soup, Cold 113

B

Bacon, and Beef Fillets 165
Bacon Garlic Cheese Grits 208
Bacon, Stuffed Mushrooms with 54
Baked Apples 227
Baked Apricot Casserole 93
Baked Beans 166
Baked Cheese Sandwich 123

299

Baked Chicken 290
Baked Chicken Sandwiches 123
Baked Eggplant 206
Baked Fish 150
Baked Oysters S.O.B. 38
Baked Spanish Eggplant 206
Baked Stuffed Eggplant 207
Baked Stuffed Mushrooms 53
Baklava 230
Banana Cake, Sour Cream 252
Banana Nut Bread, Hawaiian 78
Banana Nut Dressing 109
Bananas Foster 294
Banana Tea Bread 79
Bar-B-Q Brisket 164
Barbecue Sauce, Jiffy 143
Barbecued Shrimp 153
Basic Crêpe Batter 88
Batter Fried Squash 219
Bean Casserole, French 210
Bean Bundle, Green 210
Bean Salad, Three 106
Bean Soup 114
Bean Soup, Judge Roy 37
Bean Warm Up, Mexican Chili 199
Beans and Artichokes, Green 209
Beans and Rice, Red 200
Beans, Baked 166
Beans, Buffet Green 209
Beans, Delicious Green 210
Bechamel Sauce 139
Beef (see Meats)
Beef and Bacon Fillets 165
Beef Roll-Ups 156
Beef Stew, Delicious 121
Beef Soup, Ground 121
Beef Stroganoff I 157
Beef Stroganoff II 157
Beer Muffins 86
Beets, Orange 200
Bermuda Crush 65
Bernice McNeill's Fresh Apple Cake . . . 250
Better Brussels Sprouts 202
BEVERAGES
  Bermuda Crush 65
  Bloody Marys 71
  Brandied Cider 65
  D.J.'s Delight 65
  Eggnog 66
  Fog Cutter 66
  Frozen Margaritas 67
  Fruit Punch Tropicana 66
  Glögg 67
  Golden Summer Punch 67
  Hot Buttered Rum 68
  Hot Chocolate 68
  Hot Mulled Party Punch 68
  Hot Spiced Cider 69

  Kahlua 69
  Milk Punch 69
  Orange Flip 70
  Orange Julius 70
  Sangria 70
  Spiced Tea 71
  Rum Wassail 71
Big-Mama's Apple Pancake 88
Bing Cherry Salad 94
Biscuit Coffee Cake 84
Biscuits on Creamy Chicken 181
Biscuits, Pork Chops and Cheese 175
Biscuits, Quick 83
Biscuits, Rolls a la Canned 83
Black Bottom Cupcakes 268
Black-Eyed Pea Dip 47
Black-Eyed Peas 214
Bleu Cheese Dressing 109
Blueberry Muffins, Jordon Marsh 87
Blueberry Pie Supreme 243
Blueberry Salad 95
Bloody Marys 71
Bobbie's Broccoli 200
Bran Muffins 87
Brandied Cider 65
Brandy Alexander Souffle 232
Brandy Balls 280
BREADS
  Breads, Batter and Quick
    Apple Bread 78
    Banana Tea Bread 79
    Basic Crêpe Batter 88
    Beer Muffins 86
    Big-Mama's Apple Pancake 88
    Biscuit Coffee Cake 84
    Bran Muffins 87
    Cinnamon Fruit Crunchies 80
    Corn Spoon Bread 81
    Cranberry Coffee Cake 84
    Date Nut Bread 78
    Favorite Apple Muffins 87
    French Toast 86
    Glazed Orange Bread 79
    Hawaiian Banana Nut Bread 78
    Herbed Rolls 82
    Hush Puppies 85
    Indian Fry Bread 81
    Jordan Marsh Blueberry Muffins . . . 87
    Mexican Cornbread 85
    Popovers 89
    Pumpkin Bread 80
    Quick Biscuits 83
    Quick Cinnamon Coffee Cake 84
    Rolls a la Canned Biscuits 83
    Sausage Bread 81
    Shortbread 82
    Sour Cream Coffee Cake 85
    Speedy Crescents 83

Strawberry Bread 80
Super Easy Muffins 88
Waffles 89
Yorkshire Pudding 82
Breads, Yeast
Crescent Rolls 75
Dilly Bread 75
Donuts 86
Homemade Rolls 75
Monkey Bread 76
Pizza Shell 89
Refrigerator Rolls 76
Simple Croissants 77
Whole Wheat Bread with Honey 77
Bread and Butter-Pickles 141
Brisket, Bar-B-Q 164
Brisket, Roast, Company-is-Coming ... 164
Broccoli and Chicken Casserole 181
Broccoli Casserole 201
Broccoli, Bobbie's 200
Broccoli Casserole, Swiss 289
Broccoli Cauliflower Salad 100
Broccoli Souffle 201
Broiled Lemon Fish Fillet 151
Brownie Mix, Have-On-Hand 270
Brownie Torte, Mocha 236
Brownies 269
Brownies, Chocolate Peppermint 269
Brussels Sprouts, Better 202
Bubba's Favorite Hot Sauce 140
Buffet Green Beans 209
Butter Baked Peaches 228
Butter Cookies 273
Butter Nut Ice Cream 240
Butter, Whipped 139
Buttered Rum, Hot 68

C

Cabbage Rolls 166
Cabbage, Stir-Fry 202
CAKES
Cakes
Apricot Nectar Cake 251
Bernice McNeill's Fresh
Apple Cake 250
Carrot-Pineapple Cake 253
Cheesecake 25
Chocolate Cake Pudding 253
Chocolate Cheesecake 256
Chocolate Pound Cake 267
Coca Cola Cake 260
Coconut Cake Supreme 259
Coconut Rum Cake 258
Excellent Pound Cake 265
Extra-Moist Lemonade Cake 262
Festive Cake 258
Feud Cake 261

Five-Flavor Pound Cake 267
Fresh Apple Cake 251
Frozen Fruit Cake 261
German Apple Cake 250
Gooey Cake 264
Grandma Ward's Fruit Cake 260
Grasshopper Cake 257
Italian Cream Cake 257
Kaluha Cake 255
Milky Way Cake 259
Oatmeal Cake 262
Old-Fashioned Chocolate Cake ... 254
One-Hour Chocolate Cake
and Frosting 255
Orange-Raisin Cake 263
Piña Colada Cake 254
Pineapple Delight 263
Pineapple Jam Cake 264
Prune Cake 266
Sour Cream Banana Cake 252
Strawberry Cake 266
Strawberry Delight 265
Vanilla Crumb Cake 256
Very Special Lemon Cake 265
Cake Squares
Apricot Date Bars 268
Black Bottom Cup Cakes 268
Brownies 269
Caramel Layer Chocolate
Squares 270
Chocolate Chip Bars 270
Chocolate Peppermint Brownies .. 269
Cream Cheese Cupcakes 271
Have-On-Hand Brownie Mix 270
Lemon Squares 274
Maple Bars 271
Quick Chewy Bars 272
Camerones Cancun 23
Canapé Spread, Olive-Tuna 57
Candied Wild Duck 147
CANDIES
Apricot Balls 280
Brandy Balls 280
Caramel Corn 280
Chocolate Covered Bon-Bons 281
Date Loaf Candy 281
Divinity 281
Easy Fudge, Microwave 295
Easy Peanut Brittle, Microwave 295
English Toffee 284
Million Dollar Fudge 282
Millionaires 282
Olympia Cream 283
Orange Sugar-Coated Nuts 282
Peanut Brittle 283
Peanut Butter Bars 283
Peanut Butterscotch Turtles 284
Sue's Pecan Pralines 284

Cajun Mistakes 56
Caramel Corn 280
Caramel Ice Cream Dessert 239
Caramel Layer Chocolate Squares 270
Caramel Nut Slices 273
Carrot Casserole 203
Carrot Pineapple Cake 253
Carrot Ring 203
Carrot Soup, Cream of 116
Carrots, Aunt Thelma's Cold 202
Carrots, Sunshine 203
Catalina Salad Dressing 109
Cauliflower Casserole 204
Cauliflower, French Fried 204
Cauliflower Salad, Broccoli 100
Cauliflower, Tangy Mustard 289
Chalupas 167
Charlie's Cherries 227
Cheese and Eggs (see Eggs and Cheese)
Cheese and Onion Quiche 288
Cheese Ball 44
Cheese Ball, Dried Beef 44
Cheese Ball, Ham 45
Cheese Ball, Jalapeño 45
Cheese Ball, Pineapple 46
Cheese Biscuits, Pork Chops and 175
Cheese Buns, Tuna 125
Cheesecake 25
Cheesecake, Chocolate 256
Cheese Casserole, Potato, Ham and . . 174
Cheese, Cream 43
Cheese Dip 47
Cheese Dip, Jalapeño 48
Cheese Dip, Mexico Chiquito 51
Cheese Dip with Crabmeat, Hot 48
Cheese Grits, Bacon Garlic 208
Cheese Krispies 61
Cheese Noodles, Grecian Beef with . . . 158
Cheese Peta 133
Cheese Pie, Chiffon 244
Cheese Puffs 62
Cheese Sandwiches, Baked 123
Cheese Souffle' 133
Cheese Soup 113
Cheese Spread, Smoked Salmon 58
Cheese Squares, Jalapeño 45
Cheese Stuffed Pork 175
Cheesy Sour Cream Enchiladas 132
Cherries, Charlie's 227
Cherries Jubilee 294
Cherry Salad, Bing 94
Chicken (see Poultry)
Chicken Almond Pita Sandwiches 123
Chicken and Green Chili Pepper
    Casserole 183
Chicken and Stuffing Scallop 186
Chicken and Wild Rice Casserole 186
Chicken Breast Piquant 180

Chicken Breasts in Wine 182
Chicken Breasts-St. Louis 184
Chicken Hélène 185
Chicken Kiev 185
Chicken Liver and Water Chestnuts
    Hors D'Oeuvre 62
Chicken Parmesan 291
Chicken Roll-Ups 187
Chicken Romano 184
Chicken Salad, Hot 107
Chicken Salad, Polynesian 107
Chicken Sandwiches, Baked 123
Chicken-Sausage Casserole 182
Chicken Sherlen 182
Chicken with Chipped Beef 180
Chicken with Dumplings 183
Chicken with Zucchini and Corn 187
Chiffon Cheese Pie 244
Chili 113
Chili Bean Warm-Up, Mexican 199
Chili Beefsteak 160
Chili Egg Puff 131
Chili, Helen's 114
Chipped Beef, Chicken with 180
Chinese Egg Roll Crêpes 62
Chism Special 169
Chocolate Angel Pie
    with Meringue Crust 244
Chocolate Cake, Old Fashioned 254
Chocolate Cake, One-Hour 255
Chocolate Cake Pudding 253
Chocolate Cheesecake 256
Chocolate Chip Bars 270
Chocolate Covered Bon-Bons 281
Chocolate Dessert, Layered 234
Chocolate Drop Cookies 273
Chocolate, Hot 68
Chocolate Mousse 31
Chocolate Peppermint Brownies 269
Chocolate Pound Cake 267
Chocolate Squares, Caramel Layer . . . 270
Chocolate Tortilla Torte 235
Chowder, Corn 115
Chowder, Fish 117
Chowder, Sheepshead 33
Christmas Cookies 274
Christmas Cranberry Salad 95
Christmas Party Punch, Glögg 67
Christmas Ribbon Salad 96
Chuck Wagon Pepper Steak 158
Cider, Brandied 65
Cider, Hot Spiced 69
Cinnamon Coffee Cake, Quick 84
Cinnamon Fruit Crunchies 80
Cobbler Supreme, Peach 228
Coca Cola Cake 260
Cocktail Dip, Delicious 49
Cocktail Sauce, Shrimp 143

Cocktail Weiners 60
Coconut Cake Supreme 259
Coconut Cream Pie 245
Coconut Pudding, Angel 234
Coconut Rum Cake 258
Coffee Cake, Biscuit 84
Coffee Cake, Cranberry 84
Coffee Cake, Quick Cinnamon 84
Coffee Cake, Sour Cream 85
Cold Avocado Soup 113
Cold Meat Sauce 142
Company-Is-Coming Brisket Roast 164
CONDIMENTS
    Bechamel Sauce 139
    Bread and Butter Pickles 141
    Bubba's Favorite Hot Sauce 140
    Cold Meat Sauce 142
    Debbie's Marinade for Shiskabob . . . 143
    Hot Mustard 144
    Jalapeño Pepper Jelly 141
    Jezebel Sauce 140
    Jiffy Barbecue Sauce 143
    Pickled Squash 141
    Raisin Sauce 139
    Salsa 140
    Slang-Jang 142
    Shrimp Cocktail Sauce 143
    Super Easy Pickler 142
    Sweet and Sour Mustard 144
    Whipped Butter 139
COOKIES
    Adventure Cookies 272
    Almond Cookies 272
    Butter Cookies 273
    Caramel Nut Slices 273
    Chocolate Drop Cookies 273
    Christmas Cookies 274
    Frosted Pumpkin Spice Cookies 278
    Grandmother's Peanut Butter
        Cookies 276
    Holiday Cookies 274
    Lemon Cookies 275
    Molasses Cookies 275
    Oatmeal Crispies 276
    Old Fashioned Sugar Cookies 278
    Pecan Pie Cookies 277
    Peanut Blossoms 276
    Praline Candy Cookies 277
    Sesame Wafers 278
    Wedding Cookies 279
Corn, Caramel 280
Corn Casserole, Squash and 220
Corn, Chicken with Zucchini and 187
Corn Chowder 115
Corn, Creole 204
Corn Crisp Chicken 188
Corn Fremont 205
Corn Pudding 205

Corn Salad 100
Corn Spoon Bread 81
Cornbread, Mexican 85
Cornish Game Hens with Rice Stuffing . 188
Country Chicken 187
Crab (See Fish and Shellfish)
Crab, Deviled 39
Crab Meat Dip 48
Crab Meat, Hot Cheese Dip with 48
Crab Meat Remick 152
Crab Sandwich, Creamy 124
Crab Stuffed Avocado 108
Crab Stuffing 39
Cranberry Coffee Cake 84
Cranberry Salad, Christmas 95
Crawfish Etouffee 34
Cream Cheese 43
Cream Cheese Cupcakes 271
Creamed Chicken in Avocado Shell . . . 188
Cream of Artichoke Soup 115
Cream of Carrot Soup 116
Cream of Lettuce Soup 116
Creamy Chicken, Biscuits on 181
Creamy Crab Sandwich 124
Creole Corn 204
Creole, Oven Fried Chicken a la 192
Creole, Shrimp 155
Crêpe Batter, Basic 88
Crêpes, Chinese Egg Roll 62
Crêpes, Quiche 135
Crêpes, Special Chicken 195
Crescent Casserole, Zesty Italian 173
Crescent Chicken Roll-Ups 189
Crescent Chicken Squares 189
Crescent Rolls 75
Crescents, Speedy 83
Croissants, Simple 77
Crustless Sausage Quiche 293
Cucumber Dip 49
Cucumber Sandwiches 56
Cucumber Vichyssoise, Iced 118
Curried Hot Fruit 96
Curried Mushrooms 53
Curried Tuna Spaghetti 151
Curry Dip 49
Curry, Shrimp 155
Custard Pie, Egg 245

D

D. J.'s Delight 65
Darby's Deviled Eggs 132
Date Bar, Apricot 268
Date Loaf Candy 281
Date Nut Bread 78
Date Torte, Pumpkin 236
Debbie's Marinade for Shiskabob 143
Deep Delta Shrimp 154

Deep Dish Pizza 168
Delicious Beef Stew 121
Delicious Cocktail Dip 49
Delicious Fried Onion Rings 214
Delicious Green Beans 210
DESSERTS (Also see Cakes, Cookies,
    Candies and Pies)
  Angel Coconut Pudding 234
  Apple Crisp 227
  Baked Apples 227
  Baklava 230
  Bananas Foster 293
  Brandy Alexander Souffle' 232
  Butter Baked Peaches 228
  Butter Nut Ice Cream 240
  Caramel Ice Cream Dessert 239
  Charlie's Cherries 227
  Cherries Jubilee 293
  Chocolate Mousse 31
  Chocolate Tortilla Torte 235
  Double Lemon Fruit Cup 233
  Florendines 229
  Frozen Peppermint Pie 238
  Fruit Pizza 229
  Graham Cracker Sandwiches 231
  Heavenly Hot Fudge Sauce 241
  Layered Chocolate Dessert 234
  Lemon Cake Top Pudding 235
  Milky Way Ice Cream 240
  Mocha Brownie Torte 236
  Mocha Fudge Sauce 241
  Oreo Frozen Dessert 239
  Peach Cobbler Supreme 228
  Pecan Tassies 231
  Piña Colada Ice Cream 240
  Pretzel Jell-O 233
  Pumpkin Date Torte 236
  Strawberry French Torte 237
  Strawberry Torte 238
  Toffee Dessert 232
  Vanilla Ice Cream 241
Deviled Chicken 189
Deviled Crab 39
Deviled Eggs, Darby's 132
Dieter's Special Soup 116
Dilly Bread 75
Dinner Casserole 212
Dip for Raw Vegetables 50
Divinity 281
Dixie Pork Chops 176
Donuts 86
Dora's Chicken Pot Pie 190
Double Lemon Fruit Cup 233
Dressing (See Salads)
Dressing, Grandmother's Rice 216
Dressing, Mallard with Rice 148
Dried Beef Cheese Ball 44
Drop Cookies, Chocolate 273

Drunken Meat Balls 59
Duck (See Wild Game)
Duck Casserole 147
Ducks in Sherry 147
Dumplings, Chicken with 183
Dumplings with Sauerkraut, Roast
    Pork and 179

E

Easy Fudge 295
Easy Gazpacho 117
Easy Muffins, Super 88
Easy Orange Pork Chops 176
Easy Peanut Brittle 295
Easy Pickler, Super 142
Easy Salmon Patties, Quickend 151
Egg Brunch 130
Egg Casserole 131
Egg Custard Pie 245
Eggnog 66
Eggplant, Baked 206
Eggplant, Baked Spanish 206
Eggplant, Baked Stuffed 207
Eggplant Casserole 208
Eggplant Parmigiano 32
Eggplant, Shrimp Stuffed 207
Egg Roll Crêpes, Chinese 62
Egg Soup 117
EGGS AND CHEESE
  Arkansas Omelette 129
  Asparagus Quiche 134
  Cheese and Onion Quiche 288
  Cheese Peta 133
  Cheese Souffle' 133
  Cheesy Sour Cream Enchiladas 132
  Chili Egg Puff 131
  Crustless Sausage Quiche 293
  Darby's Deviled Eggs 132
  Egg Brunch 130
  Egg Casserole 131
  Eggs Benedict 130
  Fettuccine 132
  Fettuccini, The Villa's 40
  Good Morning Casserole 129
  Manicotti with Spinach 133
  Mushroom Scramble 131
  Quiche 134
  Quiche Crêpes 135
Eggs Benedict 130
Enchiladas, Cheesy Sour Cream 132
English Toffee 284
Escargot 22
Espagnole Sauce 28
Excellent Pound Cake 265
Extra Moist Lemonade Cake 262
Eye of Beef, Peppered 160

304

F

Favorite Apple Muffins 87
Festive Cake 258
Fettuccine 132
Fettuccini, The Villa's 40
Feud Cake 261
Fiesta Appetizer Pie 50

FISH AND SHELLFISH
    Baked Fish 150
    Baked Oysters S.O.B. 38
    Barbecued Shrimp 153
    Broiled Lemon Fish Fillet 151
    Camerones Cancun 23
    Crab Meat Dip 48
    Crabmeat Remick 152
    Crawfish Etoufee 34
    Curried Tuna Spaghetti 151
    Deep Delta Shrimp 154
    Deviled Crab/Crab Stuffing 39
    Escargot 22
    Hot Cheese Dip with Crab Meat 48
    Oysters Bienville 15
    Party Shrimp and Asparagus 156
    Pasta with White Clam Sauce ... 32
    Pezcado a la Veracruzano
        Chuachinango 29
    Quick and Easy Salmon Patties 151
    Scalloped Oysters 152
    Seafood Casserole 153
    Sheepshead Chowder 33
    Shrimp and Noodle Casserole ... 156
    Shrimp Creole 155
    Shrimp Curry 155
    Shrimp Gumbo (See Soups)
    Shrimp Ring 154
    Smoky Salmon Cheese Spread 58
Fish Chowder 117
Five-Flavor Pound Cake 267
Flip, Orange 70
Florendines 229
Fog Cutter 66
French Bean Casserole 210
French Fried Cauliflower 204
French Onion Scallop 213
French Onion Soup 118
French Toast 86
French Torte, Strawberry 237
Fresh Apple Cake 251
Fresh Apple Cake, Bernice McNeill's .. 250
Fried Chicken, Guaranteed Crispy 190
Fried Okra 213
Fried Onion Rings, Delicious 214
Fried Rice, Oriental 217
Fried Squash, Batter 219
Frito Salad 100
Frosted Nuts 54
Frosted Pumpkin Spice Cookies 278

Frozen Fruit Cake 261
Frozen Fruit Salad 96
Frozen Ham Sandwiches 124
Frozen Margaritas 67
Frozen Peppermint Pie 238
Frozen Strawberry Salad 97
Fruit Cake, Frozen 261
Fruit Cake, Grandma Ward's 260
Fruit Casserole, Hot 97
Fruit Crunchies, Cinnamon 80
Fruit, Curried Hot 96
Fruit Pizza 229
Fruit Punch Tropicana 66
Fruited Rice 17
Fudge, Easy 295
Fudge Pie 246
Fudge Sauce, Heavenly Hot 241
Fudge Sauce, Mocha 241
Fudge, Million Dollar 282
Fry Bread, Indian 81

G

Game (See Wild Game)
Garlic Dressing 39
Gazpacho, Easy 117
German Apple Cake 250
German Potato Salad 105
Glazed Clove Onions 214
Glazed Orange Bread 79
Glazed Pecans 55
Glögg 67
Golden Summer Punch 67
Good Morning Casserole 129
Good Seasons Italian Dip 50
Gooey Cake 264
Gooey Chicken 190
Goulash, Hamburger 168
Graham Cracker Sandwiches ... 231
Grandma Ward's Fruit Cake 260
Grandmother's Peanut Butter Cookies . 276
Grandmother's Rice Dressing 216
Granola 55
Grape Salad, White Seedless 101
Grasshopper Cake 257
Grecian Beef with Cheese Noodles 158
Green Bean Bundle 210
Green Beans and Artichoke 209
Green Beans, Buffet 209
Green Beans, Delicious 210
Green Chili Pepper and Chicken
    Casserole 183
Green Peas and Onions, Scalloped ... 215
Green Peppercorn Sauce,
    Steak du Chef with 24
Green Peppers, Stuffed 211
Green Tomato Pie, Sliced 223
Grilled Chicken, Mason Searcy's 191
Grilled Marinated Duck Breasts ... 148

Grilled Oriental Flank Steak 159
Grits, Bacon Garlic Cheese 208
Ground Beef (See Meats)
Ground Beef Soup 121
Guacamole Dip 51
Guaranteed Crispy Fried Chicken 190
Gumbo, Rosemary's Shrimp 120
Gumbo, Seafood Okra 120
Gumbo, Shrimp 121

H

Ham (See Meats, Pork)
Ham Ball 44
Hamburger Goulash 168
Hamburger Pie 168
Hamburger Vegetable Soup 122
Ham, Cheese, and Potato Casserole .. 174
Ham Cheese Ball 45
Ham Loaf 174
Ham Sandwiches, Frozen 124
Hash, Veal Artichoke 293
Have-On-Hand Brownie Mix 270
Hawaiian Banana Nut Bread 78
Hearty Vegetable Soup 122
Heavenly Hot Fudge Sauce 241
Helen's Chili 114
Herbed Rolls 82
Holiday Cookies 274
Holiday Scallop 101
Homemade Party Salami 57
Homemade Rolls 75
Hominy Casserole 211
Honolulu Spareribs 178
Hors D'Oeuvres (See Appetizers)
Hot Buttered Rum 68
Hot Cheese Dip with Crab Meat 48
Hot Chicken Loaf with Mushroom Sauce 35
Hot Chicken Salad 107
Hot Chocolate 68
Hot Dogs 61
Hot Fruit Casserole 97
Hot Fruit, Curried 96
Hot Fudge Sauce, Heavenly 241
Hot Mulled Party Punch 68
Hot Mustard 144
Hot Sauce 53
Hot Sauce, Bubba's Favorite 140
Hot Spiced Cider 69
Hot Spiced Meat Balls 59
Hush Puppies 85

I

Ice Cream (See Desserts)
Ice Cream, Butter Nut 240
Ice Cream, Caramel Dessert 239
Ice Cream, Milky Way 240
Ice Cream, Piña Colada 240

Ice Cream, Vanilla 241
Ice Box Pie, Strawberry 249
Iced Cucumber Vichyssoise 118
Impossible Pumpkin Pie 296
Indian Fry Bread 81
Italian Cream Cake 257
Italian Crescent Casserole, Zesty 173
Italian Dip, Good Seasons 50
Italian Meat Sauce for Spaghetti 171

J

Jalapeño Cheese Ball 45
Jalapeño Cheese Dip 48
Jalapeño Cheese Squares 45
Jalapeño Pepper Jelly 141
Jambalaya Salad 107
Jam Cake, Pineapple 264
Jell-O Delight, Strawberry 99
Jell-O Pretzel 233
Jell-O Salad, Orange 98
Jelly, Jalapeño Pepper 141
Jezebel Sauce 140
Jiffy Barbecue Sauce 143
Jordan Marsh Blueberry Muffins 87
Judge Roy Bean Soup 37

K

Kahlua 69
Kahlua Cake 255
Korean Spiced Beef 159
Krispies, Cheese 61

L

Lasagne 169
Layered Chocolate Dessert 234
Layered Chocolate Squares, Caramel . 270
Layered Lettuce Salad 101
Lemon Cake Top Pudding 235
Lemon Cake, Very Special 265
Lemon Chicken 191
Lemon Cookies 275
Lemon Fish Fillet, Broiled 151
Lemon Squares 274
Lemon Fruit Cup, Double 233
Lemonade Cake, Extra-Moist 262
Lettuce Soup, Cream of 116
Lime Salad 97
Little Links in Oriental Sauce 61
Little Rock Club Special Steak 27
Liver and Water Chestnut
    Hors D'Oeuvre, Chicken 62
London Broil Marinade 160

M

Macaroni, Ragland 212
Magic Mennefee Stew 122
Mallard with Rice Dressing 148

Manicotti 170
Manicotti, Quick 170
Manicotti with Spinach 133
Maple Bars 271
Margaritas, Frozen 67
Marinade for Shiskabob, Debbie's 143
Marinade, London Broil 160
Marinade, Vegetables in 106
Marinated Duck Breasts, Grilled 148
Marinated Mushrooms 212
Marinated Vegetable Salad 103
Mason Searcy's Grilled Chicken 191
Meatballs 171
Meatballs, Sweet and Sour 60
Meatballs, Sweet and Sour 291
Meatballs, Drunken 59
Meat Balls, Hot Spiced 59
Meat Loaf 167
Meat Loaf, Microwave 292
Meat Loaf, Venison 150
Meat Sauce, Cold 142
Meat Sauce for Spaghetti, Italian 171
MEATS
  Beef
    Bar-B-Q Brisket 164
    Beef Roll-Ups 156
    Beef Stroganoff I 157
    Beef Stroganoff II 157
    Chili Beefsteak 160
    Chuck Wagon Pepper Steak 158
    Company-Is-Coming
      Brisket Roast 164
    Dried Beef Cheese Ball 44
    Grecian Beef with
      Cheese Noodles 158
    Grilled Oriental Flank Steak 159
    Korean Spiced Beef 159
    Little Rock Club Special Steak 27
    London Broil Marinade 160
    New York Roast 164
    Oriental Roast and Vegetables . . . 163
    Party Pot Roast 165
    Peppered Eye of Beef 160
    Pooh's Shish Kabobs 161
    Savory Beef 161
    Savory Pepper Steak 162
    Steak du Chef with Green Peppercorn
      Sauce 24
    Swiss Steak 162
    Veal with Artichoke Hearts 163
  Ground Beef
    Baked Beans 166
    Beef and Bacon Fillets 165
    Cabbage Rolls 166
    Cajun Mistakes 56
    Chalupas 167
    Chism Special 169
    Deep Dish Pizza 168

Drunken Meat Balls 59
Hamburger Goulash 168
Hamburger Pie 168
Homemade Party Salami 57
Hot Spiced Meat Balls 59
Italian Meat Sauce for Spaghetti . . 171
Lasagne 169
Manicotti 170
Meatballs 171
Meat Loaf 167
Meat Loaf, Microwave 292
Mexican Casserole 292
Mother's Spaghetti 172
Quick Manicotti 170
Sloppy Joes 294
Spaghetti Sauce 173
Stuffed Tomato Cups 167
Susan's Spaghetti Sauce 172
Sweet and Sour Meatballs 60
Sweet and Sour Meatballs,
  Microwave 291
Veal Artichoke Hash 293
Zesty Italian Crescent Casserole . . 173
Pork
  Andean-Style Sweet Roast Pork . . . 16
  Cheese Stuffed Pork 175
  Dixie Pork Chops 176
  Easy Orange Pork Chops 176
  Ham Ball 44
  Ham and Cheese Ball 45
  Ham Loaf 174
  Honolulu Spareribs 178
  Pineapple Pork Chops 176
  Pork Chops 174
  Pork Chops and Cheese Biscuits . 175
  Pork Chops with Rice and Wine . . . 177
  Pork Roast and Dumplings with
    Sauerkraut 179
  Pork Tenderloin 180
  Pot Pork Chop Supper 177
  Potato, Ham and
    Cheese Casserole 174
  Sausage Balls 60
  Stuffed Pork Chops 178
  Sweet and Sour Pork Chops 177
Meringue Crust, Chocolate Angel Pie . . 244
Meringue, Mile-High 242
Mexican Casserole 292
Mexican Chili-Bean Warm Up 199
Mexican Cornbread 85
Mexican Pizza Dip 51
Mexico Chiquito Cheese Dip 51
MICROWAVE
  Baked Chicken 290
  Bananas Foster 294
  Cheese and Onion Quiche 288
  Cherries Jubilee 294
  Chicken Parmesan 291

Crustless Sausage Quiche 293
Easy Fudge 295
Easy Peanut Brittle 295
Impossible Pumpkin Pie 296
Meat Loaf 292
Mexican Casserole 292
Microwave Zucchini 290
Nuts and Bolts 287
Potato Casserole 289
Rice and Cheese Bake 288
Sloppy Joes 294
Squash Casserole 290
Sweet and Sour Meatballs 291
Swiss Broccoli Casserole 289
Tangy Mustard Cauliflower 289
Veal Artichoke Hash 293
Vegetable Soup 292
Microwave Zucchini 290
Mile-High Meringue 242
Mile-High Pie 247
Milk Punch 69
Milky Way Cake 259
Milky Way Ice Cream 240
Millionaires 282
Million Dollar Fudge 282
Mocha Brownie Torte 236
Mocha Fudge Sauce 241
Molasses Cookies 275
Monterey Jack Cheese and Rice 217
Monkey Bread 76
Mother's Spaghetti 172
Mousse, Chocolate 31
Muffins, Beer 86
Muffins, Bran 87
Muffins, Favorite Apple 87
Muffins, Jordon Marsh Blueberry 87
Muffins, Super Easy 88
Mushroom Scramble 131
Mushroom Sauce,
  Hot Chicken Loaf with 35
Mushrooms, Baked Stuffed 53
Mushrooms, Curried 53
Mushrooms, Marinated 212
Mushrooms, Stuffed 54
Mushrooms Stuffed with Bacon 54
Mushrooms Stuffed with Spinach 213
Mustard Cauliflower, Tangy 289
Mustard, Hot 144
Mustard, Sweet and Sour 144

N

New Orleans Potato Salad 104
New York Roast 164
Nix-Nax Party Mix 55
Nut Bread, Date 78
Nut Bread, Hawaiian Banana 78
Nuts and Bolts 287

Nuts, Frosted 54
Nuts, Orange Sugar Coated 282
Nuts, Party 56
Noodle Casserole, Shrimp, and 156
Noodles, Grecian Beef with Cheese . . . 158

O

Oatmeal Cake 262
Oatmeal Crispies 276
Okra, Fried 213
Okra Gumbo, Seafood 120
Old-Fashioned Chocolate Cake 254
Old-Fashioned Sugar Cookies 279
Olive Nut Sandwiches 124
Olive-Tuna Canapé Spread 57
Olive Wreath Mold 98
Olympia Cream 283
Omelette, Arkansas 129
One Hour Chocolate Cake and
  Frosting 255
Onion Quiche, Cheese and 288
Onion Rings, Delicious Fried 214
Onion Scallop, French 213
Onion Soup Duck 149
Onions, Glazed Clove 214
Onion Soup, French 118
Onions, Scalloped Green Peas and . . . 215
Orange Beets 200
Orange Bread, Glazed 79
Orange Flip 70
Orange Jell-O Salad 98
Orange Julius 70
Orange Lettuce Salad 102
Orange-Mallow Gelatin 98
Orange-Raisin Cake 263
Orange Sugar-Coated Nuts 282
Oreo Frozen Dessert 239
Oriental Chicken 191
Oriental Flank Steak, Grilled 159
Oriental Fried Rice 217
Oriental Roast and Vegetables 163
Oriental Sauce, Little Links in 61
Oven Fried Chicken á la Creole 192
Oven Potatoes 216
Oysters Bienville 15
Oysters, Scalloped 152
Oysters S.O.B., Baked 38

P

Pancake, Big-Mama's Apple 88
Paradise Pie 21
Parmesan Chicken 192
Party Nuts 56
Party Mix, Nix-Nax 55
Party Pot Roast 165
Party Punch, Christmas Glögg 67
Party Punch, Hot Mulled 68

Party Rye Bread 57
Party Shrimp and
   Asparagus Casserole 156
Pasta with White Clam Sauce 32
Pate' 58
Peach Cobbler Supreme 228
Peas and Onions, Scalloped Green . . . 215
Peas, Black-Eyed 214
Pea Dip, Black-Eyed 47
Peanut Blossoms 276
Peanut Brittle 283
Peanut Brittle, Easy 295
Peanut Butter Bars 283
Peanut Butter Cookies,
   Grandmother's 276
Peanut Butter Creme Pie 246
Peanut Butterscotch Turtles 284
Pecan Pie Cookies 277
Pecan Pie, Southern 247
Pecan Pralines, Sue's 284
Pecan, Glazed 55
Pecan Tassies 231
Peppercorn Sauce, Steak du Chef with,
   Green 24
Peppered Eye of Beef 160
Pepper Jelly, Jalapeño 141
Peppermint Brownies, Chocolate 269
Peppermint Pie, Frozen 238
Pepper Steak, Chuck Wagon 158
Pepper Steak, Savory 162
Peppers, Stuffed Green 211
Peta, Cheese 133
Pezcado a la Veracruzano
   Chuachinango 29
Pheasant 149
Pickled Squash 141
Pickler, Super Easy 142
Pickles, Bread and Butter 141
PIES
   Apple Creme Pie 243
   Apple Pie Filling 36
   Blueberry Pie Supreme 243
   Chiffon Cheese Pie 244
   Chocolate Angel Pie with Meringue
      Crust 244
   Coconut Cream Pie 245
   Egg Custard Pie 245
   Frozen Peppermint Pie 238
   Fudge Pie 246
   Impossible Pumpkin Pie 296
   Mile-High Meringue 242
   Mile-High Pie 247
   Paradise Pie 21
   Peanut Butter Cream Pie 246
   Praline Pumpkin Pie 248
   Pumpkin Cream Pie 18
   Raspberry Pie 248
   Southern Pecan Pie 247

Strawberry Icebox Pie 249
Sweet Potato Pie 249
Vinegar Pie Crust 242
Piña Colada Cake 254
Piña Colada Ice Cream 240
Pineapple Cake, Carrot 253
Pineapple Cheese Ball 46
Pineapple Chicken 192
Pineapple Delight 263
Pineapple Jam Cake 264
Pineapple Pork Chops 176
Pita Sandwiches, Chicken Almond 123
Pizza, Deep Dish 168
Pizza Dip, Mexican 51
Pizza, Fruit 229
Pizza Shell 89
Pizza Spread 58
Polynesian Chicken Salad 107
Pooh's Shish Kabobs 161
Popcorn Duck 148
Popovers 89
Poppy Seed Dressing 110
Pork Chops 174
Pork Chops and Cheese Biscuits . . . 175
Pork Chops with Rice and Wine 177
Pork Roast and Dumplings with
   Sauerkraut 179
Pork Tenderloin 180
Potato Casserole 215
Potato Casserole, Microwave 289
Potato, Ham and Cheese Casserole . . . 174
Potato Salad 104
Potato Salad, German 105
Potato Salad, New Orleans 104
Potato Soup 119
Potato Strips 215
Potatoes, Oven 216
Pot Pie, Dora's Chicken 190
Pot Pork Chop Supper 177
Pot Roast, Party 165
POULTRY
   Aunt Mary's Chicken-Rice
      Casserole 181
   Baked Chicken 290
   Biscuits on Creamy Chicken 181
   Broccoli and Chicken Casserole 181
   Chicken and Green Chili Pepper
      Casserole 183
   Chicken and Stuffing Scallop 186
   Chicken and Wild Rice Casserole . . . 186
   Chicken Breasts in Wine 182
   Chicken Breast Piquant 180
   Chicken Breasts-St. Louis 184
   Chicken Hélene 185
   Chicken Kiev 185
   Chicken Liver and Water Chestnut
      Hors D'Oeuvre 62
   Chicken Roll-Ups 187

Chicken Romano 184
Chicken-Sausage Casserole 182
Chicken Sherlen 182
Chicken with Chipped Beef 180
Chicken with Dumplings 183
Chicken with Zucchini and Corn 187
Corn-Crisp Chicken 188
Cornish Game Hens with
    Rice Stuffing 188
Country Chicken 187
Creamed Chicken in Avocado Shell . 188
Crescent Chicken Roll-Ups 189
Crescent Chicken Squares 189
Deviled Chicken 189
Dora's Chicken Pot Pie 190
Gooey Chicken 190
Guaranteed-Crispy Fried Chicken ... 190
Hot Chicken Loaf with
    Mushroom Sauce 35
Lemon Chicken 191
Mason Searcy's Grilled Chicken 191
Oriental Chicken 191
Oven Fried Chicken á la Creole 192
Parmesan Chicken 192
Pineapple Chicken 192
Robb's Special Chicken 193
Rolled Chicken Breasts 193
Sherried Chicken 193
Special Chicken Crêpes 195
Stuffed Chicken Breasts 194
Teriyaki Chicken 194
Pound Cake, Chocolate 267
Pound Cake, Excellent 265
Pound Cake, Five-Flavor 267
Praline Candy Cookie 277
Praline Pumpkin Pie 248
Pretzel Jell-O 233
Prune Cake 266
Pudding, Angel Coconut 234
Pudding, Chocolate Cake 253
Pudding, Corn 205
Pudding, Lemon Cake Top 235
Pudding, Yorkshire 82
Pumpkin Bread 80
Pumpkin Cream Pie 18
Pumpkin Date Torte 236
Pumpkin Pie, Impossible 296
Pumpkin Pie, Praline 248
Pumpkin Spiced Cookies, Frosted 278
Punch, Christmas Party, Glögg 67
Punch, Golden Summer 67
Punch, Hot Mulled Party 68
Punch, Milk 69
Punch Tropicana, Fruit 66

Q

Quiche 134
Quiche, Asparagus 134
Quiche, Cheese and Onion 288
Quiche Crêpes 135
Quiche, Crustless Sausage 293
Quick and Easy Salmon Patties 151
Quick Biscuits 83
Quick Chewy Bars 272
Quick Cinnamon Coffee Cake 84
Quick Manicotti 170

R

Ragland Macaroni 212
Raisin Cake, Orange 263
Raisin Sauce 139
Raspberry Pie 248
Refrigerator Rolls 76
Red Beans and Rice 200
Reuben Sandwich 125
Rice and Cheese Bake 288
Rice and Wine, Pork Chops with 177
Rice Casserole 216
Rice Casserole, Chicken and Wild 186
Rice Casserole, Aunt Mary's Chicken .. 181
Rice Dressing, Grandmother's 216
Rice Dressing, Mallard with 148
Rice, Fruited 17
Rice, Monterey Jack Cheese and 217
Rice, Oriental Fried 217
Rice, Red Beans and 200
Rice Salad 105
Rice Salad, Shrimp and 108
Rice Stuffing, Cornish Game Hens with 188
Rice, Winning 217
Roast and Dumplings with Sauerkraut,
    Pork 179
Roast and Vegetables, Oriental 163
Roast, Company-Is-Coming Brisket ... 164
Roast Duck Bites 149
Roast, New York 164
Roast, Party Pot 165
Roast Pork, Andean Style Sweet 16
Robb's Special Chicken 193
Rolled Chicken Breasts 193
Rolls á la Canned Biscuits 83
Rolls, Cabbage 166
Rolls, Crescent 75
Rolls, Herbed 82
Rolls, Homemade 75
Rolls, Refrigerator 76
Roquefort Dressing 110
Rosemary's Borscht 119
Rosemary's Shrimp Gumbo 120
Rum Cake, Coconut 258
Rum, Hot Buttered 68
Rum Wassail 71
Rye Bread, Party 57

S

SALAD DRESSINGS
    Banana Nut Dressing 109
    Bleu Cheese Dressing 109
    Catalina Salad Dressing 109
    Garlic Dressing 39
    Poppy Seed Dressing 110
    Roquefort Dressing 110
    Thousand Island Dressing 110
SALADS
  Fruit
    Apricot Salad 93
    Apricot Salad 94
    Baked Apricot Casserole 93
    Bing Cherry Salad 94
    Blueberry Salad 95
    Christmas Cranberry Salad 95
    Christmas Ribbon Salad 96
    Curried Hot Fruit 96
    Frozen Fruit Salad 96
    Frozen Strawberry Salad 97
    Hot Fruit Casserole 97
    Lime Salad 97
    Olive Wreath Mold 98
    Orange Jell-O Salad 98
    Orange Lettuce Salad 102
    Orange-Mallow Gelatin 98
    Strawberry Gelatin Salad 99
    Strawberry Jell-O Delight 99
    Watergate Salad 99
    White Seedless Grape Salad 101
  Meat
    Crab-Stuffed Avocado 108
    Hot Chicken Salad 107
    Jambalaya Salad 107
    Polynesian Chicken Salad 107
    Shrimp Mold 108
    Shrimp and Rice Salad 108
  Vegetable
    Broccoli Cauliflower Salad 100
    Corn Salad 100
    Frito Salad 100
    German Potato Salad 105
    Holiday Scallop 101
    Layered Lettuce Salad 101
    Marinated Vegetable Salad 103
    New Orleans Potato Salad 104
    Potato Salad 104
    Rice Salad 105
    Sweet Sour Slaw 105
    Special Spinach Salad 103
    Spinach-Cheese Salad 20
    Spinach Salad 102
    Three Bean Salad 106
    Vegetables in Marinade 106
    Winter Salad 106
Salami, Homemade Party 57
Salmon Cheese Spread, Smoky 58

Salmon Patties, Quick and Easy 151
Salsa 140
SANDWICHES
    Avocado Sandwich 19
    Baked Cheese Sandwiches 123
    Baked Chicken Sandwiches 123
    Chicken Almond Pita Sandwiches ... 123
    Creamy Crab Sandwich 124
    Cucumber Sandwiches 56
    Frozen Ham Sandwiches 124
    Olive Nut Sandwiches 124
    Reuben Sandwich 125
    Stacked Sandwich 125
    Tuna Cheese Buns 125
    Twenty-Four Hour Tuna Sandwich .. 126
Sangria 70
Sauces (See Condiments)
Sauce, Spaghetti 173
Sauce, Susan's Spaghetti 172
Sauerkraut, Pork Roast and
  Dumplings with 179
Sausage Balls 60
Sausage Bread 81
Sausage Casserole, Chicken 182
Sausage Quiche, Crustless 293
Savory Beef 161
Savory Pepper Steak 162
Scallop, Chicken and Stuffing 186
Scallop, French Onion 213
Scallop, Holiday 101
Scalloped Green Peas and Onions 215
Scalloped Oysters 152
Seafood (See Fish and Shellfish)
Seafood Casserole 153
Seafood Okra Gumbo 120
Sesame Wafers 278
Sheepshead Chowder 33
Shell, Pizza 89
Sherried Chicken 193
Sherried Sweet Potato Casserole 222
Sherry, Ducks in 147
Shish Kabob, Debbie's Marinade for ... 143
Shish Kabobs, Pooh's 161
Shortbread 82
Shrimp (See Fish and Shellfish)
Shrimp and Noodle Casserole 156
Shrimp and Rice Salad 108
Shrimp Ball 46
Shrimp, Barbecued 153
Shrimp, Cocktail Sauce 143
Shrimp Creole 155
Shrimp Curry 155
Shrimp Dip 52
Shrimp Gumbo 121
Shrimp Gumbo, Rosemary's 120
Shrimp Log 46
Shrimp Mold 108
Shrimp Ring 154

Shrimp-Stuffed Eggplant 207
Slang-Jang 142
Slaw, Sour Sweet 105
Sliced Green Tomato Pie 223
Sloppy Joes 294
Smoky Salmon Cheese Spread 58
Souffle, Brandy Alexander 232
Souffle, Broccoli 201
Souffle, Cheese 133
SOUPS
   Bean Soup 114
   Cheese Soup 113
   Chili 113
   Cold Avocado Soup 113
   Corn Chowder 115
   Cream of Artichoke Soup 115
   Cream of Carrot Soup 116
   Cream of Lettuce Soup 116
   Delicious Beef Stew 121
   Dieter's Special Soup 116
   Easy Gazpacho 117
   Egg Soup 117
   Fish Chowder 117
   French Onion Soup 118
   Ground Beef Soup 121
   Hamburger Vegetable Soup 122
   Hearty Vegetable Soup 122
   Helen's Chili 114
   Iced Cucumber Vichyssoise 118
   Judge Roy Bean Soup 37
   Magic Mennefee Stew 122
   Potato Soup 119
   Rosemary's Borscht 119
   Rosemary's Shrimp Gumbo 120
   Seafood Okra Gumbo 120
   Sheepshead Chowder 33
   Shrimp Gumbo 121
   Vegetable Soup, Microwave 292
Sour Cream Banana Cake 252
Sour Cream Coffee Cake 85
Sour Cream Enchiladas, Cheesy 132
Sour Sweet Slaw 105
Southern Pecan Pie 247
Spaghetti, Curried Tuna 151
Spaghetti, Italian Meat Sauce for 171
Spaghetti, Mother's 172
Spaghetti, Sauce 173
Spaghetti Sauce, Susan's 172
Spareribs, Honolulu 178
Special Chicken Crêpes 195
Special Spinach Salad 103
Speedy Crescents 83
Spice Cookies, Frosted Pumpkin 278
Spiced Beef, Korean 159
Spiced Cider, Hot 69
Spiced Meat Balls, Hot 59
Spiced Tea 71
Spinach and Artichoke Casserole 218

Spinach Cheese Salad 20
Spinach, Manicotti with 133
Spinach Salad 102
Spinach Salad, Special 103
Spinach Squares 218
Spinach Supreme 218
Spoon Bread, Corn 81
Squash á la Fruit 219
Squash and Corn Casserole 220
Squash, Batter Fried 219
Squash Casserole 219
Squash Casserole, Microwave 290
Squash, Pickled 141
Stacked Sandwich 125
Steak du Chef with Green Peppercorn
   Sauce 24
Steak, Little Rock Club Special 27
Steak, Savory Pepper 162
Stew, Delicious Beef 121
Stew, Magic Mennefee 122
Stew, Venison 150
Stir-Fry Cabbage 202
Strawberry Bread 80
Strawberry Cake 266
Strawberry Delight 265
Strawberry Gelatin Salad 99
Strawberry Icebox Pie 249
Strawberry Jell-O Delight 99
Strawberry Salad, Frozen 97
Strawberry French Torte 237
Strawberry Torte 238
Stroganoff I, Beef 157
Stroganoff II, Beef 157
Stuffed Chicken Breasts 194
Stuffed Eggplant, Baked 207
Stuffed Eggplant, Shrimp 207
Stuffed Green Peppers 211
Stuffed Mushrooms 54
Stuffed Mushrooms, Baked 53
Stuffed Mushrooms with Bacon 54
Stuffed Mushrooms with Spinach 213
Stuffed Pork, Cheese 175
Stuffed Pork Chops 178
Stuffed Tomato Cups 167
Sue's Pecan Pralines 284
Sugar-Coated Nuts, Orange 282
Sugar Cookies, Old Fashioned 279
Sunshine Carrots 203
Super Easy Muffins 88
Super Easy Pickles 142
Susan's Spaghetti Sauce 172
Sweet and Sour Meatballs 60
Sweet and Sour Meatballs, Microwave . 291
Sweet and Sour Mustard 144
Sweet and Sour Pork Chops 177
Sweet Potato Casserole I 221
Sweet Potato Casserole II 221
Sweet Potato Casserole, Sherried 222

Sweet Potato Pie 249
Swiss Broccoli Casserole 289
Swiss Steak 162

T

Tamale Dip 52
Tangy Mustard Cauliflower 289
Tassies, Pecan 231
Tea Bread, Banana 79
Tea, Spiced 71
Tempura Vegetables 222
Tenderloin, Pork 180
Teriyaki Chicken 194
Three Bean Salad 106
Thousand Island Dressing 110
Toffee Dessert 232
Toffee, English 284
Tomato Cups, Stuffed 167
Tomato Pie, Sliced Green 223
Tomatoes Rockefeller 223
Torta Risa 43
Torte, Chocolate Tortilla 235
Torte, Mocha Brownie 236
Torte, Pumpkin Date 236
Torte, Strawberry 238
Torte, Strawberry French 237
Tuna Canape Spread, Olive 57
Tuna Cheese Buns 125
Tuna Sandwich, Twenty-Four Hour 126
Tuna Spaghetti, Curried 151
Turtles, Peanut Butterscotch 284
Twenty-Four Hour Tuna Sandwich 126

V

Vanilla Crumb Cake 256
Vanilla Ice Cream 241
Veal Artichoke Hash 293
Veal with Artichoke Hearts 163
Vegetable Plenty 224
VEGETABLES
   Acorn Squash a la Fruit 219
   Asparagus Casserole 199
   Asparagus Elegante 199
   Aunt Thelma's Cold Carrots 202
   Bacon Garlic Cheese Grits 208
   Baked Eggplant 206
   Baked Spanish Eggplant 206
   Baked Stuffed Eggplant 207
   Batter Fried Squash 219
   Better Brussels Sprouts 202
   Black-Eyed Peas 214
   Bobbie's Broccoli 200
   Broccoli Casserole 201
   Broccoli Souffle 201
   Buffet Green Beans 209
   Carrot Casserole 203
   Carrot Ring 203

Cauliflower Casserole 204
Corn Fremont 205
Corn Pudding 205
Creole Corn 204
Delicious Fried Onion Rings 214
Delicious Green Beans 210
Dinner Casserole 212
Eggplant Casserole 208
Eggplant Parmigiano 32
French Bean Casserole 210
French Fried Cauliflower 204
French Onion Scallop 213
Fried Okra 213
Fruited Rice 17
Glazed Clove Onions 214
Grandmother's Rice Dressing 216
Green Beans and Artichokes 209
Green Bean Bundle 210
Hominy Casserole 211
Marinated Mushrooms 212
Mexican Chili-Bean Warm Up 199
Microwave Zucchini 290
Monterey Jack Cheese and Rice 217
Mushrooms Stuffed with Spinach ... 213
Orange Beets 200
Oriental Fried Rice 217
Oven Potatoes 216
Potato Casserole 215
Potato Casserole, Microwave 289
Potato Strips 215
Ragland Macaroni 212
Red Beans and Rice 200
Rice and Cheese Bake 288
Rice Casserole 216
Scalloped Green Peas and Onions .. 215
Sherried Sweet Potato Casserole ... 222
Shrimp-Stuffed Eggplant 207
Sliced Green Tomato Pie 223
Spinach and Artichoke Casserole ... 218
Spinach Squares 218
Spinach Supreme 218
Squash and Corn Casserole 220
Squash Casserole 219
Squash Casserole, Microwave 290
Stir-Fry Cabbage 202
Stuffed Green Peppers 211
Sunshine Carrots 203
Sweet Potato Casserole I 221
Sweet Potato Casserole II 221
Swiss Broccoli Casserole 289
Tangy Mustard Cauliflower 289
Tempura Vegetables 222
Tomatoes Rockefeller 223
Vegetable Plenty 224
Winning Rice 217
Zucchini Casserole 220
Vegetable Salad, Marinated 103
Vegetable Soup, Hamburger 122

313

Vegetable Soup, Hearty 122
Vegetable Soup, Microwave 292
Vegetables, Dip for Raw 50
Vegetables in Marinade 106
Vegetables, Oriental Roast and 163
Vegetables, Tempura 222
Venison Meat Loaf 150
Venison Stew 150
Very Special Lemon Cake 265
Vichyssoise, Iced Cucumber 118
Vinegar Pie Crust 242

W

Waffles 89
Water Chestnut Dip 52
Water Chestnut Hors D'Oeuvres, Chicken
    Liver and 62
Watergate Salad 99
Wedding Cookies 279
Weiners, Cocktail 60
Whipped Butter 139
White Clam Sauce, Pasta with 32
White Seedless Grape Salad 101
Whole Wheat Bread with Honey 77
WILD GAME
    Candied Wild Duck 147
    Duck Casserole 147
    Ducks in Sherry 147
    Grilled Marinated Duck Breasts 148
    Mallard with Rice Dressing 148
    Onion Soup Duck 149
    Pheasant 149
    Popcorn Duck 148
    Roast Duck Bites 149
    Venison Meat Loaf 150
    Venison Stew 150
Wild Rice Casserole, Chicken and 186
Wine, Chicken Breasts in 182
Wine, Pork Chops with Rice and 177
WINING AND DINING
    Wine Guide 7-14
    Menus
        Anderson's Cajun's Wharf 15
        Andre's 16
        Capital Club, The 18
        Cheers! 19
        Country Club of Little Rock, The 20
        Coy's 22
        Gonzales' and Gertrude's 23
        Jacques and Suzanne 24
        Leather Bottle 25
        Little Rock Club 27
        Mexico Chiquito 29
        "Nu Deli" Ltd. 31
        Percito's 32
        Pleasant Valley Country Club 33
        Red Apple Inn, The 35

        Shorty Small's 37
        S.O.B. Shrimp, Oysters, and
            Beerhaus 38
        Villa, The 40
    Recipes
        Andean-Style Sweet Roast Pork ... 16
        Apple Pie Filling 36
        Avocado Sandwich 19
        Baked Oysters S.O.B. 38
        Camerones Cancun 23
        Cheesecake 25
        Chocolate Mousse 31
        Crawfish Etouffee 34
        Deviled Crab or Crab Stuffing 39
        Eggplant Parmigiano 32
        Escargot 22
        Espagnole Sauce 28
        Fettuccini 40
        Fruited Rice 17
        Garlic Dressing 39
        Hot Chicken Loaf with Mushroom
            Sauce 35
        Judge Roy Bean Soup 37
        Little Rock Club Special Steak 27
        "Pairing Wine with Food" 7
        Paradise Pie 21
        Pasta with White Clam Sauce 32
        Pezcado a la Veracruzano
            Chuachinango 29
        Pumpkin Cream Pie 18
        Oysters Bienville 15
        Sheepshead Chowder 33
        Spinach Cheese Salad 20
        Steak du Chef with Green
            Peppercorn Sauce 24
Winning Rice 217
Winter Salad 106

Y

Yorkshire Pudding 82

Z

Zesty Italian Crescent Casserole 173
Zucchini and Corn, Chicken and 187
Zucchini Casserole 220
Zucchini, Microwave 290

RAVE REVIEWS

RAVE REVIEWS PUBLICATIONS
JUNIOR LEAGUE OF NORTH LITTLE ROCK
POST OFFICE BOX 15753
LITTLE ROCK, ARKANSAS 72231

Please send_____copies of **RAVE REVIEWS** @   11.95 each _____

Postage and handling. . . . . @   2.00 each _____

Gift Wrap (_____)   Free

                TOTAL _____

☐ Check enclosed . . . We honor MasterCard and Visa (over)

Name _____

Street _____

City_____ State _____ Zip _____

All proceeds from the sale of these books shall be used for community service
projects approved or sponsored by the Junior League of North Little Rock.

RAVE REVIEWS

RAVE REVIEWS PUBLICATIONS
JUNIOR LEAGUE OF NORTH LITTLE ROCK
POST OFFICE BOX 15753
LITTLE ROCK, ARKANSAS 72231

Please send_____copies of **RAVE REVIEWS** @   11.95 each _____

Postage and handling. . . . . @   2.00 each _____

Gift Wrap (_____)   Free

                TOTAL _____

☐ Check enclosed . . . We honor MasterCard and Visa (over)

Name _____

Street _____

City_____ State _____ Zip _____

All proceeds from the sale of these books shall be used for community service
projects approved or sponsored by the Junior League of North Little Rock.

RAVE REVIEWS

RAVE REVIEWS PUBLICATIONS
JUNIOR LEAGUE OF NORTH LITTLE ROCK
POST OFFICE BOX 15753
LITTLE ROCK, ARKANSAS 72231

Please send_____copies of **RAVE REVIEWS** @   11.95 each _____

Postage and handling. . . . . @   2.00 each _____

Gift Wrap (_____)   Free

                TOTAL _____

☐ Check enclosed . . . We honor MasterCard and Visa (over)

Name _____

Street _____

City_____ State _____ Zip _____

All proceeds from the sale of these books shall be used for community service
projects approved or sponsored by the Junior League of North Little Rock.

If using Charge Card, please fill in the following:

Name _____

Address _____

City _____ State _____ Zip _____

Charge to my: ☐ VISA   ☐ MasterCard

Account Number:

_____

_____

Expiration Date: _____
                        Month   Year

Customer's Signature: _____

If using Charge Card, please fill in the following:

Name _____

Address _____

City _____ State _____ Zip _____

Charge to my: ☐ VISA   ☐ MasterCard

Account Number:

_____

_____

Expiration Date: _____
                        Month   Year

Customer's Signature: _____

If using Charge Card, please fill in the following:

Name _____

Address _____

City _____ State _____ Zip _____

Charge to my: ☐ VISA   ☐ MasterCard

Account Number:

_____

_____

Expiration Date: _____
                        Month   Year

Customer's Signature: _____